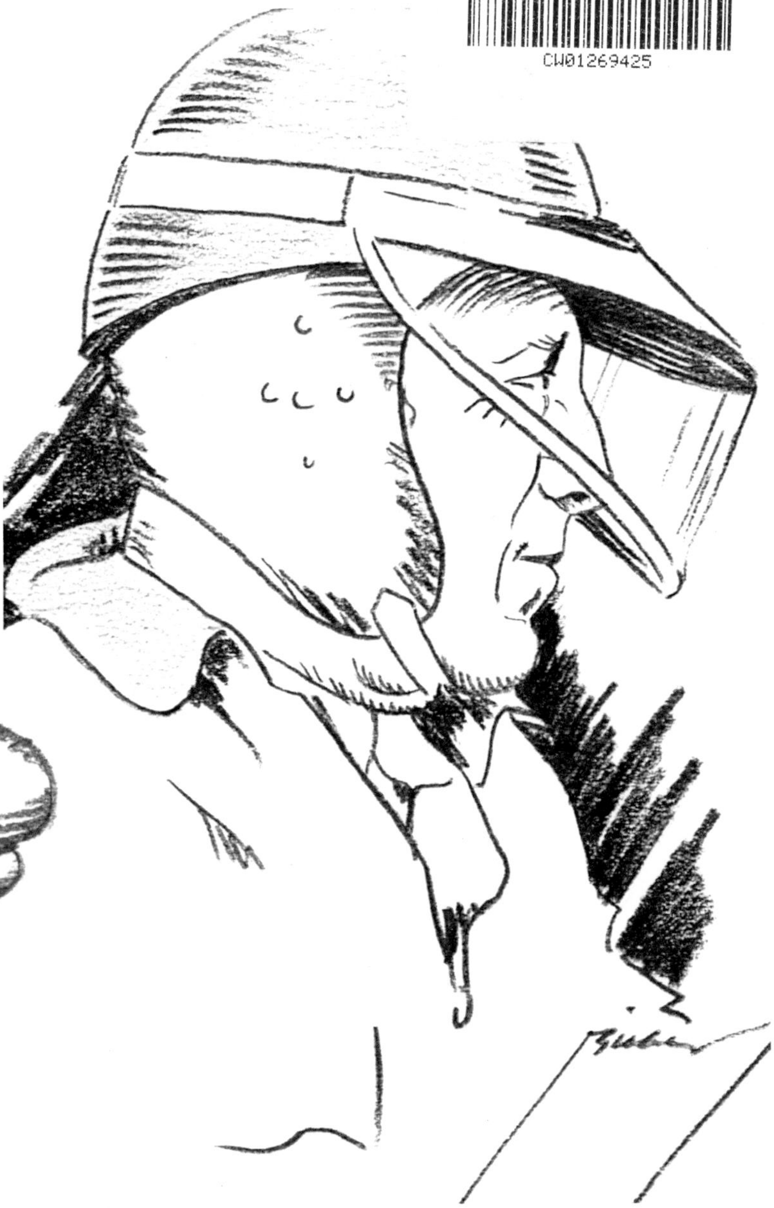

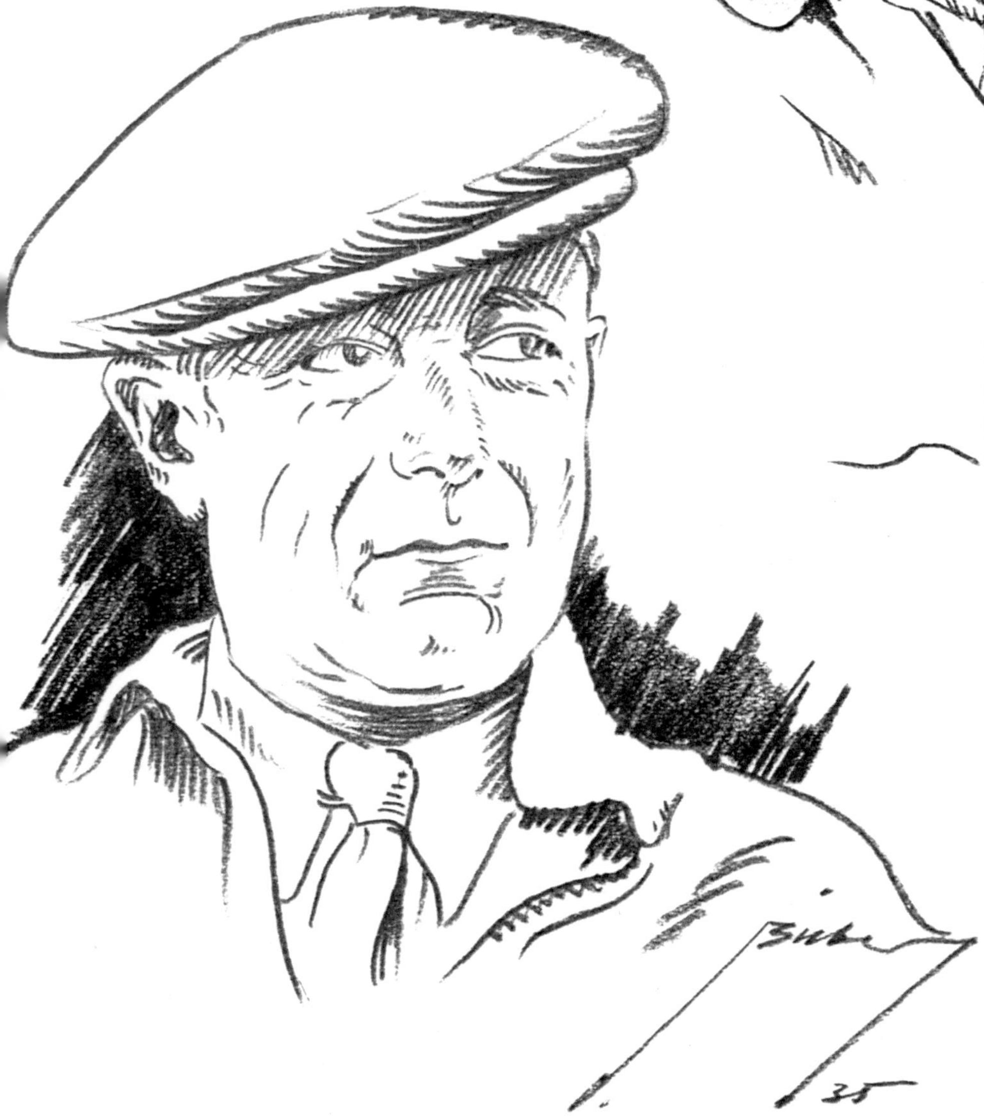

Francis Howe
Motor Man Par Excellence

Francis Howe
Motor Man Par Excellence

by
Tim May

GMS Publications

© text 2011 Tim May
© photographs 2014 Individual photographers per caption credit

First published 2014 by GMS Publications
c/o Chateau Impney, Droitwich Spa, Worcestershire WR9 0BN
email: orders@howebook.co.uk
www.howebook.co.uk

ISBN 978 0 9928680 0 0

All rights reserved. No part of this publication may be reproduced,
stored in a retrieval system, or transmitted, in any form or by any means, electronic,
mechanical, photocopying, recording or otherwise, without prior permission of the authors.

The reproduction of any part of the text or any of the illustrations in whole
or in part is forbidden without written permission from the copyright holders.

Designed and printed by Quorum Print Services Ltd, Cheltenham
www.quorumprint.co.uk

All profits from the sale of this book
will go to the Motor Neurone Disease Association

Motor Neurone Disease Association
PO Box 246
Northampton
NN1 2PR
www.mndassociation.org

Best wishes Margaret Measures
11.11.18

All the very best — Howe drove my old Lagonda EPE 97 at the TT.

David.

Robin
You are a wonderful man, I have so many fond memories of you in Ireland &
Chest...

Contents

Editor's Note	viii
Foreword by the Rt. Hon. the Earl Howe PC	ix
Acknowledgments and Photographic Credits	x
Background and Beginnings	1
Naval Man	15
Political Man	23
Sports Car Racing	37
The Grand Prix Years	79
The Voiturette Years	131
Motor Racing Man – Organising The Sport	161
Appendix One	182
Appendix Two	189
Appendix Three	198
Index	199

Editor's Note

Before his untimely death in September 2011 Tim May had spent more than a decade researching the life of Francis, Earl Howe. He was able to complete the text of the book, as published here. He had, however, only managed to do preliminary work on the list of Howe's racing appearances (Appendix 1) and on the photographs to be included in the book. With the aid of Guy Spollon I have completed these tasks along with the captions to the photographs. I hope that the finished product stands as a memorial to Tim's enthusiasm for the subject, and for motor racing history in general.

Adam Ferrington
February 2014

Foreword by the Rt. Hon. the Earl Howe PC

When Tim May approached me a few years ago with his plan for a full-scale biography of Francis Howe, I was truly delighted: not only on behalf of enthusiasts for motor racing history, in which Francis's career occupies such a prominent place, but also on behalf of my own family. The story of Francis's exploits and successes on the track was long overdue. But a book that would also do justice to the man and the forces which motivated him would serve to put his racing career into the wider context of his many-faceted life.

That Tim should have died when on the finishing straight to completing this book is indeed tragic. He left behind a meticulously researched piece of work: one that was so well organised that his wife and close friends were able, without too much difficulty, to tie up the few loose ends that were left. They are to be congratulated for making Tim's vision a reality in the way that I am sure he would have wished.

This is a portrait of a most remarkable man who lived life to the full. His legacy from a very different era of motor racing lives on through the B.R.D.C., which he started, and through the many vintage racing events which now flourish around the country and which provide an opportunity to view and touch the very cars in which Francis Howe and his contemporaries raced with such success.

Howe
March 2013

The current Earl Howe as a passenger in Nick Pellett's ex-Howe Talbot 105 works team car at Kop Hill hillclimb, Buckinghamshire. *Photograph courtesy of Nick Pellett*

Acknowledgments and Photographic Credits

As is noted on the previous page, at the time of his death Tim May had largely completed the manuscript of this book. However, as far as can be ascertained, he had not compiled a list of acknowledgements. What follows is the editor and publisher's list of people we are aware of who helped Tim in his researches plus those who have helped in the subsequent editing process. We apologize in advance if anybody has been inadvertently omitted.

Acknowledgments

The Howe Family
B.R.D.C. Archive
The late Alan Burnard
Bob Cooper
Simon Davis
Tim Dutton of Ivan Dutton Ltd.
James Fack
Paul Gibbons
Willie Green
Clive Harrington
Terry Harrison

The late Mike Hawke
John Humphries
The late Mark Joseland
Yves Kaltenbach
Julian Majzub
John Moody
Simon Moore
Doug Nye
Nick Pellett
Ian & John Polson
Barrie Price

Peter Putterill
Emmanuel Rault
The late A F Rivers Fletcher
David Sewell
Alessandro Silva
Simon Thomas
Barry Walker
David Weguelin
Ted Widgery

Photographic Credits

Brooklands Society
Terry Cardy
Richard Crump
Arnold Davey
Ferret Fotographic – Ted Walker
Adam Ferrington Collection
Getty Images – Amba Horton
Goddard, Monkhouse and Zagari Archives – Matt and Di Spitzley
GP Library – Doug Nye
Tim Houlding
Howe Family Archive, via Clive Harrington
Image Restore – Neil Rhodes
Jarrotts – Martin Jordan
M R Kenneth Archive, via Roger Clark
The Klemantaski Collection – Peter Sachs
LAT Archive – Kevin Wood, Zoe Schafer and Kathy Ager

Leicestershire Record Office
Simon Lewis
John Maitland
Midland Automobile Club Archive – David Moore
David Morris – Reggie Tongue Archive
Mark Morris
Motoring Picture Library at the National Motor Museum – Jon Day
National Portrait Gallery – Elizabeth Taylor
Science and Society Picture Library – Zoltan Glass Archive – Sophia Brothers
John Pearson
Nick Pellett
REVS Institute – Mark Patrick
Graeme Simpson
Guy Spollon Collection
David Venables
Jeremy Wood

1

Background and Beginnings

- The origins of the Howe family
- Family traditions – the services
- Family traditions – politics
- Francis' grandparents and parents
- From the nineteenth century to the twentieth – declining family fortunes?
- Francis Howe and his background: how much impact?
- Early life and education
- Early motoring experience
- Family and personal life

Chapter 1

Background and Beginnings

The origins of the Howe family

In shaping an individual's character few would dispute that both heredity and environment are important. The argument is *much* more about how much each shapes personality – and this is an unresolved and perhaps irresolvable conundrum. Virtually all biographers devote some space to their subject's family because it provides clues both about heredity and about the first significant 'environment' which individuals experience. What kind of family was Francis Richard George Penn Curzon born into on May 1st, 1884?

Although the earldom was of relatively recent creation (1821), the family's origins in the middle ranges of the British aristocracy can be traced back a great deal further. The Curzon-Howe name signals the fusion of two main lines of descent. The Howe family were landowners in Nottinghamshire living at Langar House which was south east of the modern city of Nottingham. In the late seventeenth and early eighteenth century Scrope Howe was an M.P. at three different times, amounting to twenty years service in the House of Commons. He was a prominent figure in supporting the 'Glorious Revolution' of 1688 which invited William of Orange to replace James II as King and his part in this process was recognised by the grant of two Irish peerages – Lord Glenawly and Viscount Howe.

One of Scrope Howe's grandsons, Richard, became a famous admiral commanding the British navy at the battle of the 'Glorious First of June' in 1794. It was one of the Admiral's daughters, Sophia Charlotte, who married the Hon. Penn Assheton Curzon in 1787 and this marriage brought the two branches of the family – Curzons and Howes – together.

The Curzon line descended from the Curzons of Kedleston in Derbyshire who amassed large landholdings in Derbyshire, Staffordshire, Leicestershire and Nottinghamshire. Kedleston Hall, an outstanding Palladian mansion, was built by Nathaniel, the first Baron Scarsdale between 1759 and 1765. Lord Scarsdale's younger brother, Assheton, was the father of Penn Assheton; Assheton himself was an M.P. for nearly thirty years and was created Viscount Curzon in 1802. He lived to the great age of 90, outliving his son who died at the early age of 40.

The marriage between Sophia Howe and Penn Assheton Curzon produced a son, Richard William Penn Curzon, who was born in 1796. Shortly after inheriting the Curzon viscountcy from his grandfather he was created Earl Howe in 1821 and he altered the family name to Curzon-Howe in order to recognise fully the two families brought together by his parents' marriage. The first Earl was Francis' great grandfather but Francis would not have known him as he died in 1870. His eldest son, George Augustus, succeeded as the second Earl but as he had no male heir when he died in 1876, his brother Richard became the third Earl. He was Francis' grandfather who Francis would certainly have known as he survived until 1900 being succeeded, in turn, by Francis' father, George.

Family traditions – the services

Before taking a closer look at Francis' parents and grandparents it is useful to note a number of characteristics of the Howe family of which Francis would certainly have been aware as a child and adolescent. Two strong elements which run consistently through the generations are politics and the services. In addition to the celebrated victor of the 'Glorious First of June' there was another Admiral, Sir Assheton Curzon-Howe (1850-1911) who was the youngest of the first Earl's nine sons. The second, third and fourth Earls all had army roles and Francis' grandfather was a career soldier entering the army at 16 and reaching the rank of General at the age of 58.

Another general in the Howe family played an interesting part in the loss of the American colonies. Initially General Sir William Howe (who was the fifth and final holder of the Irish viscountcy and barony) was successful against the colonists with a victory at the battle of Bunker Hill in 1775 followed up by success at White Plains and Brandywine Creek. He could have consolidated these successes by attacking George Washington in his beleaguered winter quarters at Valley Forge but he chose not to. Howe believed he had insufficient troops and that he was being unfairly attacked back in Britain. He sent in his resignation and subsequently (in 1779) obtained a parliamentary enquiry into the conduct of the American war. The outcome of this investigation was indeterminate: "The ministers could not substantiate any charge against Howe, and he on his part failed to prove that he had not received due support" *(Dictionary of National Biography)*.

While the historical verdict on General William Howe has been at best rather mixed, that on his elder brother, Admiral Howe, has been overwhelmingly favourable. He was born in 1726, entered the navy when he was barely an adolescent and had command of his own ship by his early twenties. Later in his career he had two spells as First Lord of the Admiralty in the 1780s and commanded important actions which relieved Gibraltar in 1782 and defeated the French at the battle of the 'Glorious First of June' in 1794. His distinguished service brought numerous honours and rewards – he was created a U.K. Viscount in 1782, advanced to an earldom in 1788, and enrolled as a Knight of the Garter in 1797.

On his return to Portsmouth following the 'Glorious First of June' victory he was greeted by King George III who, together with Queen Charlotte and three of the Princesses, was rowed out to Howe's ship where the King presented him with a diamond-hilted sword. As is often the case, some historians have subsequently expressed certain reservations about Howe's 1794 victory. This criticism is based on the fact that the destruction of the French ships was less than complete and that a grain convoy, much-needed to feed Paris and which Howe had left to be shadowed by one of his Rear Admirals, successfully docked at Brest. While it is true that a few of the French ships were able to limp back to their fleet it is easy to overlook how demanding the engagement had proved, especially for Howe himself: "Howe's age and health after several days of unremitting strain must have inhibited effort at this late stage; he is said to have been on deck almost continuously for five days" (Roger Knight: *Oxford Dictionary of National Biography*, Oxford University Press (2004)). The failure to locate the grain convoy was unfortunate but Howe cannot be seen as having any direct responsibility for this error.

Whatever the judgement of history there is no doubt that the victory at the time came at a low point in the war and was widely celebrated with bonfires and the ringing of church bells.

Right at the end of Admiral Howe's career, indeed after he had actually resigned from the navy, he was asked to intervene in the naval mutiny at Spithead in May 1797. He succeeded in de-fusing the situation, aided no doubt, by the fact that "by general consent he is allowed to have been temperate, gentle and indulgent to the men under his command, who on their part adored him whether as Captain or Admiral" *(Dictionary of National Biography)*.

Thomas Gainsborough painted his portrait on more than one occasion and he also completed an outstanding portrait of Howe's wife Mary, which is on display at Kenwood House in north London.

Family traditions – politics

We have already noted Scrope Howe's part in establishing William of Orange on the English throne and subsequent generations have continued to occupy political roles of one kind or another.

The first Earl was a whip in the House of Lords and his son was M.P. for South Leicester for thirteen years before succeeding his father in 1870 and transferring from the Commons to the Lords. The third Earl, a younger son, pursued an army career and this was not compatible with political responsibilities. The third Earl's son, Francis' father, followed a similar pattern to his uncle, the second Earl.

He was elected to the House of Commons at the 1885 General Election for the Wycombe division of Buckinghamshire and remained its Conservative M.P. for fifteen years before moving into the House of Lords in 1900 when he succeeded his father.

Francis' father was also active in the Conservative Party outside parliament, chiefly through his involvement with the Primrose League. Although the League survived well into the twentieth century it was the 1880s and 1890s when it was of most political significance: "By the end of the nineteenth century hundreds of thousands of women were involved in the Primrose League…" ((editors): A. Seldon and Stuart Ball: *Conservative Century*, Oxford University Press (1994)). While the League was not part of the formal structure of the Conservative Party it undoubtedly spread a Conservative message; it also established the importance of women as Conservative Party workers and voters which were significant features of the Party throughout most of the twentieth century. From 1900-1902 the fourth Earl was 'Chancellor' of the League a role described by one of the League's historians as "(its) leading public voice; he presided at most functions and travelled round the country to address the habitations (branches)" (Martin Pugh: *The Tories and the People 1880-1935*, Basil Blackwell (1985)).

Francis' grandparents and parents

Francis' grandfather, Richard William Penn Curzon was born in 1822, the second son of the first Earl. When he was 36 he married Isabella Maria Katherine Anson who was the elder daughter of Major General the Honourable George Anson, a member of the Earl of Lichfield's family. They had two children, both boys, the elder of which was christened Richard George, but usually known by his second name. George's brother, Frederick Graham, who was nearly seven years younger, was the grandfather of the present Earl, Frederick Richard, born in 1951, who inherited the title in 1984.

As already noted the third Earl was a career soldier entering the Grenadier Guards at the age of 16 and retiring, just before his sixtieth birthday, with the rank of General. A considerable amount of his service career was spent abroad, he served in the Kaffir War in 1852, was Military Secretary to the C-in-C in India in 1854, A.D.C to Sir George Cathcart at the siege of Delhi in 1857. In 1858 he was created a C.B. most likely as recognition of his Indian service. Both before and after his retirement in 1880 he was honorary Colonel of a Leicestershire regiment and of the second Life Guards. His brother, the second Earl died at the relatively young age of 55, after suffering from heart disease, but Richard reached the age of 78 and his widow had an even longer life outliving her husband by twenty-two years.

Francis' father, George, was born in 1861. He was actually the second son, but his elder brother did not survive childhood. George was educated at Eton and Christ Church Oxford so following exactly the same path as the first and second Earls. This was not his father's pattern, of course, but his father as a younger son had followed a different kind of tradition. In 1885, at the age of 24, George was elected to Parliament and remained there until succeeding to the Earldom in 1900. He served as a whip in both Houses but did not advance to any other ministerial post.

One probable reason for not progressing further was the demands of his life as a courtier. George Howe's principal Court role was as Lord Chamberlain to Queen Alexandra from 1903 until 1925. It meant that he was the chief official in managing the Queen's household. He received the G.C.V.O. in 1903, the highest rank of the Royal Victorian Order, a decoration founded by Queen Victoria to recognise personal service to the sovereign and her family. In 1925 he received an additional honour, the Royal Victorian Chain and he was also given many foreign decorations through his role as Lord Chamberlain. When Francis Howe's son, Richard, was christened in 1908 Alexandra's husband, King Edward VII, was one of his sponsors which was a mark of the close association between his grandfather, the fourth Earl, and the royal family.

George's wife, Georgiana Spencer-Churchill, was the fifth daughter of the seventh Duke of Marlborough. The Marlboroughs have not been generously dealt with by historians who have often invoked Gladstone's dictum "There never was a Churchill from John of Marlborough down who had either morals or principles". The seventh Duke comes off rather better than some of his predecessors: Cannadine describes him as "a pious and high-minded Victorian nobleman" and Jenkins strikes the same note in saying that he "was probably the one with the highest sense of public service" (D. Cannadine: *Aspects of the Aristocracy* Yale University Press (1994) and R. Jenkins: The *Chancellors*, Macmillan (1998)). However, like his less 'high-minded' ancestors, he found it necessary to sell off various family lands and heirlooms in order to keep going. In the light of this strained financial situation and the fact that Georgiana was one of ten children it seems highly unlikely that any marriage settlement would have been generous. One of Georgiana's brothers was Lord Randolph Churchill which means that his son, Winston Churchill, and Francis Howe were first cousins.

From the nineteenth century to the twentieth – declining family fortunes?

In the 1880s an assessment of U.K. land-holding calculated that Earl Howe owned 33,699 acres generating an income of £37,032. Nearly two-thirds of this land was in Nottinghamshire or Leicestershire but there were also significant holdings in Buckinghamshire and Suffolk (approaching 5000 acres in each case). The remaining land was spread around Cheshire, Derbyshire, Essex and Warwickshire with very minor acreage in Kent, Flintshire and Worcestershire (John Bateman: *The Great Landowners of Great Britain and Ireland*, 1884). One of the important limitations of this data is that it excludes metropolitan (i.e. London) land and Earl Howe certainly owned land in London including Curzon House in Mayfair and some adjacent property in Curzon Street.

While the Howe land and its accompanying income were substantial many other aristocratic and landed families had much bigger land-holdings and correspondingly higher incomes. Using Bateman's data David Cannadine lists the forty wealthiest landowners in the 1880s all of whom had land with a gross annual value of £60,000 or more, considerably in excess of Howe's £37,000 (D. Cannadine: *Aspects of the Aristocracy*, Yale University Press (1994)).

Obviously the significance of any income depends upon what it has to support. If there is an expansive life-style and a number of different houses to maintain, or if there are major extensions or adaptations to these houses even a large income will be quickly absorbed. In the case of the Howe family the first Earl spent money on building and restoring churches, the third and fourth Earls on extending or modernising their properties. In 1901 Gopsall Hall and some of its estate properties were converted to electricity which cost £4400.

Gopsall Hall, Leicestershire – Francis Curzon's childhood home was Gopsall Hall, near Market Bosworth in Leicestershire. The Howe family sold the estate in 1919 and the hall was eventually demolished in 1952. *Image courtesy of Leicestershire Record Office.*

Gopsall Hall in Leicestershire replaced the Howe's previous principal residence which was Langar House in south-east Nottinghamshire. Langar's purchase had been facilitated by Scrope Howe's father marrying a wealthy heiress and from the latter years of the seventeenth century and throughout the eighteenth the Howes lived there. Admiral Howe, the victor of the 'Glorious First of June', was buried in Langar parish church when he died in 1799 (though he had mostly lived elsewhere) as his father and grandfather had been before him.

From the early years of the nineteenth century until the end of the First World War family life was centred on Gopsall. Francis would certainly have been familiar with this house and the surrounding countryside during his childhood and adolescence. The estate was on the borders of Leicestershire and Warwickshire, close to the villages of Twycross and Congerstone which are about five miles north of Atherstone, a small town lying directly on Watling Street only a short distance before that Roman road turns decisively southwards.

The parish church in Twycross has a celebrated east window which "is worth a pilgrimage of many miles" (N. Pevsner: *The Buildings of England: Leicestershire and Rutland* (1960)). The window contains thirteenth century French glass acquired by George III during the French Revolution and given to the first Earl Howe by William IV, one of George III's sons. Howe arranged for the glass to be installed in the church in 1840. The first Earl and his second wife are buried in the church's graveyard but most of their descendants have been buried at Penn Street, the village where Penn House is situated and which became the main family residence after Gopsall was sold in 1918.

Gopsall was bought by Samuel Waring, a member of the Waring and Gillow furniture firm, who was created Lord Waring in 1922. During Lord Waring's ownership one of the Gopsall roads was used for some speed trials in the mid and late 1920s. Francis Howe's name has sometimes been associated with these events but the connection is spurious, though understandable given Howe's keenness to develop new venues for motor sport and that Gopsall was his family home until 1918. The house at Gopsall subsequently passed to the Crown Estates: it was occupied by troops during the Second World War and badly treated. It was pulled down in the early 1950s and few visible links remain with the Howe family beyond the church graves and the village pub in Twycross (still called *The Curzon Arms*).

Penn House in Buckinghamshire is a brick building of seventeenth century origins which was substantially reduced in size during the middle of the eighteenth century, although enlarged again by the third Earl in 1880. On a spur to the south of the house Admiral Howe's mainmast was preserved for many years and his flag flown every 1st June to commemorate his victory. After the Gopsall estate was sold the Penn House estate was the only remaining country house of the Howe family. The fourth Earl did have a house called Woodlands at Uxbridge but this was not retained after his death in 1929.

Penn House is situated to the south of Penn Street village. The first Earl paid for a new church, Holy Trinity, in this village which was completed in 1849. Various aspects of the church's furnishings reflect its close association with the Howe family, for example much of the church's woodwork was brought from the chapel at Gopsall when that estate was sold, Admiral Howe's flag at the 'Glorious First of June' is displayed in the chancel and there is a memorial to Francis' mother, Georgiana, in the churchyard.

The main Howe London residence was Curzon House, a substantial residence occupying nearly 11,000 square feet and containing twenty bedrooms, nine reception rooms (including a very large ballroom) and various accompanying buildings for cars, horses and servants. At the beginning of 1931 Francis Howe instructed the property agents, John D. Wood, to sell the house. Some London property was retained and Francis had a base for the remainder of his life at different houses in Curzon Street. In 1935 John D. Wood were engaged again to handle the sale of nearly 1000 acres of land between Beaconsfield and Penn which involved existing cottages in surrounding villages as well as land on which to build new properties.

These decisions to sell the Gopsall estate, Curzon House and land around Penn are examples of a general twentieth century trend which can be dramatised as the 'Decline and Fall of the British Aristocracy' (the actual title of a book by David Cannadine). This decline has a number of dimensions – economic, political and social – and, as with all general developments, there are many variations in the way it has worked out for each aristocratic family. Some of the underlying dynamics are well established, for example the impact of the agricultural depression in the late nineteenth century, the taxation system – especially taxes levied at death, the rising cost of labour, and the extension of mass democracy coupled with increasing restrictions on the role of the House of Lords.

To assess precisely how these various developments impacted on the Howe family a good deal of information would be needed which is not readily available. But the property disposals outlined above indicate clearly the general direction in which things were moving and this pattern has continued into the second half of the twentieth century.

Francis Howe and his background: how much impact?

When Francis Howe was born in 1884 his own place and that of his family appeared to be secure. As the eldest son of Viscount Curzon he was more or less certain to succeed to the Earldom in due course. While the Howe family were not among the richest aristocrats they had substantial land-holdings which yielded an assured income that removed any need to earn money from a trade or occupation. Although the forces weakening the aristocracy's position were certainly at work during Francis' youth and adolescence he reached adulthood before their impact was fully visible.

If Francis had wanted to lead a very similar life to that of his grandfather and father it would have been difficult, if not impossible. The economic base simply didn't exist and some degree of retrenchment would have been needed, whatever his own preferences. In practice his life did demonstrate some powerful elements of continuity but it was also characterised by strong elements of innovation and breaking with family tradition.

His interest in ships and the sea, especially his service in the Royal Naval Volunteer Reserve (R.N.V.R.), was one obvious element of family tradition that he absorbed and which became one of the dominant themes in his life. It is true that in purely quantitive terms military rather than naval

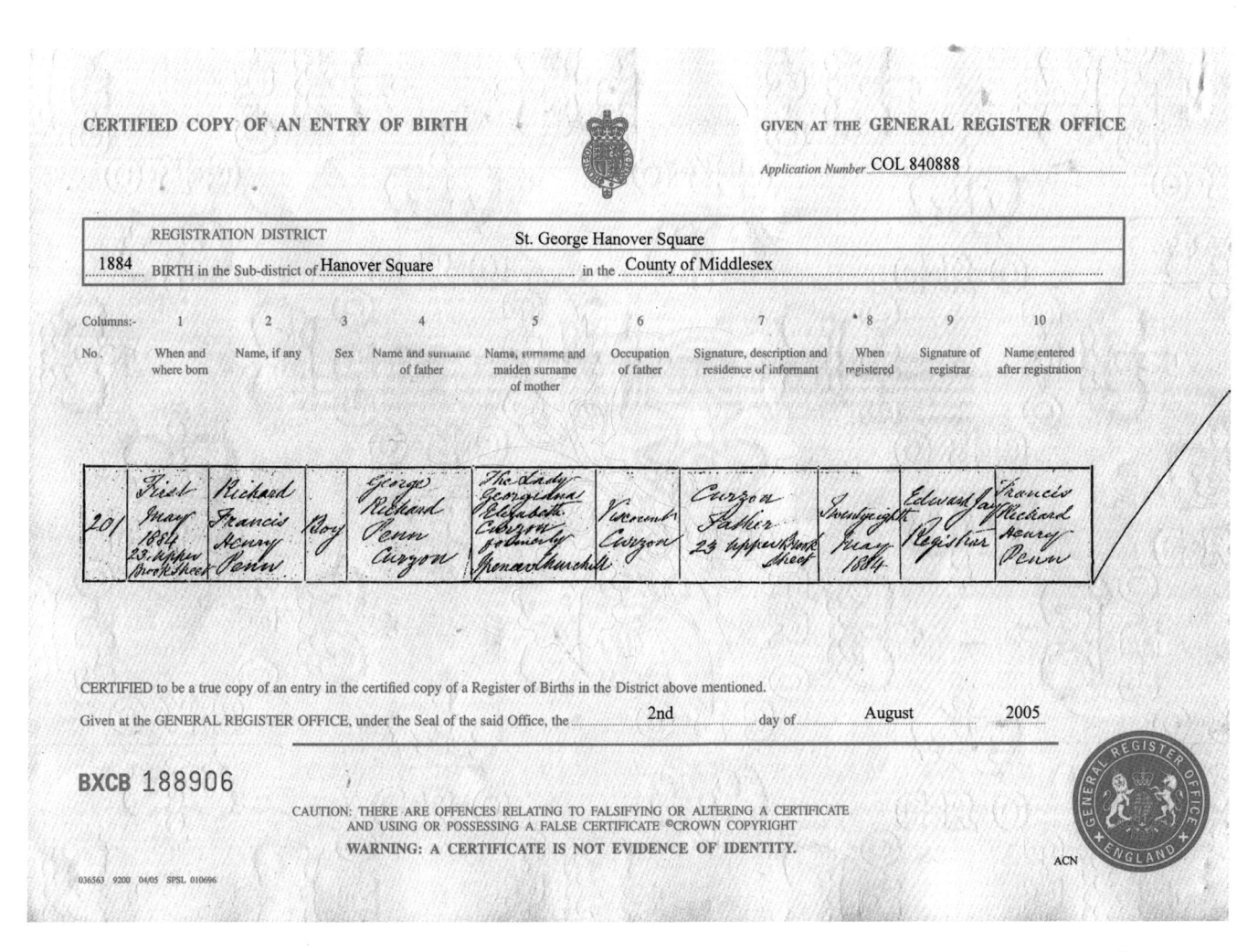

1884 – London – Francis Curzon's birth certificate showing his birth on 1st May, 1884, at 23, Upper Brook Street, Mayfair.
Photograph courtesy of Adam Ferrington Collection

connections predominate but Admiral Howe of the 'Glorious First of June' exerted a powerful hold on his imagination and there was also his great-uncle, Admiral Assheton Howe, who provided another example of a life devoted to the sea.

The pursuit of politics was another family tradition and one that Francis enthusiastically embraced with an energetic career as a Member of Parliament for ten years followed by regular attendance in the House of Lords until the end of his life. Like his father he was also involved in party organisation outside parliament by seeking to maintain Conservative support in London in a period when the full impact of universal suffrage was first experienced.

If the sea and politics were two central themes in Francis' life, the third and probably most important was the motor car. In this respect he was unquestionably pursuing a theme that had no family precedent. In part this had to be the case because the motor car was a late nineteenth century invention. It would have been possible for Francis' father to take up this cause in his thirties or forties but there is no evidence that he showed any such inclination. If he had done so, he would have been unusual and atypical of his class. Though a few members of the aristocracy did become strong advocates of the 'automobile' they were very much a minority. Far more common was indifference or outright hostility – the car often being seen as a disruptive force in society.

Francis however embraced the car from his youth and it remained an abiding passion for the rest of his life. It was not only a life-long love affair but very comprehensive in its nature. He owned many different cars both for road and racing; he served on the committees of numerous different clubs and organisations concerned with furthering the car on road and track; and he used his political position in both the Commons and the Lords to further the interests of the car producer and the car user.

Francis had no interest in horse-racing or the life of a courtier, both of which were important to his father. Nor was he committed to the life of the landed aristocrat, concerned with maintaining and preserving his estate and using it for traditional activities such as hunting and shooting. He could see the point of preserving pictures or artefacts which memorialised his ancestor Admiral Howe but was prepared to use much of the remainder to pursue his major passions such as motors and motor sport. Of course there may have been an element of making a virtue out of a necessity – if he *had* been committed to the idea of the aristocratic estate he would still

have had to rationalise it in order to cope with the changing external world. Recognising this necessity may have reinforced his own preferences which were to mobilise what remained of his inheritance in the pursuit of what interested him most.

Early life and education

We have argued that in trying to make sense of an individual's character and personality family background is very important no matter whether 'heredity' or 'environment' is emphasised. As we have seen, Francis was born into an established aristocratic family with substantial wealth through land ownership. When Francis' father registered his son's birth he filled in the 'Occupation' category on the registration form with 'Viscount Curzon'. Equally, as outlined above, Francis' father did not simply rest on his inherited laurels but was both a politician and a courtier. Previous generations had also filled various political and service roles of which Francis would certainly have become aware through childhood and adolescence.

But however important social and economic background is in understanding individuals modern biography is at least as concerned with the 'psychological' dimension. This approach involves focusing much more closely on the dynamics of the immediate family within which individuals develop. However, it is a potential minefield strewn with competing theories and frequently with data that is partial – in every sense of the word. Francis left no first-hand testimony about his family experience and all those who participated in, or were witnesses of his childhood, have long since died.

Something could be made of the fact that he was an only child – an unusual experience in a Victorian family. There would have been no competition with any siblings for his parents' affections; equally he would have been the sole focus for any hopes or ambitions they had for a child. Of course it has to be remembered that in aristocratic families relations between parents and children, especially in the early years, were formally structured with much responsibility for early upbringing delegated to household staff – nannies, governesses and the like. But such staff would have been well aware that from birth Francis was destined to inherit the Earldom and would have behaved accordingly.

As an adult Francis undoubtedly had some clear character traits – for example, he was both decisive and determined: there's little sign that he found it

Background and Beginnings

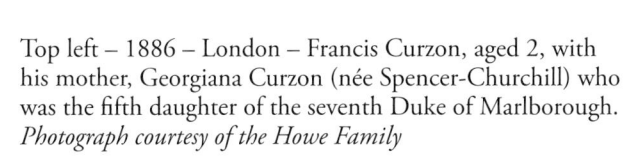

Top left – 1886 – London – Francis Curzon, aged 2, with his mother, Georgiana Curzon (née Spencer-Churchill) who was the fifth daughter of the seventh Duke of Marlborough. *Photograph courtesy of the Howe Family*

Top right – 1897 – London – Francis Curzon, aged 13, dressed in an Eton collar. *Photograph courtesy of the Howe Family*

Right – c1900 – London – Francis Curzon, aged about 18, in a portrait taken by Lafayette. *Photograph by Lafayette, courtesy of National Portrait Gallery*

9

1905 – Gopsall Hall, Leicestershire – A family group at Francis Curzon's Coming of Age festivities on 4th September, 1905. Francis is seated in the middle front, flanked by his father, George Curzon, to the left and his mother, Georgiana, to the right. *Photograph courtesy of the Howe Family*

difficult to make up his mind and once he had done so he pushed his case hard. Sammy Davis, who knew Francis well over a long period, said that he could be obstinate. All of this might be expected of a child who has only had to consider his own interests and desires and who would be customarily deferred to by many of those around him, conscious of his position and future status. Francis clearly had plenty of 'self-worth', his dress and attire – the carnation, the raked cap, the ebony cigarette-holder – demonstrated this aspect of his personality and it seems unlikely that this was some adult carapace, much more that it was an outcome of childhood certainties which powerfully shaped his adult persona.

Many references are made to his 'gentlemanly' behaviour both on and off the racing track. He was the product of an Eton education, a school well-known for emphasising such conduct. Of course many of its pupils are from rich and/or aristocratic backgrounds which provide them with an assurance about their own position in society. The corollary of their privileged position is expressed through a stress on notions of 'responsibility' and 'decency' – suggesting various appropriate ways in which to conduct themselves both socially and personally.

Francis' Eton education was followed by Christ Church Oxford, though only for a brief while. He began there in October 1903 but by the end of the academic year, in June 1904, he had left. At the beginning of the twentieth century Oxford's entry standards were fairly relaxed – some Latin and maths and a scattering of a modern language sufficed. But all students had to reach a satisfactory standard in 'Responsions' – Oxford's system of first year examinations. We don't know whether Francis failed this test or simply decided he wasn't sufficiently interested in his studies to pursue them for two further years. At that time attendance without graduating was quite common among aristocratic students.

His naval interests may have played a part. Family lore says that he would have liked to join the Royal Navy but had suffered some illnesses during childhood and adolescence which cast doubt on his suitability for such a career. As the next chapter details, an acceptable substitute presented itself in 1903 with the foundation of the Royal Naval Volunteer Reserve.

Background and Beginnings

Top left – 1928 – London – Francis Howe's first wife, Mary (née Curzon) to whom he was married for almost thirty years, from October 1907 to July 1936. *Photograph by Bassano, courtesy of National Portrait Gallery*

Top right – 1939 – London – Francis Howe's second wife, Joyce Mary Mclean (née Jack) to whom he was married from October 1937 to 1943. *Photograph by Bassano, courtesy of National Portrait Gallery*

Below – 1946 – London – Francis Howe's third wife, Sybil Boyter (née Johnson) to whom he was married from February 1944 to until his death in 1964. Francis Howe's second and third daughters Lady Frances Esmé Curzon and Lady Sarah-Marguerite (Sally) Curzon are pictured first and third from the left respectively, along with Countess Howe's two children from her previous marriage. *Photograph by Bassano, courtesy of National Portrait Gallery*

11

Although the formal demands this new force made on its recruits were modest, they could choose to devote far more time to it. Francis was an early recruit initially joining the London Division in 1904 and then later transferring to the Sussex Division.

Early motoring experience

Obviously given the centrality of the 'automobile' to his adult life it would be helpful to know how this involvement was initially sparked. However there is frustratingly little detail: Francis himself said that he worked as a mechanic in France before the turn of the century on cars using the hot tube form of ignition. He could not have been more than fourteen or fifteen and what exactly he was doing in France and what being a 'mechanic' meant are far from clear.

Neither do we know when he first saw some form of competitive motor sport. When he was elected to the House of Commons in December 1918 he was already known as a motor enthusiast but it was nearly ten years before he began motor racing himself. We know that he was present as a spectator at various events in the 1920s both at home and abroad. Following the unfortunate incident at Kop hill climb in 1925 Francis wrote a letter to *The Times* based on what he had seen; equally he was a spectator at a number of Mille Miglias as well.

A possible reason for his delayed entry to motor sport was the demands of his political career. As chapter three details, Francis was an extremely active back-bench M.P. up to October 1924 when he became an assistant whip. He was just as busy in this new role although his efforts were now directed at organising and mobilising Conservative M.P.s behind the scenes rather than speaking publicly in the Commons.

One oft-repeated account of his entry to motor sport attributes it to a magistrate before whom he was summonsed for breaking the speed limit. Francis accumulated numerous such convictions during the 1920s and lost his licence for six months in April 1924. Unsurprisingly these successive infringements attracted political and media publicity and some Labour M.P.s attacked his credibility as a law-maker when he was so frequently convicted of breaking the law. The magistrate, doubtless seeking to be helpful, suggested he should satisfy his speed instincts on the track rather than the public highway.

However, this explanation for his motor sport career seems highly dubious. A long time before his own debut Francis was fully aware of motor sport, with no need of a magistrate to guide him in that direction. It's possible that there was some family resistance though no evidence of it. His modest start in motor racing, in May 1928, came while his father was still alive. His father's death at the beginning of 1929 did result in two significant changes in Francis' life: it was the end of his career as an M.P. and his accession to the Earldom gave him full control of the family finances. As chapter four details, once he had embarked on motor sport he progressively increased his involvement. Before we turn to look at his motor racing it is necessary to say something briefly about his family and personal life.

Family and personal life

Francis married a cousin, Mary, in October 1907. Their cousinhood was slightly complicated as the first Earl Howe married twice, Francis descending from his first wife, Mary from his second. As already recounted Francis was a great grandson of the first Earl whose first wife bore him seven sons and died in 1836. The first Earl then married for a second time in 1845 and there were two further sons from this marriage, the elder of which, Colonel Montagu Curzon was Mary's father. As Montagu didn't marry until he was forty, in 1886, Mary was a granddaughter of the first Earl unlike her future husband who was a fourth generation descendant. Mary's mother was the youngest daughter of the eighth Duke of Grafton.

Mary Curzon, born in 1887, was a renowned beauty; on her death in 1962 she was described as one of the 'last legendary beauties of the first half of the twentieth century' and her obituarist recalled that Lady Cynthia Asquith similarly described her as "manifestly, indisputably beautiful" (*The Times*, 11th September, 1962). This reputation resonated through successive generations: when the noted diarist James Lees-Milne met one of her grandchildren in the mid-1980s he recorded "Mary Keen charming, with her young face and greying hair; her grandmother Lady Howe and Aunt Georgie were both beauties" (James Lees-Milne: *Beneath a Waning Moon, Diaries 1985-1987* (2003)). 'Georgie' (Georgiana) was Mary and Francis' second child, born in 1910; their first child, and Francis' heir, was Richard, born in 1908,

Francis and Mary were married for nearly thirty years before Mary was granted a divorce in July 1936. Francis had become involved with a South African lady, Joyce Mary Mclean Jack, who he met during his first trip to race in South Africa during the winter of 1935/6. Miss Jack, the daughter of Charles Mclean Jack, a mining commissioner at Klerksdorp, was 23 when she became Francis' second wife in a civil ceremony in Johannesburg in February 1937, a week after the Rand Grand Prix. A daughter, Frances Esmé, was born in June 1939.

Just prior to Francis and Mary's divorce both their children had married – Richard in July 1935 to Miss Patricia Weigall, daughter of Sir Archibald Weigall Bt. a career soldier, and Georgiana four months later to Home Kidston, the younger brother of Glen Kidston, one of the 'Bentley Boys' who had lost his life in an aeroplane accident in 1931.

During the Second World War Howe family relationships were in considerable turmoil. Francis' marriage to Joyce collapsed as did those of both his children, with all three divorcing during 1943. Equally they all subsequently re-married: Francis in 1944, Richard in 1946, and Georgiana in 1957. Francis' third marriage was another union not short of legal and financial complications at its outset. Francis' third wife was Sybil Boyter Johnson, daughter of Captain Francis Johnson R.N., who had married Major Ernest Shafto in 1939 and therefore a further divorce was necessary before she was free to marry Francis.

Francis and Sybil had one child, a daughter christened Sarah-Marguerite but always known as Sally. At the age of 21 she married Piers Courage a scion of the brewing dynasty but in the 1960s rapidly establishing himself as a front-line racing driver. Their marriage ended in June 1970 when Piers Courage was killed while competing at Zandvoort. Two sons had been born, Jason in 1967 and Amos in 1969. Jason began a career in motor sport which showed some promise but at the age of 28 he was the innocent party in a catastrophic accident in central London. He recovered sufficiently to live independently but further front-line motor sport was not possible.

2

Naval Man

- Francis Howe and the R.N.V.R.
- The R.N.V.R. in World War One and the Royal Naval Division controversy
- Pursuing naval politics in the House of Commons
- Francis Howe and the Royal National Lifeboat Institution

Chapter 2

Naval Man

In the late 1930s Howe's son, Viscount Curzon, asked him why he didn't write a book about his many adventures. Howe said that he hadn't got the time besides which "it's too mixed up with the navy" (*Old Motor*, September, 1981). This response may have been, as his son thought, "slightly mysterious" but there is no doubt that the sea and ships was an important thread running through the greater part of Francis Howe's life.

As chapter one has indicated, the services were a strong aspect of his family background and the naval strand especially prominent with the example of Admiral Howe during the Napoleonic wars. Francis' attachment to this aspect of family tradition was shown in his R.N.V.R. career, his pursuit of naval and defence issues throughout his parliamentary life and his involvement with the Royal National Lifeboat Institution (R.N.L.I.) each of which will be considered in turn.

Francis Howe and the R.N.V.R.

The Royal Naval Volunteer Reserve (henceforth R.N.V.R.) was formed in 1903. Like many ostensibly new institutions it did not come out of the blue. Various attempts at constructing a naval reserve body had been made in the nineteenth century and one called the Royal Naval Reserve (R.N.R.) was already in existence in 1903. However the R.N.R. was designed for merchant seaman who could be speedily mobilised in the event of a war or similar emergency. The R.N.V.R., by contrast, was aimed at those who were in civilian employment but were willing to undertake some naval training. At a broader level the R.N.V.R.'s launch was part of a general set of developments aimed at strengthening British naval forces whose previous dominance was under threat from other countries, Imperial Germany in particular.

Initially the demands made on recruits to the R.N.V.R. were modest – they had to commit to three years service with a minimum of forty hours training in the first year followed by twenty-four in each of the next two years. Furthermore, although they were encouraged to serve at sea with the fleet for two weeks a year to begin with it wasn't compulsory. In practice however to win acceptance, especially from the Royal Navy itself, "it was soon made plain to them that to become efficient, the official minimum level of drills was quite inadequate: in reality they would have to put in much more time – and they did. Records show that many put in an average of over ninety drills (*i.e. hours*) a year, and in some exceptional cases, anything up to 300" (Stephen Howarth: *The Royal Navy's Reserves in Peace and War*, Leo Cooper (2003)).

Even with such levels of commitment it took a few years for the R.N.V.R. to overcome the doubts among some regular R.N. officers about its seriousness. Howarth considers that such scepticism had been largely dispelled by 1910 as by then many R.N.V.R. personnel had worked alongside R.N. officers and men both ashore and afloat (Howarth: *ibid*). It was this face-to-face contact rather than high-level political or Admiralty blessing that was

c1940 – Leith, Midlothian – Howe poses in his R.N.V.R. uniform outside the Old Ship Hotel and King's Landing at Leith, with his wartime transport – a FIAT Topolino complete with headlamps adapted for the blackout. *Photograph courtesy of the Howe Family*

crucial in establishing the R.N.V.R.'s legitimacy. By the start of the First World War in 1914 it had grown to more than 30,000 officers and men.

Francis Howe initially joined the London Division of the R.N.V.R. in 1904 transferring to the command of the Sussex Division in 1907. The Sussex Division began life as a sub-unit of the London organisation but operated independently from April 1904. When the First World War began the R.N.V.R. Divisions ceased to exist and were not fully reinstated until two or even three years after the Armistice. Once re-established, Francis was actively involved with the Sussex Division until the outbreak of the Second World War. When the events of the Munich Crisis coincided with the original scheduled date of the 1938 Donington Grand Prix Francis had to scratch due to the need to join his ship at Portsmouth (reported in *The Sporting Life* and cited in Christopher Hilton: *Hitler's Grands Prix in England* (1999)). In addition to his role in the Sussex Division Francis held the post of Commodore of the R.N.V.R. from 1933-1942 by which time he was the R.N.V.R.'s longest-serving Commodore. When the Second World War ended Francis was over 60 and did not take part in any of the R.N.V.R.'s post-war work. It survived as an independent organisation until 1958 when it was merged with other naval reserve forces as part of the rationalisation of defence arrangements in the late 1950s.

Francis Howe – Motor Man Par Excellence

1943 – London – Howe in his R.N.V.R. uniform in a portrait taken subsequent to his retirement as Commodore of the Royal Naval Volunteer Reserve in 1942. *Photograph by Bassano, courtesy of National Portrait Gallery*

The R.N.V.R. in World War One and the Royal Naval Division controversy

Those serving in the R.N.V.R. did so because they were interested in ships and the sea and they expected that if war came that they would serve alongside officers and men in the Royal Navy. Although this is what many did experience there were a significant number who found they were fighting on land – effectively in the role of soldiers rather than seamen. In the earliest stages of the war Francis Howe was one of these and the decision to deploy R.N.V.R. personnel in such a manner initiated a long-running controversy.

The controversy surrounded both the creation and the deployment of what was known as the Royal Naval Division. The origins of this force lay in work done by the Committee of Imperial Defence, a key planning body set up in 1904 and consisting of senior politicians, civil servants and service personnel. It had produced plans in 1912 for a Royal Marines

Above and following page – 1918 – Scapa Flow, Orkney Isles – Howe films the surrender of the seventy-four ships of the German Hochseeflotte (High Seas Fleet) on 21st November, 1918. At this point he was an assistant gunnery officer on the battleship *H.M.S. Queen Elizabeth*. However these photographs clearly indicate that he was acting as cinematographer at this event, and it is not entirely clear in exactly what capacity he was present at this historic event. Howe was demobilized a few weeks later, at the end of 1918. The German fleet was subsequently scuttled in Scapa Flow on 21st June, 1919. *Photographs by A.R. Coster, courtesy of Getty Images*

type force "to seize, fortify or protect temporary naval bases necessary to the use of the fleet or the provisioning of any army" (Gordon Taylor: *London's Navy, A story of the Royal Naval Volunteer Reserve*, Quiller Press, London (1983)). However it is not clear at what stage the idea of drafting considerable numbers from the R.N.V.R. into this force arose.

The fact of the matter was that a few days after the outbreak of the war Francis, together with the commander of the R.N.V.R.'s London Division, were summoned by the First Lord of the Admiralty – Winston Churchill – to be told that the R.N.D. was to be established with many R.N.V.R. personnel seconded to it. The London Division commander thought Churchill wanted him to endorse this plan but "I am afraid I said I thought it rotten" (quoted in Taylor: *ibid.*). Many years later Francis maintained that the R.N.V.R. personnel transferred to the R.N.D. were effectively the only conscripts in the British forces at this stage of the war and that a corps less loyal "might not have stopped at deep and bitter cursing" (Taylor: *ibid*). In a similar retrospective article Francis said the deployment of R.N.V.R. personnel to the R.N.D. was a "retrograde step" that "has never been justified" (quoted in Howarth: *op. cit.*).

Churchill was the central political figure of the time and some months before the war started he had expressed doubts about whether it would be possible to absorb the whole of the R.N.V.R. into the Royal Navy in the early stages of any war given their lack of sea training and experience. But Churchill's contribution did not stop at the creation of the Royal Naval Division; he also took the decision to deploy it in October 1914. It was despatched to Belgium to thwart the German advance which was threatening the important port of Antwerp. A battle was fought in which sixty R.N.D. officers and men were killed, 138 injured and a large number of the remainder were captured or interned.

The action was unpopular at home and Churchill was criticised for pursuing "a bold strategy with inadequate means" (A.J.P. Taylor: *English History 1914-1945*, Oxford (1965)). Nonetheless the action is judged to have had an important impact in deflecting the German advance to the sea and re-directing it inland. Whatever Francis Howe's reservations about the involvement of the R.N.V.R. in the R.N.D. he had no doubt that the Antwerp expedition was a success and spoke publicly in those terms more than fifteen years later when presiding over a re-union of the R.N.V.R. at which Churchill was a guest (*The Times*, 17th November, 1930).

Francis himself did not remain for very long in the R.N.D. On 7th December, 1914 he joined the battleship *H.M.S. Queen Elizabeth* as assistant gunnery officer and continued there until his demobilisation just after the 1918 General Election.

Pursuing naval politics in the House of Commons

By the time Francis entered the Commons he had extensive experience of naval life: ten years of peacetime activity in the R.N.V.R. and then, with the outbreak of war, brief service in the R.N.D. followed by nearly four years as a gunnery officer. With that background it was hardly surprising that various forms of 'naval politics' was a major area of interest for him as an M.P. and it remained one of his central concerns when he moved to the House of Lords in 1929.

Francis Howe and the Royal National Lifeboat Institution

This was another organisation with which Francis Howe was involved for a very long period. He joined its Committee of Management in the immediate aftermath of the First World War and had an active association with it for the remainder of his life. In 1931 he took up the role of Deputy Treasurer (a post he held until 1947) and the following year, 1932, became Chairman of the General Purposes and Publicity Committee. This chairmanship was held until 1956 when he was made overall Chairman of the R.N.L.I. Ill health obliged him to relinquish this post in 1964 and the R.N.L.I., which had made him a Vice-President in 1936, created a special post of 'Chairman for Life' which as it turned out he only held for the few months preceding his death in July 1964.

3

Political Man

THE HOUSE OF COMMONS
- Getting elected – and re-elected – as M.P. for Battersea South
- Francis Howe as an M.P. – the active back-bencher
- Francis Howe's parliamentary causes
- Francis Howe as a party whip

THE HOUSE OF LORDS
- Francis Howe's activity in the Lords

ORGANISING FOR THE CONSERVATIVE PARTY

THE POLITICS OF MOTORING
- The basis of motoring politics
- The key issues in motoring politics in the first half of the twentieth century
- Paying for the roads
- The road network and the problem of parking
- Why accidents occur and how to avoid them
- What did he achieve?

Chapter 3

Political Man

As was made clear in the first chapter 'politics' in various shapes and forms was one of the three central strands running through Francis' public life. The main elements involved were his ten years as M.P. for South Battersea (1918-1929) followed by membership of the House of Lords for the remainder of his life. There was also a brief but important period from the late 1920s until the early 1930s when he was active in the Conservative Party's organisation.

Although Francis spoke on a variety of topics, especially when he was first in the Commons, his major long-term concern was motoring policy. Whether measured by the number of speeches or by his extensive involvement in the detailed amendment of legislation there is no doubt that motors and motoring was his dominant policy preoccupation. Accordingly the discussion that follows falls into four main parts: his career as an M.P.; his life in the Lords; his role in the organisation of the Conservative Party and finally his contribution to motoring policy.

THE HOUSE OF COMMONS

Getting elected – and re-elected – as M.P. for Battersea South

There must have been some degree of patronage or influence to promote Francis' adoption as the parliamentary candidate for South Battersea. He did little or no canvassing as he was still on active service right up to polling day itself. The December 1918 contest, often dubbed the 'coupon' election, was fought in unusual circumstances – the war had barely ended and the coalition government endorsed (or issued a 'coupon') to approved candidates. The practical effect of the 'coupon' was to diminish greatly the normal party conflict in most constituencies as candidates endorsed by the coalition attracted the majority of Conservative and Liberal votes. This is what happened in Francis' case where he emerged with a majority of 12,287 – far larger than at his three subsequent contests when he had to campaign as a straightforward Tory candidate.

The early 1920s were a period of considerable turmoil in party politics with four general elections in less than six years. Following his initial success in 1918 this meant Francis had to defend his seat in three successive elections – 1922, 1923 and 1924. In 1923 the seat became very marginal as Francis' majority fell to 1118 votes. He suffered, as did many other Conservative candidates in this election, from the Conservative espousal of tariff reform, or what would these days be called import duties. Voters feared – women especially (according to *The Times*) – that tariffs meant dearer food and accordingly did not support Conservative candidates. Francis loyally took the party line in 1923 despite making it clear

1919 – London – Francis Curzon photographed in Naval uniform just after his election as Conservative Member of Parliament for South Battersea in December 1918. *Photograph by Walter Stoneman, courtesy of National Portrait Gallery*

that he was basically a free-trader "but it cannot be obtained under present conditions" (*The Times*, 29th November, 1923). When the 1924 election took place, only ten months later, the Conservatives had backed away from tariffs and Francis' majority recovered to just over 5000 votes.

Francis' campaigning was robust, never hesitating to take the fight to 'the enemy'. He was helped by the fact that in the neighbouring constituency of North Battersea a communist, Shapurji Saklatvala, stood as the Labour candidate at the 1922 election and then under the Communist Party's own colours in 1924. Francis saw little to distinguish Labourites and Communists and said that he was fighting "Socialism and Bolshevist doctrines" (*The Times, ibid.*). In May 1924 he took part in a debate with Saklatvala and a Liberal on the theme of 'The Socialist Government in Theory and Practice' during the course of which he said that the Labour government hadn't "put a single man or woman into work" and that "the Socialist Party is founded on misery and discontent" (*The Times*, 19th May, 1924).

Such verbal fisticuffs are one thing, physical violence a rather different matter. In the 1924 election campaign Francis had a meeting at a school in his constituency which was peaceful. However, when he emerged from the meeting he was met by 'a large crowd of hooligans'. A blow with a stick was aimed at him but actually hit one of his supporters who required medical attention. Francis' car was attacked and 'severely damaged' although he was still able to drive it away under police protection (*The Times*, 28th October, 1924).

Quite what occasioned this incident the report did not explain but some strong clues can be found in a remarkable Commons speech Francis made earlier in the year. He alleged that in the 1923 election campaign "my life and the life of my Liberal colleague (*the M.P. for North Battersea*) were directly threatened". He repeated this claim in even more emphatic terms at the end of his speech: "They would have taken the life of my Liberal colleague...if they could – they made no secret of it – and they would have had me too". Who were 'they'? Francis believed that "behind the forces of Labour such as we see represented on the benches in this House there are far more sinister forces ranged". He singled out two groups in particular – the first being the I.R.A. of which "there are in my constituency on the register no fewer that 1000 known members"; secondly there was a group of people "who are well known to be down and out who were going round with sums of £15 and £20 on them. Where did they get it?" (Commons, *Debates*, 17th January, 1924, cols. 373-6).

This speech was made only a few days before the first-ever Labour government took office. Although the heightened atmosphere this prospect generated might have led Francis to some exaggeration the attack on him during the 1924 election demonstrates that physical intimidation was an aspect of his constituency politics.

When Francis inherited the earldom there was a by-election to replace him in the Commons and the Conservatives lost the seat to Labour by 500 votes. Had Francis built up a personal vote which didn't transfer to his Conservative replacement? It's possible but the Conservatives had been losing votes and seats in virtually all by-elections between 1925 and 1929. Additionally the Conservative candidate at the by-election faced both Labour and Liberal opposition, unlike Francis who had straight fights with Labour in 1922-3-4.

Francis Howe as an M.P. – the active back-bencher

Once a candidate has fought a successful election and become an M.P. he has to carry out his parliamentary duties. But what exactly do those comprise? One crucial job is to support the party in the division lobbies even if the party 'line' is not wholly to one's liking. M.P.s also 'represent' their constituencies, for example if they contain a significant economic interest then the M.P. is expected to protect and promote it. Individually constituents have various encounters with the state as taxpayers, welfare recipients and so forth and when there are grievances M.P.s are expected to intervene. Constituents also have interests which are not located geographically – motoring would be one obvious example – and lobby or pressure groups seek out M.P.s and Peers to speak on their behalf. M.P.s respond to these demands in different ways. When first elected many are politically ambitious wanting to climb what Disraeli dubbed 'the greasy pole' and become ministers. Those less bothered about such matters will be more ready to veer away from the party 'line' and embrace unpopular causes.

How did Francis Howe spend his years in the Commons? The first thing to note is that he was extremely active: during six years as a back-bencher (1919-1924) he made nearly three thousand interventions, i.e. either by asking questions or contributing to debates. This high visibility came to an end in

October 1924 when he was appointed an Assistant Whip, his first step on the ministerial ladder, and a post he held until he was 'translated' to the Lords in January 1929. The tradition is that whips do not speak or only on a very limited basis and as they are bound by the convention of collective responsibility they must maintain the government's official line.

What sense can be made of Francis' intense activity during his six years as a back-bencher? Part of the answer is that it reflected his temperament – he was an activist anxious to play a full part in the work of the Commons which he was able to do because his assured income meant he didn't have the 'distraction' of an outside job. He was also active because he believed that for any problem there was always a clear solution; he did not suffer from philosophical doubt or hesitation.

It's likely, too, that he was ambitious, anxious to build a political career. His father had held minor office in both the Commons and the Lords an example which would have had some impact on his son. Another inescapable form of paternal influence was that on his father's death Francis' Commons career would cease so he knew that he didn't have unlimited time in which to make his mark.

Francis Howe's parliamentary causes

Some of the issues he concentrated on he pursued for the remainder of his parliamentary career – not just in the Commons but the Lords as well. The previous chapter has explored one important example – naval politics – and later in this chapter another key area – motoring politics – will be examined.

Other matters in which he was interested, such as the Irish settlement of the early 1920s and Indian self-government though not life-long preoccupations were the subject of considerable controversy at the time, not least within the Conservative Party itself. On both these issues Francis was on the right of the Conservative Party being fundamentally hostile to Lloyd-George's 1921 legislation partitioning Ireland and highly sceptical about any movement towards Indian self-government.

When a bill on Irish affairs was being debated in 1924 he recalled that he had "voted against the Treaty (*of 1921*) on every occasion that it was possible to record a vote against it. I voted against it because I did not believe that in any sense of the word did it contain the seeds of settlement between Northern and Southern Ireland" (Commons, *Debates*, 1st October, 1924, col. 176). He was echoing what he had said two and a half years earlier when he maintained that the 1921 Government of Ireland Act was "no settlement but only the seeds of future difficulties, and even war" (Commons, Debates, 8th March, 1922, cols. 1919-20). One could say Francis was being remarkably prescient insofar as four years after he died major conflict did begin in Ireland, albeit not in any simple sense between the 'North' and the 'South'.

On Indian affairs he found himself in a similar position to Irish policy, opposing the Lloyd George coalition government by voting against the Government of India Act in 1919, described by one historian as "generous in British eyes but slight to the Indians" (C.L. Mowat: *Britain Between the Wars*, Methuen (1955)). Francis Howe was certainly one of those who deemed it too generous and he was hostile to those anti-imperial, pro-nationalist forces who did indeed find the 1919 Act too 'slight'. Gandhi was prominent among the latter and Francis was asking critical questions about his activities in 1921 followed, three years later, but a strong attack in which he alleged Gandhi was "responsible for the loss of many hundreds of lives {*Honorary Members:* "No, No!"}"(Commons, *Debates*, 15th April, 1924, col. 1256). When he made that claim he had begun his speech by declaring that he would refrain from "passing any party remarks" but in fact he attacked various Labour ministers for their association with Gandhi and their sympathy for nationalist aspirations. He ended a highly combative speech by declaring that "whatever party is in power I hope it will assert and give effect to the principle that Great Britain will, in no circumstances, relinquish her responsibility to India" (Op. cit. col. 1265). In fact official policy throughout the inter-war period was engaged in doing precisely what Francis didn't want culminating in full independence in 1947. However the issue was a troubling one in the Conservative Party and Francis was involved at a later stage of his political career with some of the fall-out.

Francis Howe as a party whip

There are two important requirements for a party whip, firstly personal acceptability to parliamentary colleagues and secondly a capacity for sustained hard work. The first quality is important because a key component of the whips' job is to act as a two-way channel of communication: ministers expect the whips to explain and justify current government policy and back-benchers want the whips to make clear to ministers where their policies are inadequate.

'Selling' government policy may not always be easy and whips therefore need to be people who are at least respected and, if possible, liked. Equally when back-benchers have doubts about a minister and a department they need to feel their anxieties will be taken seriously. Being a whip is emphatically not a sinecure but requires a commitment to constant activity.

The hard work demanded of a whip would not have been a problem for Francis whose assiduous activity as a back-bencher has been noted. Francis did have strong opinions on certain issues and these might have influenced his appointment, i.e. that he would be well regarded by fellow Tory M.P.s who shared such views. A more cynical interpretation would see his appointment as a way of diminishing his critical voice because a whip is very restricted in what he can say publicly. While not ignoring such considerations the main factor in his selection is likely to have been 'technical' or 'organisational' – could he be relied upon for the hard work of mobilising the government's majority when the votes were needed?

The work of the whips is a part of Parliament that is 'hidden', and therefore it is difficult to comment on how anybody undertakes it. At the broadest level he was a whip during a government that had a comfortable parliamentary majority and which did not face any major rebellions – actual or threatened – during its life. The General Strike occurred in May 1926 and although there were different opinions in the Conservative Party about how that should be handled and, in particular once it was over, how trade union law should be altered, these differences were relatively easily dealt with among Tory M.P.s.

THE HOUSE OF LORDS

Francis Howe succeeded his father as the fifth Earl Howe on 10th January 1929 and just over two weeks later he took his seat in the House of Lords. Some who inherit titles have little interest in politics and no wish to contribute to the work of the second chamber. At the other end of the spectrum there are a handful who have embarked on serious political careers in the Commons and resent being 'kicked upstairs'. Francis was obviously closer to the latter than the former group. The option to disclaim a peerage – and hence continue as an M.P. – lay more than thirty years in the future so Francis had to accept his fate.

For the majority of the time Francis was a member of the Lords it was in something of a political limbo. The 1911 Parliament Act had not only reduced its power but also indicated that there would be a further stage of reform to establish a popular rather than heredity basis for its membership. However although no such changes were actually made until 1958 when life peerages were introduced, the obvious supremacy of the Commons together with uncertainty about the ultimate status of the Lords did not make for a very attractive or compelling assembly. Lords attendances were quite small – in the 1940s it was calculated that out of a total membership of 800 only 100 were regular attenders. Once some significant reform did get under way the long-term impact, at least on attendance, was substantial: by the late 1980s the average attendance was 300 (Norton: *Does Parliament Matter?* (1993)).

Francis Howe's activity in the Lords

When Francis began his life in the Lords it was as a back-bench peer, a status he retained as he never held a government post or served as an official opposition spokesman. In some ways this is surprising given his ten years Commons experience including four years as an assistant whip. Governments always contain some ministers from the Lords and it incorporates a whipping system of approximately the same kind as the Commons. Why didn't he become a minister or serve in the Lords' whips' office?

As we don't have any direct evidence it is impossible to be sure but one or two factors are worth mentioning. He may not have wanted to be either a minister or an Opposition spokesman: his motor-racing activity increased markedly in 1931 when he bought the Delage and the Bugatti to compete in continental events. Even with the more relaxed Lords time-table it would have been very difficult to sustain both political office and motor sport. During the early and mid-1930s there was a form of coalition government, admittedly chiefly weighted to the Conservatives. Howe's robust Conservatism could have been a disqualification in a political climate where the emphasis was on softening party differences rather than heightening them. In the post-war period he would have been contending with younger peers and by the time the Conservatives returned to office in October 1951 he was 67 years old which might have gone against him.

As a back-bench peer there was decidedly no return to his behaviour as an M.P. between 1919 – 1924. In 1957 he recalled that when he had first come into the Lords he had been "strongly advised by everybody who knew about it never to open my mouth on a subject unless I knew something about it" (Lords, *Debates*, 2nd April, 1957). He said this in a debate about the development of nuclear power which, as he admitted, was *not* an area in which he could claim any expertise. But it was one of the few exceptions to his normal practice in the Lords which was to concentrate on areas he did know 'something about'.

The two broad areas to which he devoted most of his time were motoring policy and naval and defence issues. Francis' focus was sometimes very specific, on other occasions it ranged over broad principles. His contribution to motoring policy is examined later in this chapter and naval and defence matters have already been dealt with in Chapter 2.

Outside of these two areas Francis occasionally worked up a head of steam on other things, for example in the mid-1930s he was exercised about the crisis in Abyssinia and in the early 1950s he wanted the re-introduction of corporal punishment for violent crime. Francis was strongly pro-Italian, enthusiastic about the people and the motor sport they sustained and he had significant long-term friendships with Italians such as Giovanni Lurani. He did not want to see Britain drifting into conflict with Italy on the Abyssinian issue and was critical of policy that appeared to tolerate, or indeed encourage, such hostility.

His support for corporal punishment is a slight puzzle, not so much for the principle which many of his generation readily endorsed but for his *public* identification with the cause. He made no claim to "expert knowledge", declaring that he was speaking "simply as a member of the public". He thought the issue was "largely a question of theory *versus* realism and, if I may say so without offence, common sense". He had little or no sympathy with the view that "you can reform the gangster" on the contrary he believed "the gangster is a bully: that he looks upon any sign of leniency as a sign of weakness and will never be able to take his place in society until he has a dose of his own medicine" (Lords, *Debates*, 22nd October, 1952, cols. 840 and 912). As the Lord Chancellor made clear in his reply, Francis was not just arguing for a reversal of the 1948 Act but for a much wider discretion to be given to judges and magistrates to order corporal punishment for violent crime. Although there would have been some sympathy among the general public with Francis' views there was little parliamentary support and Francis only raised the issue on one further occasion, in 1957.

ORGANISING FOR THE CONSERVATIVE PARTY

Quite apart from his work in the South Battersea constituency party Francis took on some national roles within the Conservative Party. At the beginning of 1927 he became the London Whip to the Conservative and Unionist Central Office. Central Office's primary function was to maximise the Conservative vote at both local and general elections. When Francis' father was first elected to the Commons in 1885 five million people were entitled to vote; by 1918, when Francis was first elected, this had increased to twenty million. Faced with this massive increase political parties had to devote much greater resources – of time, money and personnel – to mobilising support. During Francis' time at Central Office the final major extension of voting took place in 1928 when all women under thirty were enfranchised adding another seven million voters to the electorate. During the 1920s it also became clear that the Labour Party was replacing the Liberals as the Conservative's main rival.

Before the First World War Central Office had been quite a small organisation but by 1928 there were 180 people working in its London headquarters and another sixty based in its regional outposts (always referred to as Area Offices). It was the London Area that was the focus of Francis' activities from his appointment in 1927 until he resigned his appointment in June 1932. When he gave up the job the Conservative leader Stanley Baldwin said that 'warm thanks' were due to him for the 'splendid work which he has done on behalf of the Party organisation in London, the efficiency of which is, in no small measure, due to his able direction' (*The Times*, 4th June, 1932). Following the Conservative defeat in the 1929 General Election the Conservatives had reviewed their Area machinery and Francis' work was transferred to party members in particular those on the Metropolitan Area Council.

Conservative Central Office has always worked closely with what is called the National Union which is the Conservative organisation for its rank and file membership. For the great majority of Tories belonging to the Party means belonging to a particular constituency party and working to sustain local councillors, a parliamentary candidate or an M.P. But the Party provides some machinery for the rank and file both at area and national level. The Party's Annual Conference is organised by the National Union and provides an opportunity for members to express their view about Party policy. There is also an annual meeting of the National Union's Central Council which is a smaller body than the Annual Conference but another opportunity for members to express their opinion. However most historians and political analysts have concluded that the views of the membership are not very influential in forming party policy, it's the parliamentary party and especially the leadership that carry most weight. Francis Howe was Chairman of the National Union from March 1932 to March 1933. One of the main tasks for the holder of that post is to chair the debates at the Party's annual conference and at the Central Council meeting.

The fact that Francis was anything but an 'ordinary' rank and file member of the Party is an example of how the Conservatives attempted to 'manage' rank and file opinion, using figures with considerable social and political status who would usually be sympathetic to the parliamentary and leadership point of view. However there are occasions when the parliamentary party, and indeed the leadership, is divided about issues and on these occasions the conflict can spill over into arguments among the ordinary members. One such example was the Indian issue, a topic already noted as troubling Francis Howe when he was an M.P.

The issue became highly controversial within the Party in the early 1930s and intertwined with the fate of its leader, Stanley Baldwin. Baldwin was in favour of Indian self-government but he faced significant opposition from other prominent Tories and from some rank and file members. At the 1934 Annual Conference Baldwin's policy was only just approved with a hostile amendment failing by only a few votes on a ballot (itself unusual and indicating the strength of feeling). The matter was then raised again at the Central Council meeting held a few weeks later when Baldwin's policy was approved by a much more generous margin.

Francis was among Baldwin's critics as he made clear in a speech just after the Central Council meeting. It was delivered in a Lords debate on proposals to move India in the self-governing direction. Francis said "It seems to me that to give a fully fledged Western democracy to such people with all the machinery of elections and everything else is simply to risk the most appalling disaster". He was highly sceptical about certain 'safeguards' that were built into the proposals recalling that similar arrangements had accompanied the Irish Treaty and that they had nearly all been swept aside: "Surely we ought to be warned by such an experience". Quite apart from the content of the proposals he was very unhappy that they had not been flagged up in any way in the 1931 general election: "The country…never understood and certainly never realised at the last General Election that if they returned a Government to deal with the urgent economic situation…that Government would be likely to deal with the question of India without consulting the electors". He certainly didn't accept that consulting the Conservatives' own Central Council had been an adequate substitute especially as he alleged it had been "carefully packed" (Lords, *Debates*, 17th December, 1934, cols. 478-482). He made it clear that he could not support the government and would vote in favour of the Marquess of Salisbury's critical amendment.

THE POLITICS OF MOTORING

The basis of motoring politics

Francis Howe's life spanned a transport revolution: when he was born motor vehicles were unknown in Britain but by the time of his death there were literally millions on the roads. It would have been amazing if this transformation had not aroused controversy. In fact almost with the first spark of the internal combustion engine 'motoring politics' was ignited. This 'politics' persisted throughout the twentieth century and shows no sign of diminishing in the twenty-first.

Politics and the motor car are inextricably interwoven because the motor car has very widespread consequences for the economy and society and there is disagreement about how these should be dealt with. It falls to politicians – both at national and local level – to settle many of these disagreements. Such 'settlements' are often temporary, after a few years old battles are re-fought or new ones arise, often as a result of changing technology. Politicians determine some very important and fundamental aspects of motoring – such as the law on the construction and use of vehicles and the design and upkeep of the roads. To fund such activities a variety of taxes are levied on motorists which provide a perpetual source of argument as to their type, level and incidence.

Although motoring politics is often an intense activity arousing strong feelings on all 'sides' these have rarely corresponded to conventional party divisions. In some ways this is surprising because for most of Francis' life the private car was an upper and middle class prerogative and it wasn't until 1970 that a majority of British households owned a car. Given what is known about party support that might have led the Conservatives to favour the car and Labour to oppose it. Although there are occasional echoes of this alignment motoring politics makes little sense viewed through this particular pair of spectacles.

Motoring politics in fact reflects a multitude of differences and distinctions. In theory motorists do have certain shared interests but in practice differences quickly arise when specific objectives have to be agreed upon, even more when it's necessary to formulate strategy and tactics to pursue these objectives. Francis Howe was a leading member of the R.A.C. which certainly thought of itself as representing the motorist but he didn't always support the R.A.C.'s position and neither did the R.A.C. and the A.A. always make common cause. There were frequent differences between the private motorist and those chiefly concerned with lorries and buses. Equally among those sceptical about the motor vehicle there was a wide range of opinion about how far it could, and should, co-exist with the environment, both natural and man-made.

The key issues in motoring politics in the first half of the twentieth century

During the time Francis Howe was in parliament, from 1918 until 1963, motoring politics was preoccupied with three main issues: how motoring was to be financed; the question of vehicle movement – especially the need for roads and for parking; and the problem of accidents. Before looking at Francis' attitude to these three areas it is useful to outline what was at issue in each case.

Motoring finance involved the two classic sides of the coin – how money was to be raised and how it was to be spent. On the revenue side British practice always involved some payment by vehicle-owners and some allocation from general taxation with endless debate about their relative contributions. On the spending side the arguments were about how any given sum should be allocated (e.g. building new roads or repairing existing ones) and who (i.e. which state body) should share it out. In 1909 the Liberal government had set up something called the Road Fund which contradicted the usual principle for British public finance of collecting all taxes, however levied or raised, in one large undifferentiated fund. The Road Fund, by contrast, collected all the money from vehicle duties, principally licence fees and petrol taxes, with the idea that the proceeds should be spent specifically on the roads.

However when Churchill was Chancellor of the Exchequer in the mid-1920s he carried out a 'raid' on the Road Fund by appropriating some of the accrued money for non-road expenditure. The Fund was finally abolished in 1937 but the underlying issue of whether the motorist was receiving a 'fair' share of public expenditure in return for the duties and taxes paid continued to resonate for many years after its abolition. These duties and taxes were also much argued over especially the 'horsepower tax', originally introduced in 1909 and further strengthened in 1920. It was the basis of the licence fee and the subject of much debate as to its impact on the design and performance of British cars.

The second basic issue, 'Vehicle movement', is rather a bland description for something that raised a great deal of passion. The growth in motor vehicles was never matched by the development of the road network or of parking provision. This was an area where the motoring and environmental lobbies conflicted most of the time, nearly always pulling in opposite directions. Because the growth in vehicles wasn't matched by a proportionate increase in roads and parking, both local and central government rationed the available space by increasing regulation. Inevitably there was continuing argument both about the lack of roads and parking and about the detail of regulation.

Road safety, or rather its absence, was the final major issue. Horse and carriage travel was not accident free but when the internal combustion engine replaced it there was a price to pay for its speed and convenience. It killed and injured not only drivers and passengers but pedestrians as well. The very rapid expansion of vehicles during the 1920s was accompanied by a steep rise in deaths and injuries – so much so that by 1934 over seven thousand were killed and more than a quarter of a million injured. As it turned out this was the peak year, these figures not reached again in peace-time until 1955 – by which time vehicle numbers had greatly increased. An important element in the two major Road Traffic Acts of 1930 and 1934 was measures aimed at making road travel less hazardous. This legislation may have helped to reduce accidents but it didn't significantly diminish parliamentary concern about road safety. Debates and inquiries continued for the remainder of the 1930s and were resumed again in the post-war years. Almost everyone agreed 'that something must be done' but there was far less agreement about just what that should be. In particular there were arguments about the role of speed in causing accidents (and therefore the relevance of speed limits), about the state of the roads, the respective responsibilities of motorists and pedestrians, about the definitions of 'careless' and 'dangerous' driving and the appropriate penalties for such offences.

Having outlined the three major areas of debate about motoring policy in the first half of the twentieth century we can now examine Francis' views on these issues.

Paying for the roads

Francis had no doubt whatever that more roads were needed and he was equally certain that they should not be paid for by specific taxes levied on the motorist as his references to 'soaking', 'milking' and 'fleecing the overtaxed motorist' demonstrate. In part therefore he was a straight-forward motoring lobbyist arguing that governments should spend far more money on roads – and that the money should come from general taxation. In 1934 he became President of a major pressure group the British Road Federation which, as its name suggests, was an umbrella group campaigning for new and improved roads. However, Francis was also a committed Conservative and the Party has always stressed that public spending is limited by what can be raised through taxes and borrowing. Francis attempted to reconcile these two imperatives in different ways. For example in the summer of 1939 he was urging the importance of new roads as an essential element of war preparation but even if war was avoided the country would still benefit "in increased transport facilities and a reduction of loss through congestion. Industry would be stimulated, the general yield of taxation would be increased and a disastrous toll of road accidents would be greatly reduced" (*The Autocar*, July, 1939). In effect he was arguing that any cost would be more than recouped by the economic stimulus provided by the construction and operation of the new roads.

He was attempting to put a Keynesian argument before such ideas had been fully accepted. Unfortunately even in the post-1945 period when they did come to guide economic policy, they weren't of much help to the road programme. In a situation where governments faced many demands on the public purse there were other priorities, at any rate until the late 1950s. In the early and mid-1950s Francis was drawn to the idea of a special loan fund and to toll roads as ways of raising money and he mooted the possibility of a National Roads Authority to take over the work of the Ministry of Transport. These ideas were all directed at raising additional funds for road expenditure and to prising the roads away from direct government control. Although Francis had some support from other peers in the Lords, mainstream parties and politicians showed little interest.

However, expenditure on roads did begin to rise appreciably from the mid-1950s and Francis was able to greet enthusiastically the first stretches of the motorway network which were one of the more obvious signs of this increased spending.

The road network and the problem of parking

As we have just noted, Francis wanted a great deal more money spent on the roads. His starting point was that "roads should be made to fit the traffic, not traffic to fit the roads" (Lords, *Debates*, 17th February, 1949). That meant not just improving existing roads but designing and building an entirely new system – a network of motorways as they came to be called. Francis was arguing in favour of such a system in the mid-1930s, twenty years before they eventually became a reality. He wanted the U.K. to follow American practice and similar schemes in various European countries. He emphasised that a motorway network would not only provide much safer roads – with two or three carriageways in each direction – but it would be cheaper than the alternative of patching and adapting the existing main roads.

He acknowledged that a motorway system would permit increased speed but far from making travel more dangerous, as some of his parliamentary critics maintained, Francis claimed the precise opposite. He argued that poor roads resulted in endless congestion and frustration encouraging drivers to take risks and increasing the chance of accidents. A radically improved system would therefore reduce costs of all kinds for both individuals and for companies. He also believed that the motor industry would benefit from improved roads as travel would be easier and safer which would boost the demand for cars.

As someone who always had a house in central London and who represented a south London seat when he was an M.P., he was particularly attuned to the traffic issues in the capital city. Although he accepted that on-street parking had to be regulated and rationed he thought the failure to provide a proper system of car parks was a fundamental weakness and greatly exacerbated the on-street problem. He didn't approve of the parking meter as a device to ration space and argued unsuccessfully for the Parisian system of parking discs.

Why accidents occur and how to avoid them

Francis maintained a remarkable degree of consistency in his views about road safety. When he made his maiden speech in the Lords on what became the 1930 Road Traffic Act he developed a set of arguments which he pursued over the following thirty years. Central to his analysis of road safety was the need to improve driving standards. A driving test – but administered by bodies like the A.A. or the R.A.C. with the state endorsing their work – plus a Highway Code would be two ways to improve things. On the vexed subject of the speed limit which was still 20 mph (originally fixed in 1909 and never subsequently amended) while he was in favour of its revision (not abolition) he argued that any change should be conditional on the introduction of driving tests.

He always rejected the idea that speed was the major cause of accidents. Speed was perfectly appropriate providing the road conditions and the driver's skill could cope with it. Hence his emphasis on the need for a road system that allowed for 'safe' speed and the constant effort to increase the capability of the average driver. As the discussion above indicates he considered the British road system was woefully inadequate and a significant contributor to accidents – many of his speeches vividly rehearsed the deficiencies of major roads such as the A1 and the A5.

Another major concern was the behaviour of pedestrians. Francis argued that accidents were not solely attributable to motorists; irresponsible pedestrians certainly caused some of them and therefore, in principle, should be just as much subject to regulation as motorists were. On two or three different occasions Francis told the Lords of his experience in Germany where he had been caught and fined by a traffic policeman for not observing the crossing regulations. Francis thought many British pedestrians deserved similar admonishment repeatedly characterising their behaviour as 'heedless' and 'reckless'. Cyclists too, though less often inveighed against than pedestrians, were another group of road users he thought should be brought fully within the compass of the law.

His emphasis on the role of pedestrians and cyclists in contributing to accidents was part of his campaign to shift the focus away from what he saw as a disproportionate concern with the private motorist. Cars were only one element within the whole traffic system and targeting their drivers distorted this reality. In similar vein Francis often criticised 'street furniture': he didn't like the proliferation of signs and he thought placing them along the edge of the road, rather than overhead as in many other countries, distracted drivers and diverted their attention from the view ahead.

He believed that it was too easy to keep adding new laws to the statute book, thereby creating more and more motoring offences – and offenders. Francis wanted much more emphasis on advice and persuasion in order to improve driving standards and reduce the accident rate. He was a member of the committee that produced the original Highway Code and he maintained an interest in its various revisions and re-issues. On one occasion, while continuing to endorse it, he wondered if it could be made 'a little less dry' and to this end suggested that it should incorporate some of the humorous cartoons of Russell Brockbank, a well-known artist at that time (Lords, *Debates*, 24th November, 1954). Just prior to the war a pilot system of advisory police patrols achieved encouraging results and Francis backed this scheme very strongly urging the government to fund it nationally (it refused to do so); twenty years later when the London-Birmingham section of the M1 opened he was advocating the use of a similar system to familiarise drivers with this new form of motoring.

What did he achieve?

Having outlined Francis Howe's approach to some of the key aspects of motoring politics in the first half of the twentieth century it's worth asking whether his views had any impact on public policy. This is quite a complicated question but the simplest way to begin is to compare what Howe wanted with the way policy actually developed. In these terms Francis eventually had some success because the amount of money devoted to road construction was appreciably increased from the mid-1950s and the modern motorway system began to appear from 1958 onwards. He had, of course, been urging such policies for many years but campaigns often have to take the long view, seeing their work rather like water dripping on to a stone which is eventually worn away.

So Francis could point to some ultimate success but it's difficult to measure the significance of his particular contribution. It's here that some of the complications just referred to arise because Francis was only one element among many pushing for more money to be spent on roads. One writer who examined the various individuals and organisations involved thought the crucial impetus came from an agreed front between the employers associations and the major trade unions – an unusual phenomenon and therefore especially significant (S.E. Finer: *Political Quarterly* (1958)).

Other factors weighed in favourably as well. By the mid-1950s economic restraint which had suppressed both maintenance work on existing roads and the building of new ones was less pressing. Economic growth in the 1950s led to rising living standards and boosted car purchase far in excess of official estimates. Consequently the inadequacy of the road system to cope with these increases was more apparent than ever and its effects were correspondingly experienced by more people – who, of course had votes to cast.

If Francis could derive some satisfaction from this major expansion of the road system, the picture is more mixed on some of his other concerns. His desire for a lighter touch from the state with less emphasis on law and regulation and more on advice and persuasion was not satisfied. Over the thirty years from 1930-1960 the most frequent response to motoring issues was to pass new laws or to allow the Ministry or local authorities to make additional regulations. Even in those cases where Francis agreed with the case for new laws, such as on-street parking and the compulsory testing of 'old' cars, he disagreed with the way such schemes were implemented.

On the matter of accidents the very rapid growth in the numbers of those killed and injured throughout the 1920s and the early 1930s was reversed from 1935; it was not until 1955 with 4 million more vehicles on the roads that the 1934 figures were reached and exceeded. How was a steep rise in deaths and injuries avoided with so many more vehicles? A distinguished transport planner, Colin Buchanan, thought it was due to: "small road improvements... life-saving devices such as pedestrian crossings and better street lighting but a substantial part must be due to better road behaviour, prompted, no doubt, by propaganda and road safety training for children" (Colin Buchanan: *Mixed Blessing: the Motor in Britain*, Leonard Hill (1958)). Howe was a strong advocate of all that Buchanan mentions and also shared one of the latter's central beliefs about the "disastrous results of mixing pedestrians, cyclists and motor vehicles on the same track" (*ibid.*)

Francis Howe wasn't always directing his fire at major objectives such as more spending on roads or reducing the accident rate but at various points of detail which, although of limited impact, were important to particular categories of road-users. On some of these issues he was representing a particular interest such as commercial vehicle manufacturers. Francis was a director of A.E.C., a substantial manufacturer of buses and commercial vehicles: as one would expect he 'declared his interest' when engaged in such activity. Some of this activity did bear fruit – ministers listened to the representations made and subsequently modified the legislation or regulations in some degree. Even when the there was no change Francis Howe ensured that the claims of certain interests were voiced and such advocacy formed part of the overall context in which policy was made and implemented.

Whether he was arguing the case on a narrower or broader front his speeches were carefully prepared, making much use of specialised information and they were delivered in a rapid no-nonsense style. On one occasion when road safety was being debated Lord Chorley said he wished he had a pedestrian crossing "by which I could escape from the high powered criticism of the noble Earl delivered with all the velocity for which he is so famous" (Lords, *Debates*, 6th April, 1949). Although he continued to take the Conservative whip it did not inhibit him from criticising Conservative ministers: when Harold Watkinson was Transport Minister and made some remarks which appeared critical of the private motorist Francis attacked him in forthright terms. Francis did not have a particularly high regard for civil servants either, preferring to trust the work of various specialists or special investigations. One such inquiry, by a House of Lords Select Committee in 1939, chaired by Lord Alness, was repeatedly and fulsomely praised by Francis: the "really wonderful work of this Committee" and "one of the most able Committees that has ever been set up" (Lords *Debates*, 3rd May, 1939 and 21st November, 1945). As these remarks suggest, Francis' judgements were customarily emphatic, very much black or white with little room for any shades of grey.

When he was in the Commons and relentlessly accumulating speeding convictions he was attacked as a 'law breaker'. Similar sentiments were occasionally voiced when he transferred to the Lords: in 1937 one of his fellow-peers dubbed him a 'super-scorcher' alleging that Francis' only interest in new roads was to provide more opportunities for him to travel at ever-higher speeds. But ministers and front-bench spokesman did not follow suit, on the contrary acknowledging his arguments deserved a serious response.

4

Sports Car Racing

- Starting competition work with the Type 43 Bugatti
- Beginning on the circuits: the case of Brooklands
- Road racing at Ards with the Bugatti
- Another kind of racing: on the sand at Southport
- Experience with the 6C Alfa: fifth at Le Mans in 1930
- The 38/250 Mercedes at Shelsley Walsh
- The Mercedes in long distance races: the Tourist Trophy and the Irish Grand Prix
- The 8C Alfa and victory at Le Mans
- More Le Mans, more Alfas, but only retirements
- Howe and the Tourist Trophy: variety is the spice...
- Lord Howe and the Mille Miglia: the background
- M.G. and the Mille Miglia: the role of Lord Howe
- The Mille Miglia races of 1933 and 1934
- A bizarre episode: a Marendaz at the 1936 French Grand Prix

Chapter 4

Sports Car Racing

Starting competition work with the Type 43 Bugatti

Francis Howe began his competition career with a T43 Bugatti which, at the time of its launch in 1927, was one of the most advanced sports cars in the world. Its design drew from the T38 for its chassis and certain other components, and from the T35 for its engine. The latter was one of the most celebrated of Ettore Bugatti's many models and certainly the most successful in terms of its competition record. Although it had originally appeared as an unsupercharged car many of its rivals were adopting blowers to boost output and Bugatti had supercharged the T35 engine in 1926.

A sports or grand touring car with a blown engine as a standard part of its specification was most unusual in the late 1920s, and immediately singled out the T43 as a distinctive motor car. Subsequently, many other manufacturers adopted the same principle so that the T43 appeared to be a more 'normal' sports car by the late 1930s. The blower boosted the top-end performance and one of the T43's defining characteristics was its ability to comfortably exceed 100 mph which was quite exceptional for a road car in 1927.

Given the T43's pedigree it is not surprising that it provoked much debate on whether it should be regarded as a racing or a sports car. W.F. Bradley, a celebrated writer on Bugatti, ran a T43 himself, and in the light of his own experience, declared that it "has all the characteristics of a racing car, and is indeed a racing car with a touring body..." (*Autocar*, 26th July, 1929). Critics of the car have seen this mixed identity as a source

1928 – Brooklands – Howe (still known as Viscount Curzon) leans on his Type 43 Bugatti outside the Brooklands Clubhouse, before his first competition event in the Essex 6 Hour Race on 12th May 1928. Photograph by Planet News, courtesy of Getty Images

1928 – Brooklands – Howe adjusts the side screen of his Bugatti Type 43 before the Essex 6 Hour Race at Brooklands in May 1928. *Photograph courtesy of Geoffrey Goddard Archive*

of considerable weakness: Anthony Blight argued that it was not successful either as a touring car or in competition and that most of its troubles "derived from the compromises implicit in its dual function" (A. Blight: *The French Sports Car Revolution* (1996) pp.35-6).

Blight actually uses Howe's experience in the 1929 Tourist Trophy (T.T.) to illustrate his critique: Howe had modified the exhaust system, lowering it in order to reduce heat in the cockpit. Unfortunately Howe struck a kerb and this "sent him clattering like a newly-wed into early retirement" (Blight: *op. cit.*). There is obviously room to argue about whether the problem was really the T43's or the driver's – after all the car didn't mount the kerb off its own bat! However it is true that Howe had various mechanical problems with his T43s which were sufficiently serious to force him into a number of retirements.

As we have already emphasized, Howe's main interest was in long-distance races rather than in sprints or short handicap events. The Double Twelve and the Tourist Trophy were leading examples of distance events and Howe used his Bugatti in the 1928 and 1929 T.T. races as well as for the 1929 and 1930 Double Twelve. He retired from both T.T.s, on the first occasion with a leaking fuel tank and on the second, as noted above, with a defective exhaust. In the two Double Twelve races while the results were somewhat better, on both occasions there were considerable delays with pit stops and on-track repairs.

In the 1930 Double Twelve he co-drove the T43 with Malcolm Campbell and they were delayed by hub problems. Initially Howe, baulked by another car, slid into a sandbank which resulted in a bent wheel. The wheel was replaced but the damage to the hub was not apparent, or not identified, at that stage. When it was Howe carried out the repair on the circuit and his efforts are memorialized both in a photo – often reproduced – which shows him lying full length under the off-side rear wheel, and by

39

Sammy Davis' depiction of his efforts: "From our car it looked as though Howe was rebuilding the entire machine, for first he was met running from the pit with a huge jack, and then with the world's biggest blow-lamp included in a complete bucketful of tools" (S.C.H. Davis: *Motor Racing* (1932)) Count Giovanni Lurani, a close friend of Howe, was also a fellow competitor and remembers "his characteristic figure pacing along the track to and from his pit to the stationary car. Every time I passed he waved cheerily to me and it was with real pleasure that I saw him restart just over an hour later" (G. Lurani: *Racing Round the World* (1953)).

Beginning on the circuits: the case of Brooklands

Howe's experience in the Double Twelve and the T.T. took place on tracks that could hardly have been more different. All racing drivers are interested in the tracks they compete on because their skill lies in working out how to make a particular car go round a circuit in the minimum time. But drivers differ a good deal in judging what they regard as good and bad circuits and even more on how important the track is in influencing the pleasure – or occasionally the pain – they derive from racing. Howe was one of those who attached great importance to the tracks on which he raced and he was always interested in opening up new opportunities for racing, or in trying to revive those where it had been stopped – such as Donington after the Second World War.

The Double Twelve was run at Brooklands and the T.T. on the Ards circuit in Northern Ireland. Brooklands forms the 'book-ends' to Howe's racing career – it was the scene both of his first and his final appearance as a racing driver. Because it was the only mainland circuit in continuous use throughout the inter-war years it inevitably had a big influence on British motor racing. It is not surprising that there is much disagreement about whether that influence was good or bad. Sir Henry 'Tim' Birkin was a particularly harsh contemporary critic: "I think that it is, without exception, the most out-of-date, inadequate and dangerous track in the world...The surface is abominable; to those who have never had any experience of it at high speed, it would be incredible. There are bumps, which jolt the driver up and down out of his seat and make the car leave the road and travel through the air. I am absolutely amazed that this has not caused far more fatal accidents". (H.R.S. Birkin: *Full Throttle*, Foulis (1943)).

Birkin was strongly committed to road racing and there was no way in which Brooklands was going

1929 – Brooklands – Howe and Leslie Callingham's Bugatti Type 43 (No.14) can be seen third in this group of cars speeding along the Railway Banking during the J.C.C. Double Twelve in May 1929, At the front of the group are Sir Ronald Gunter's Bentley (No.6) and Ivanowsky's Alfa Romeo (No.54). *Photograph by Autocar, courtesy of LAT Archive*

1930 – Brooklands – Howe in his Bugatti Type 43 on his way to his first race victory at Brooklands, in the First Mountain Handicap during the B.A.R.C. Opening Meeting in March 1930. *Photograph by Autocar, courtesy of LAT Archive*

Above – 1929 – Brooklands – Howe climbs into the cockpit of his Lea Francis before the B.R.D.C. 500 in October 1929. He finished ninth in the race, with co-driver Sir Ronald Gunter. *Photograph courtesy of Geoffrey Goddard Archive*

Below – 1930 – Brooklands – Two views of Howe and his Bugatti Type 43 in the pits at Brooklands during the J.C.C. Double Twelve which he eventually won giving him his first major race victory, sharing the car with Malcolm Campbell. *Photograph by* Autocar, *courtesy of LAT Archive*

Top – 1930 – Brooklands – Howe's Bugatti Type 43 (No.25) crashes through an earth retaining bank during the 1930 J.C.C. Double Twelve. *Photograph by* Autocar, *courtesy of LAT Archive*

Below left – 1930 – Brooklands – Howe attends to repairs at the trackside to his Bugatti Type 43 during the J.C.C. Double Twelve on 9th May, 1930. *Photograph by Imagno, courtesy of Getty Images*

Below right– 1930 – Brooklands – Howe takes a nap during the J.C.C. Double Twelve in May 1930. Howe and his co-driver Malcolm Campbell won the race in Howe's Bugatti Type 43. Note that Campbell is the name mentioned on the pit counter label, no doubt because he was the better known driver at the time. *Photograph courtesy of Terry Cardy Collection*

Above – 1934 – Brooklands – Howe made a rare appearance in a car not owned by him in the 1934 B.R.D.C. 500. He and Dudley Froy competed in Woolf Barnato's Barnato Hassan Bentley (No.41 – third from left). They retired on lap 49. Of the other cars No.37 is the Marker Jackson Bentley of Marker and Bevan, followed by No.5 Dodson & Denly's M.G., with No.8 Samuel & Ashton-Rigby's M.G. behind the B-H Bentley. *Photograph by* Autocar, *courtesy of LAT Archive*

Below – 1936 – Brooklands – Hon. Brian Lewis in the Lagonda he was sharing with Howe (No.21) is flanked by the Pacey-Hassan of Pacey and Baker-Carr (No.22) and the Duesenberg of Jack Duller (No.20) at the start of the 1936 B.R.D.C. 500. Howe can be seen behind the Lagonda, with his hands on his hips whilst two to the right of Howe, in the light overalls, is Donald Wilcockson, Fox & Nicholl's chief mechanic. Howe and Lewis finished third in the race. *Photograph courtesy of Arnold Davey*

to measure up to that kind of criterion. Although Howe did not openly criticize Brooklands in the same way as Birkin, there is no doubt that he shared his view about road racing as the most desirable form of motor sport. In his Foreword to *Full Throttle* Howe distinguished between those who excel on the track and on the road. Although he acknowledged that it required "great courage and an iron nerve" to drive a car like Birkin's single-seater Bentley at Brooklands, he considered road racing was a "far more supreme test of the individual". He maintained this view throughout his life: in 1955, he referred to the "artificial conditions" of tracks like Silverstone or Aintree, compared to the "natural conditions" of road racing, where the "standard and skill of driving required are much higher and the test to which the vehicle is subjected is much more considerable" (House of Lords *Debates*, 19th July, 1955).

However, like anyone who wished to circuit race on the British mainland, Howe knew that it was Brooklands or nothing, at any rate until 1933, when Donington started up, followed by Crystal Palace four years later. Those better disposed to Brooklands have pointed out that when it did face competition its meetings still had good entries, as well as continuing support from spectators. Birkin's remarks also overlook other aspects of the track, such as its importance as a test facility for both racing and road cars. Howe himself placed a lot of emphasis on this latter role, recalling in the early post-war years, that Dunlop had two cars permanently based at Brooklands for continuous tyre testing.

1928 – Ards – Howe, still Viscount Curzon and dressed largely in street clothes, except for a linen helmet, seems to be dealing with some administrative matters in front of an interested crowd of spectators prior to unofficial practice for the R.A.C. Tourist Trophy in August 1928. The Type 43 Bugatti visible is his road car (PH 9397) not the car he was to drive in the T.T. *Photograph by* Autocar, *courtesy of LAT Archive*

Road racing at Ards with the Bugatti

The Ards circuit was as pure a road racing circuit as anyone could wish for. Harry Ferguson, subsequently known both for tractors and for a successful four wheel drive racing car, was the moving force in reviving the T.T. on this new circuit near Belfast. It covered 13⅔rds miles and was widely admired: Anthony Blight, for example, describes the circuit as "the finest ever seen in the British Isles and...among

1928 – Belfast – Howe poses in his Bugatti Type 43, with Percy Thomas alongside him in the cockpit, in Ferguson's Belfast garage where his team was based for his first international motor race, the R.A.C. Tourist Trophy in August 1928. To the left, the rightmost of the group in front of the car, is Sir Malcolm Campbell. On the extreme right is Harry Ferguson, later of Ferguson tractor fame. *Photograph courtesy of Terry Cardy Collection*

Top left – 1929 – Ards – Howe's Type 43 Bugatti (No.52) follows "Williams" Bugatti through Quarry Corner, during the R.A.C. Tourist Trophy in August 1929. Behind Howe is Woods' Lea Francis. *Photograph by* Autocar, *courtesy of LAT Archive*

Top right – 1928 – Ards – Howe sits in his Type 43 Bugatti in the pits before his first R.A.C. Tourist Trophy race. His riding mechanic Percy Thomas can be seen in the background to Howe's left. *Photograph by HF Davis, courtesy of Getty Images*

Right – 1928 – Ards – Howe and his Bugatti Type 43 pass into Conway Square in Newtownards during the 1928 R.A.C. Tourist Trophy. Howe retired after twenty laps with a split fuel tank. This was the first of Howe's nine participations in the Ards T.T.s. *Photograph courtesy of Geoffrey Goddard Archive*

Left – 1929 – Shelsley Walsh – Howe drives his Mercedes SS 38/250 up a crowded Shelsley hill during the September 1929 M.A.C meeting, where he won his class. *Photograph by* Autocar, *courtesy of LAT Archive*

Below – 1928 – Ards – Howe passes the large crowds exiting Dundonald Hairpin during his drive in the 1928 R.A.C. Tourist Trophy. *Photograph courtesy of Geoffrey Goddard Archive*

the most difficult and testing in the world" (Blight: *Georges Roesch and the Invincible Talbot*, Grenville, (1970)). He notes that some of its features – such as limited straights, some very narrow stretches of road and high banks – might be seen as unsuitable for competition work, but, in fact, such elements were characteristic of all true road circuits. Committed though Howe was to road racing, he recognized its dangers, especially the limited visibility. After the death of Clive Dunfee on the Outer Circuit at Brooklands, he told Rivers Fletcher that he didn't find that track 'frightening' because you could always see a long way ahead – it was blind corners on road racing circuits that were far more hazardous.

In the 1928 T.T. Howe made a good start but soon suffered a leaking fuel tank which forced his retirement. He could at least console himself that he avoided Malcolm Campbell's fate. From the earliest stages of the race Campbell's T43 was leaking fuel and when he came into the pits to lower his hood, the petrol ignited in a large sheet of flame. The attempts of marshals and others to extinguish the fire were largely unsuccessful and the car was badly damaged. In 1929 Howe also retired after running for less than an hour of the five hour race. It left him plenty of time to watch, and to admire, the remarkable performance of Rudolf Caracciola driving the 7 litre 38/250 Mercedes-Benz. Although Caracciola is best remembered for his record in grand prix races between 1934 and 1939, he had some outstanding results long before then, of which his 1929 T.T. victory was one of the very best. Howe was so impressed by the Mercedes that he made a substantial offer for the car as soon as the race was finished. No doubt Caracciola was amply rewarded for his win by the prize money, but he could have claimed a bonus as a successful salesman for the 38/250! Howe's offer was accepted and within a month he made his debut with it at Shelsley Walsh.

Another kind of racing: on the sand at Southport

While Howe's ideal event was a road race he was interested in sampling other opportunities for competitive motoring, especially in the early years. This interest led him to Lancashire in May 1929 for the 100 mile race on Southport sands. Sand racing had a significant role in inter-war motor sport and deserves more recognition than it has received from historians. Little of it survived into the second half of the twentieth century with the proliferation of new venues after 1945 but between 1920 and 1939 it offered another outlet for competition in a world where those possibilities were strictly limited, especially for speed events.

Howe used his T43 Bugatti for the race and he appears to have had some preparatory problems: "There was some delay on the starting line for Earl Howe's Bugatti which apparently he had decided to re-build after arrival at the paddock..." (*The Autocar*, 24th May, 1929). Whatever the problems, the car lasted through the race though it wasn't among the leaders as it was competing alongside faster and more suitable cars. Initially the two leaders were Thistlethwayte in a 38/250 Mercedes and Raymond Mays in the Vauxhall Villiers. The latter was one of many retirements that allowed the survivors, such as Howe, to move up the order. Out of the thirty cars that started only eleven survived the hour and a half it took to complete the thirty-five laps, one of whom was Howe in sixth place Although the Southport races continued throughout the 1930s Howe did not return, so one must conclude that he didn't find the experience sufficiently compelling to venture north again.

Experience with the 6C Alfa: fifth at Le Mans in 1930

A small consolation for his own retirement from the 1929 T.T. was that his Alfa Romeo finished second in its class, driven by Leslie Callingham. This car was a 6C model with a 1750 cc engine. The 6C was one of Vittorio Jano's classic designs, first emerging in 1926 and originally fitted with a single o.h.c., unsupercharged 1½ litre engine. Over the next three years it was developed in various ways – with the single o.h.c. unit becoming a twin o.h.c. unit, enlarging the engine to 1750 cc and adding a Roots type supercharger. The day before the T.T. Leslie Callingham used Howe's car at the Craigantlet hill climb where he won his class. In the following year, 1930, Howe added another 1750 Alfa to his stable: this was the GS model, mainly distinguishable from his first 6C (the SS model) by a larger supercharger. Howe followed his 1929 T.T. precedent by purchasing the GS car, driven by Achille Varzi which had finished third in the 1930 T.T.

With the important exception of the 1930 Le Mans, Howe himself did not make much competitive use of either of his 6C Alfas. At Le Mans, co-driving with Leslie Callingham, he finished fifth overall and fourth on the Index of Performance. This was the first time an Alfa competed at Le Mans

Above – 1929 – Le Mans – Howe and Bernard Rubin lean on their Bentley in the Le Mans pits before the 1929 24 Heures du Mans. They retired on the seventh lap with a broken magneto cross shaft. This was the first of Howe's six appearances at Le Mans. *Photograph courtesy of Geoffrey Goddard Archive*

Below – 1929 – Le Mans – The Bentley pits with Howe's car (No.11) and the car of Dudley Benjafield (No.10) behind. *Photograph by* Autocar, *courtesy of LAT Archive*

but it wasn't Howe's first Le Mans. He had partnered Bernard Rubin the previous year in a 4½ litre Bentley, but it had not given him much experience of the race as the car retired early on with plugs and magneto problems.

For the 1929 race there was a slight modification to the original Le Mans circuit which had been used since the event began in 1923. Three years later, in 1932, a major change was made when it was shortened from just over ten miles to the lap to eight and a half – the Esses and the two Dunlop bridges date from that year. Howe thought the circuit "on the whole an easy one" but with one or two points of potential danger, particularly the S bend at Arnage and White House corner.

Howe had some modifications made to his Alfa 6C SS for the 1930 race, the main visible evidence of which was a re-routing of the exhaust system which ran alongside the car in an extended S shape. The main competition for the Alfa came from the two Talbot 90s entered by Fox and Nicholl which finished third and fourth overall. The Alfa and the Talbots were closely matched with the Italian car quicker on the straights and the Talbot, helped by better brakes, gaining ground on the twistier parts of the circuit.

Above – 1929 – Le Mans – Howe's 4½ litre Bentley during a pit stop at the 24 Heures du Mans in June 1929. Howe can be seen changing the magneto. The regulations only allowed drivers to work on their car, and during Howe's repairs a crucial gasket was omitted. After rejoining the race the cross-shaft gears stripped leading to the car's retirement. This was the first of Howe's six participations at Le Mans.
Photograph courtesy of Tim Houlding

Left – 1930 – Le Mans – Howe and Callingham attend to their Alfa Romeo during a pit stop during the 1930 24 Heures du Mans in June 1930. They eventually finished fifth overall, and fourth in the Index of Performance.
Photograph by Autocar, *courtesy of LAT Archive*

Top – 1930 – Le Mans – Howe and Callingham pose after their drive to fifth place in the 1930 24 Heures du Mans. *Photograph by* Autocar, *courtesy of LAT Archive*

Above – 1930 – Brooklands – Howe leans on his Talbot 90 in the Brooklands paddock before the B.R.D.C. 500 in October 1930. Howe shared the car with Hon. Brian Lewis, finishing fourth. The two Talbots of Hindmarsh/Wolfe (No.31) and Rose-Richards/Saunders-Davies (No.32) can be seen to the rear left of the photo. *Photograph by Central Press courtesy of Guy Spollon Collection*

Left – 1930 – Brooklands – The Talbot 90 of Howe and Hon. Brian Lewis passes the Riley of "S. Bird" during the B.R.D.C. 500 in October 1930 in which they finished in fifth place. *Photograph by* Autocar, *courtesy of LAT Archive*

Both had to make some unscheduled pit stops – the Alfa to replace its plugs, and the Talbots to secure loose wings and lamps. The Roesch-designed Talbots made a considerable impression on Howe and after the race he approached Arthur Fox about the possibility of having a competitive drive.

Fox responded to Howe's interest with a particularly interesting proposition. Fox and Nichol had decided to add a single seater to their three orthodox Talbot entries for the 500 Miles Race at Brooklands in October 1930. Howe was invited to share this car with Hon. Brian Lewis, their principal driver. They proved an effective combination, finishing fourth, only eighty seconds behind the third-placed Sunbeam driven by Cushman and Purdy.

The 38/250 Mercedes at Shelsley Walsh

The ex-Caracciola Mercedes featured to a much greater extent than the Alfas in Howe's 1929-30 racing programme. It was used for long-distance events like the Irish Grand Prix as well as for short races at Brooklands and for hill climbs such as Shelsley Walsh. He also owned a Barker bodied Mercedes 36/220 which he occasionally used for competition work.

The 38/250 Mercedes was a remarkable car that provoked strong opinions, both positive and negative. Accommodating a 7 litre engine was bound to result in a car of some 'presence': D.B. Tubbs remarked that "If Thor, the god of Thunder owned a sports car it would be a 38/250 Mercedes", describing it as "stark brutal and imposing, so altogether Wagnerian". But its power and sheer bulk could give a misleading impression. Blight says "it was light for its size, and everything about it – including its supercharger characteristics – was designed first and foremost for acceleration" (Blight: *op. cit.* (1970)). The supercharger provided one of the car's defining features as Mercedes favoured a system that was only activated when near maximum revs were reached. The result was a "tremendous screaming noise and, if it made little difference to the very moderate performance, at least encouraged the occupants to imagine they were going a lot faster" (C. Clutton and J. Stanford: *The Vintage Motor Car*, Batsford, (1954)). As these remarks suggest, Clutton and Stanford are among the 38/250's sceptics, noting its inordinate fuel thirst, the risk of cylinder head gasket failure, uncertain brakes and unsuitability for English roads.

Unsuitable or not, Howe was one of those who did use the car on the road and, according to Rivers Fletcher, with great enjoyment: "He was perpetually in love with the 38/250, he always kept it in touring trim and used it extensively even for business trips to the City of London" (Rivers Fletcher: *Mostly Motor Racing*, Haynes, (1986)).

Howe's first competitive outing with the 38/250 was at Shelsley Walsh in September 1929. It wasn't, however, his first experience of a speed hill climb. A month before Shelsley he had competed at Craigantlet in Northern Ireland, a hill that had been first tried before the First War and then revived for a small event in 1925. The 1929 fixture was deliberately pitched to attract those coming over for the T.T., a week later. No racing cars were allowed and Howe's two entries, his 36/220 Mercedes and the T43 Bugatti set first and second fastest times, admittedly against opposition of less powerful cars. Unlike the rest of the U.K. there was no problem about closing public roads in Northern Ireland and the Ulster Automobile Sports Club used a stretch of one and a third miles which Howe climbed in ninety-nine seconds.

1930 – Wilson Avenue, Brighton – In 1929 and 1930 a speed trial was held on a newly-constructed section of road on the eastern outskirts of Brighton. In the 1930 event, which was run in conjunction with the Brighton Motor Rally, Howe won his class and he is seen here on during one of his runs in his Mercedes SS 36/220. *Photograph courtesy of Motoring Picture Library, Beaulieu*

Above – 1930 – Shelsley Walsh – Howe and his Mercedes Benz SS 38/250 power up the Shelsley hill during a murky day at September 1930 MAC meeting, where Howe won his class in both the Mercedes and in his Bugatti Type 43. *Photograph by* Autocar, *courtesy of LAT Archive*

Right – 1931 – Shelsley Walsh – Howe powers his Mercedes-Benz SS 38/250 up the Shelsley hill during the July 1931 meeting. Howe won his class, setting a best time of 46.8 seconds. *Photograph courtesy of Midland Automobile Club Archive*

1934 – Shelsley Walsh – Howe drives his Mercedes Benz SS 38/250 to class victory at the June 1934 Shelsley Walsh meeting
Photograph by Autocar, *courtesy of LAT Archive*

Shelsley Walsh's prominence owed much to its longevity and its singularity. It had been used continuously since 1905 and it was on private land, the importance of which had been increased by the R.A.C.'s refusal to allow any hill climbs or sprints on public roads following the accident at Kop Hill in 1925. Howe succeeded in getting the Mercedes to the top in 47.6 which was an excellent time for someone with no previous experience of either the hill or the car. The car was at best a mixed blessing for climbing Shelsley: while the 38/250's acceleration was certainly an asset, the sheer bulk of the Mercedes on Shelsley's narrow track, and its less than perfect brakes, were distinct drawbacks.

Another measure of the merits of Howe's time was that Raymond Mays, in setting a new outright hill record, was only two seconds ahead of the Mercedes, at 45.6. A few months later, at the first Shelsley of 1930, Caracciola drove a 38/250 recording a best time of 46.8. Howe equalled this time in the following year and at his final Shelsley appearance with the Mercedes, in June 1934, he shaved another fraction off with a best time of 46.2. By then there was a larger gap between this time and the outright hill record of 40.0, due to the combined efforts of Hans Stuck, Raymond Mays and Whitney Straight.

The Mercedes in long distance races: the Tourist Trophy and the Irish Grand Prix

Howe used Mercedes cars for the 1930 T.T. and for the Irish Grands Prix of 1930 and 1931 (in the 1930 Irish race he drove a works entered car). Unlike his two previous T.T.s with the Bugatti, he did reach the finishing line in 1930, albeit in last place. There were two problems, the first of which was the handicapping. This might be dubbed the penalty of success for Caracciola's victory in 1929 had led to some very harsh targets for the largest cars like Bentley and Mercedes. The second difficulty was the weather. After the first ten laps in the dry the rain began and Howe found coping with the Mercedes in such conditions almost impossible. Blight notes that he "virtually gave up racing, slowing two minutes a lap and oiling up his plugs in consequence". Even if it had remained dry the handicap would have ruled out finishing in one of the first few places but, without the rain, he would certainly have been much higher up the order. At least he had the satisfaction of setting the fastest lap at 77.2 which was slightly quicker than Birkin's best in the 4½ litre Bentley (76.24).

The first Irish Grand Prix took place in 1929 on a circuit in Phoenix Park, a very large urban park two

Above – 1930 – Phoenix Park, Dublin – The Works Mercedes SSKs of Malcolm Campbell (No.1) and Howe (No.2) lead the field away from the start of the Irish Grand Prix in July 1930. Howe finished fourth in the race. *Photograph by* Autocar, *courtesy of LAT Archive*

Left – 1930 – Phoenix Park, Dublin – Howe's Mercedes SSK, followed by the short chassis car of the eventual winner, Rudolf Caracciola, passes the Wellington Monument in Phoenix Park during the Irish Grand Prix in July 1930. The Monument was built to commemorate the victories of the Duke of Wellington. *Photograph by* Autocar, *courtesy of LAT Archive*

Bottom left – 1930 – Ards – Howe's Mercedes SSK passes through the streets of Comber during the 1930 R.A.C. Tourist Trophy. Behind him is 'Tim' Birkin's Bentley which later crashed at Ballystockart. Howe finished eighteenth and second in class. *Photograph courtesy of Guy Spollon Collection*

1930 – Ards – Howe passes the Central Bar in Dundonald in his ex-Caracciola Mercedes SSK during the 1930 R.A.C. Tourist Trophy. Howe finished eighteenth overall and second in his class. He is followed by the Lea Francis of Dan Higgin. *Photograph courtesy of Geoffrey Goddard Archive*

miles from the centre of Dublin. The circuit was D shaped with one very long straight and a lap distance of 4½ miles; like the Ards circuit it had received the prior enthusiastic endorsement of two prominent Irish racing drivers, Kenelm Lee Guinness and Henry Segrave. The government of the Irish Free State strongly supported the race and agreed to the removal of the Phoenix monument which was fortunate as it stood right in the middle of the main straight! Although entitled a 'grand prix', the race was for sports cars and it was subject to handicap. It was actually two races divided according to capacity with the line drawn at 1500 cc; each race had its own trophy with the Phoenix Trophy awarded to the driver who completed either of the races in the shortest possible time.

In the 1930 race Howe and Campbell had orthodox SSK models, whereas Caracciola had a special short-chassis car. The race was chiefly memorable for the duel the latter waged with Tim Birkin, driving one of the supercharged 4½ litre Bentleys. It was resolved in Caracciola's favour and later in the race Birkin had lubrication problems which dropped him down the field. Howe drove a very steady race finishing third in the Eireann Cup, and was classified fourth in the Phoenix Trophy. As in the T.T., which came a month later, the weather was mixed with the race starting in the dry but, after a few laps, heavy rain set in. Despite his reputation as the 'regenmeister', these conditions caught out Caracciola who spun his Mercedes a number of times on the back straight although he managed to avoid hitting anything and scarcely reduced his speed.

Despite his problems in the T.T. Howe didn't have any difficulty coping on this occasion and a similar mixed pattern of weather the following year left him equally unruffled. Unfortunately this third Irish G.P. was beset by various administrative and financial problems. The entry was weakened somewhat and it meant the support of people such as Howe was more important than ever. Initially, despite the weather, Howe was running strongly and he received a round of applause for a rapid pit stop, taking on thirty gallons of fuel in thirty seconds. However, soon after the pit stop problems arose: "Perceptive onlookers began to notice something different about the noise from Earl Howe's Mercedes...and it was soon apparent that it had lost the distinctive whine from its supercharger" (Bob Montgomery: *The Irish International Grands Prix* (1999)). In fact the blower casing had developed a crack and Howe lost speed and began to drop down the field, finally finishing fifth in the Eireann Cup race; he had also set the fastest lap at 91.6 mph.

Above – 1931 – Phoenix Park, Dublin – The leading drivers competing in the Eireann Cup, (l-r) Howe, 'Tim' Birkin, George Eyston and Giuseppe Campari pose in the pits front of Howe's Mercedes SSK at the Irish Grand Prix meeting in June 1931. *Photograph by Popperfoto, courtesy of Getty Images*

Below – 1931 – Phoenix Park, Dublin – Howe puts on his racing overalls on the pit counter at the Irish Grand Prix meeting in June 1931, watched by an appreciative crowd. *Photograph by Popperfoto, courtesy of Getty Images*

1931 – Phoenix Park, Dublin – The parkland characteristics of the Phoenix Park circuit are well illustrated by these three photographs showing Howe's Mercedes at Mountjoy Corner during the 1931 Eireann Cup. Howe finished fifth. *Photograph by Autocar, courtesy of LAT Archive*

1931 – Phoenix Park, Dublin – Howe – Howe's Mercedes at speed on Phoenix Park's main straight during the 1931 Eireann Cup. *Photograph by* Autocar, *courtesy of LAT Archive*

The 8C Alfa and victory at Le Mans

Vittorio Jano had already designed two outstanding Alfa successes, the P2 and the 6C. He now produced the 8C engine which he said, many years later, was "not a masterpiece" (quoted in *Classic and Sports Car* (2000)) Without getting bogged down in a debate about what is a 'masterpiece' the engine has been widely admired ever since its introduction and, in various forms, it powered all Alfa sports and racing cars until 1939. Such cars continue to be very highly valued, both financially, and in terms of their aesthetic and driving appeal.

The 8C model was originally produced in two different chassis lengths, the Corto (short) and the Lungo (long); subsequently, in 1932, a third, slightly shortened version of the Corto chassis was used for the Monza racing cars. The Lungo was designed for a four-seater body to comply with current A.I.A.C.R. regulations for sports car racing and it was the type chosen by Sir Henry Birkin and Lord Howe – the first British customers for the 8C. Birkin's car appeared for the first time at the Irish Grand Prix, held the weekend before the Le Mans race; it was only ready just in time and was driven straight to Ireland from the Alfa factory at Portello by Clive Gallop. Birkin had a good race winning the Eireann Cup and he only failed to win the overall Irish G.P. through a shortage of fuel. Birkin therefore went to Le Mans, where he was to share Howe's new 8C, with some valuable race experience of the new model.

Howe had originally intended to compete at Le Mans with the ex-works 1750 GS Alfa he had bought from Achille Varzi the previous year, but once the 8C model was announced he substituted the new car for the 1750. He did not see his car until he arrived at Le Mans for the practice sessions – all the preparation work was carried out by the Alfa factory alongside their two works entries. Alfa's assault on the 1931 Le Mans was extremely impressive: "The Alfa Romeo equipe stayed at the Hotel Moderne, former headquarters of the victorious Bentley teams, and consisted of three racing cars, two practice cars, one lorry, seven drivers, thirteen mechanics and a team manager" (Peter Hull and Roy Slater: *Alfa Romeo: A History* (Revised Edition, 1982)).

Alfa's planning reflected the opportunity presented by the disappearance of Bentley from Le Mans. In 1931 the chief contestants were Alfa, Bugatti and Mercedes Benz and the outcome turned, as much as anything, on tyres. All three marques experienced tyre problems but, fortunately for Alfa, it had sorted out its difficulties before going to Le Mans, and its main practice anxiety revolved around fuel rather than rubber.

The fuel issue concerned the mixture of petrol and benzole – which was originally combined in proportions of 70:30. Because of the difficulties this caused in obtaining smooth running it was decided that the cars should run on benzole alone. This decision meant that lower compression pistons were needed and urgent messages were sent to the factory

1931 – Le Mans – Two views of Howe's Alfa Romeo 8C 2300, which he shared with 'Tim' Birkin, in the pits during their drive to victory in the 1931 24 Heures du Mans. They also won the Coupe Bienniale and the Index of Performance. This was Howe's first continental race win. *Photograph by* Autocar, *courtesy of LAT Archive*

requesting suitable replacements for all three cars. After some hectic scrambling round they were fitted on Friday evening but one of new pistons failed as soon as the car was started up. Any repair at that late stage was impossible, so the Alfa starters were reduced to Howe's private entry and the remaining works car of Marinoni and Zehender

The main opposition to the two Alfas came from a team of three Type 50 Bugattis and a single 38/250 Mercedes and these three makes dominated the opening laps of the race. Tim Birkin succeeded in getting the Alfa into third position in the early stages, but then dropped down the field after a visit to the pits to change one of the plugs and to adjust the shock-absorbers. Marinoni and Zehender then took over the lead from the Mercedes of Stoffel and Ivanowsky. The Mercedes was displaced due to tyre problems and these difficulties began to dictate the progress of the race. Shortly after the Mercedes came in to change its tyres, Chiron in one of the Bugattis had to do the same. Rost, in another of the Bugattis, had a spectacular accident when a stripped tyre tread wrapped itself round the brake mechanism, locking the wheels and over-turning the car. Although Rost himself was not seriously hurt, the Bugatti struck some spectators, one of whom was killed. Unsurprisingly, after consulting with his drivers, Jean Bugatti decided that the other Bugattis should withdraw from the race.

With the withdrawal of the Bugattis the lead passed to the works Alfa followed by the Mercedes and two of the Roesch-designed Talbot 105s. Howe and Birkin were still making up ground lost earlier on by their enforced pit stop, but once their plug

Above – 1931 – Le Mans – Howe's Alfa Romeo 8C 2300 leaves the short-lived Route du Circuit section onto the Mulsanne straight on its way to victory in the 1931 24 Heures du Mans. The Route du Circuit section of the circuit was only used from 1929 to 1931, being used to bypass the Pontlieue hairpin until the Tertre Rouge modification was made in 1932. *Photograph courtesy of Geoffrey Goddard Archive*

Below – 1931 – Le Mans – Approaching the end of the race, Howe watches as Birkin passes with a newspaper attached to the radiator of the soon-to-be victorious Alfa Romeo. *Photograph by Autocar, courtesy of LAT Archive*

1931 – Le Mans – Howe and Birkin celebrate their victory. *Photograph by* Autocar, *courtesy of LAT Archive*

problems had been overcome they began to speed up and moved up the order. Just after midnight they took over the lead from the works 8C. The Mercedes challenge had been weakened by its tyre problems, the Engleberts seemingly not able to cope; Ivanowsky and Stoffel were very fortunate in being able to swap to Dunlops half-way through the race, for without this change they would probably have been forced into retirement.

What might have been a one-two victory for Alfa was sacrificed to Zehender's over-enthusiasm at Arnage where he mounted the bank. When the car was checked over at the pits, it appeared to be alright but subsequently it became apparent the damage was more serious and it was unable to continue. The rate of attrition in this Le Mans was very high. At noon on the Sunday with four hours still to go only six cars remained from the twenty-six that started the race.

Despite some last-minute anxiety on Lord Howe's part as he saw Birkin circulating with a newspaper that had attached itself to the radiator grille, his 8C took the chequered flag at 4 pm to register a convincing victory. It finished more than 100 kilometres ahead of the Mercedes, and for the first time in the race's history the winning car had covered over 3000 kilometres. Its overall average speed was 78.13, which was 2½ mph beyond the previous best established by the 6 litre Bentley in 1930. Although Birkin was a more experienced Le Mans driver than Howe, he was full of praise for Howe's contribution: "He drove beautifully during the whole time he was in the car, steering it safely during the most difficult hour of the race, when a thunderstorm passed in the night and made the road into a river" (Birkin: *Full Throttle*).

Birkin and Howe's pleasure in their victory was slightly diluted by the unavoidable acknowledgement that it had been secured in an Italian car. The officials at Le Mans underlined this by playing the Italian national anthem at the end of the race, which *The Autocar* complained was "interminably long". Birkin notes, somewhat ruefully, a telegram they received from Mussolini, congratulating them on their victory "for Italy".

More Le Mans, more Alfas, but only retirements

The 1931 result was no flash in the pan for Alfa Romeo who became the dominant make at Le Mans for the next few years. Although Howe participated in three out of the next four Le Mans races – only missing the 1933 race due to an eye injury – he was not able to repeat his 1931 victory and, indeed, failed to finish in all three races.

1932 promised to be a repeat of the preceding year with Howe's car – a new 8C – prepared alongside the three works cars at Portello and delivered to him on the eve of practice. There was a slight concession to the car's English owner as it had been finished in Howe's blue paint, unlike his 1931 car which was red – although Howe had worn his blue overalls to strike his characteristic note! Birkin and Howe were again teamed together and when they went round to close the circuit to ordinary traffic (the victor's prerogative from the previous year) it was clear that in places the very hot sun had melted the road surface. This knowledge helped them to avoid the off-circuit excursions that afflicted other competitors but they did suffer mechanical bothers of exactly the same kind as the previous year, with some of the plugs not working properly. By midnight they were holding third place but shortly afterwards Birkin came into the pits with steam coming out of the engine which singled a blown cylinder head gasket and the end of their race.

1932 – Brooklands – Howe sits in his Alfa Romeo 8C 2300, with a very dapper 'Tim' Birkin, his co-driver, alongside before the J.C.C. 1000 in June 1932. They retired in the race with a broken con-rod. Behind the car to the right is Howe's mechanic, Percy Thomas. *Photograph courtesy of Guy Spollon Collection*

Above – 1932 – Brooklands – Howe waits trackside whilst his mechanic attempts running repairs to his Alfa Romeo 8C 2300 during the J.C.C. 1000 Miles race in June 1932. *Photograph by Autocar, courtesy of LAT Archive*

Right – 1933 – Shelsley Walsh – Howe passes the crowded spectator banks at the September 1933 hillclimb meeting in his newly-acquired Alfa Romeo 8C 2300 on the way to setting a best time of 47.6 seconds, finishing eighth in class. *Photograph courtesy of Midland Automobile Club Archive*

Below – 1932 – Le Mans – The Howe/Birkin Alfa Romeo 8C 2300 (No.8) leads Minoia's works car at the start of the 1932 24 Heures du Mans. They retired after 110 laps due to gasket trouble. *Photograph by Autocar, courtesy of LAT Archive*

By the time of Howe's next Le Mans, Birkin was dead so other co-drivers were needed. In 1934 it was Tim Rose-Richards, and the following year, Hon. Brian Lewis. Both were experienced and talented drivers providing Howe with an excellent chance of repeating his 1931 victory. And, indeed, his Alfa did lead the race for some hours in 1934 and 1935 before mechanical problems intervened forcing its retirement on both occasions.

In 1934 Tim Rose-Richards inherited the lead from Sommer's 8C, when the latter's engine caught fire. Another of the works Alfas, driven by Etancelin and Chinetti, was in close pursuit and, with a quicker pit stop than the Howe/Rose-Richards equipe, the works car went into the lead. Howe gave chase, and got closer and closer to Chinetti. Barrie Lyndon, who was present at the race, vividly described the duel between the two Alfas: "Howe gained steadily, travelling hard down the Mulsanne straight, holding his speed until the last moment before braking at the corner. He came through White House turn absolutely flat out, so that the machine presented a magnificent sight as it flashed past the grandstands and ran on to the banking of the curve beyond…Chinetti did his utmost to keep him behind but Howe gained until the two were racing side by side at fully 125 mph, for Howe to be just ahead when they were forced to use their brakes at Mulsanne" (Lyndon: *Grand Prix* (1935)).

The two Alfas continued to travel in close

Top – 1934 – Le Mans – Howe and his Alfa Romeo 8C 2300 pass Arnage corner during the 1934 24 Heures du Mans. Howe shared the Alfa with Tim Rose-Richards but retired after eighty-five laps with clutch problems. It appears that the tents in the background belong to officials. *Photograph by* Autocar, *courtesy of LAT Archive*

Left – 1934 – Le Mans – Howe and his Alfa Romeo 8C 2300 make a pit stop during the race. Howe's co-driver, Tim Rose-Richards can be seen standing on the pit counter. *Photograph courtesy of Geoffrey Goddard Archive*

1935 – Le Mans – Howe, wearing his CSI official armband (see page Appendix 3), watches a discussion in the Fox & Nicholl pit. Behind the winning Lagonda of Hindmarsh & Fontes to the left can be seen John Hindmarsh (second from left) and Arthur Fox (fourth from left, wearing glasses). The photograph is taken early in the race on the Saturday. *Photograph courtesy of Arnold Davey*

company until the next fuel stop. The Chinetti car was then considerably delayed because of a leak in the fuel tank and this enabled Howe's car to build up a comfortable lead. However, as midnight approached, problems began. Initially it was the lighting which forced a stop on the circuit to repair a broken wire. Once rectified the car began to pick up places – having dropped down to eleventh – but clutch trouble then set in which delivered the final coup de grâce.

Some consolation for this retirement came two months later when Howe, again partnered by Rose-Richards, won the Campari cup in the Targa Abruzzo. This race held over the Pescara circuit, one of Howe's favourite, was run, for the first time in 1934, over 24 hours. A large entry of 8Cs was remorselessly whittled away by retirements and Howe's own car "was limping along slowly to keep an ailing back axle intact, and with only bottom and top gears working" (Hull and Slater). Fortunately this nursing of the car was successful but it did mean Howe and Rose-Richards had to give best in the overall classification to the 6C unsupercharged Alfas.

In many respects Howe's final Le Mans in 1935 followed a similar pattern to the preceding year. His co-driver, Hon. Brian Lewis, led the race in the early stages but the engine began to misfire which meant a pit stop and the loss of several places. Once the trouble was rectified the car began to move up the order again and by the early hours of Sunday was back in the lead, but at 5.30 a holed piston forced its retirement. As in the Targa Abruzzo, there was a high rate of attrition among the 8Cs, with three out of the four failing to finish; the one survivor finishing as runner-up to the winning Lagonda. Howe did not come away entirely empty-handed as he set the fastest lap of the race at 86.751, though this didn't break Raymond Sommer's record of 90.959, set in 1933.

Howe and the Tourist Trophy: Variety is the spice...

Nine T.T. races were held on the Ards road circuit between 1928 and 1936 and Howe competed in all of them driving two different models of Bugatti and four other makes of car. For his first two entries he used the T43 Bugatti and retired on both occasions. In 1930 he did finish the race, driving his 38/250 Mercedes, albeit in last place. In 1931 he swapped horses again entering the 8C Alfa, to which he was faithful in the next two years as well. In 1931 with his Le Mans win of two months before he had good reason to think he could finish among the leading cars. To begin with he was indeed among the frontrunners, duelling closely with Campari, also in an 8C. Unfortunately he then made a spectacular exit from the race: "...on the descent of Bradshaw's Brae he tried to overtake where there was no room to do so, touched the kerb, spun backwards across the road towards a telegraph pole, missed it by inches and vanished tail first through the hedge, to drop heavily into a potato field some eight feet below" (Blight: *George Roesch and the Invincible Talbots*).

Fifteen years later Howe put the blame on a car that slowed unexpectedly forcing him to brake suddenly and spin into the bank (*Motor Sport* – January 1946). But in the immediate wake of the accident he told Arthur Fox it was "my wild and bad driving" which suggests Blight's account is more accurate (letter to Arthur Fox, 1st September, 1931). Howe claimed in his 1946 account that as the car went into the air "it cleared a low brick wall and sailed over the heads of three very surprised people who were climbing a bank to take photographs". Very fortunately the Alfa landed in the potato field the right way up. Howe told *Motor Sport* that he considered it was his "most frightening experience in motor racing" (*ibid*). A number of subsequent racing accidents will be chronicled in the following pages from all of which, save one, Howe extricated himself with minimal damage. The Ards accident, in terms of possible consequences for the driver, passenger, and for various spectators, must come near the top of any list of his 'phenomenal avoidances'.

1931 – Ards – Howe's Alfa Romeo 8C 2300 is seen in entering Conway Square, Newtownards during the R.A.C. Tourist Trophy in August 1931. *Photograph by* Autocar, *courtesy of LAT Archive*

Top left – 1931 – Ards – Howe's Alfa Romeo 8C 2300 (No.10) passes through the streets of Newtownards, heading for the Railway Bridge, during the R.A.C. Tourist Trophy in August 1931. *Photograph by* Autocar, *courtesy of LAT Archive*

Middle left – 1932 – Ards – Howe exits Dundonald Hairpin in his Alfa Romeo 8C 2300 during the 1932 R.A.C. Tourist Trophy in which he finished fourth, winning his class. Note the presence of only one mudguard, which was used as a driver's stone guard. *Photograph courtesy of Guy Spollon Collection*

Bottom left – 1932 – Ards – Howe's Alfa Romeo 8C 2300 passes the Central Bar at Dundonald Hairpin during the 1932 R.A.C. Tourist Trophy in which he finished fifth. *Photograph by* Autocar, *courtesy of LAT Archive*

Bottom right – 1933 – Ards – Howe greets Tazio Nuvolari before the start of the 1933 R.A.C. Tourist Trophy. Nuvolari won the race, driving Whitney Straight's M.G. K3. George Manby-Colegrave's similar car (No.18) is visible to the left in the photo, behind Straight's pit manager, Hugh McConnell. *Photograph courtesy of Jarrotts*

Above – 1933 – Ards – Howe (No.4) leads the three Alfa Romeo 8C 2300s away from the pits at the start of the 1933 R.A.C. Tourist Trophy, cars being started in Class batches. Howe finished fifth. The No.3 Alfa was driven by Hon. Brian Lewis and the No.5 car by Tim Rose-Richards. *Photograph courtesy of Geoffrey Goddard Archive*

Right – 1934 – Ards – Howe's Talbot 105 is followed by John Hindmarsh's Lagonda through Quarry Corner during the R.A.C. Tourist Trophy in September 1934. Howe finished thirteenth, second in his class. *Photograph by* Autocar, *courtesy of LAT Archive*

Bottom right – 1935 – Ards – Howe and his works Bugatti Type 57T are seen passing the Central Bar at Dundonald Hairpin during the 1935 R.A.C. Tourist Trophy. *Photograph courtesy of Geoffrey Goddard Archive*

Above – 1935 – Ards – The works Bugatti Type 57Ts of Hon. Brian Lewis (No.4) and Howe (No.5) lead Eddie Hall's Bentley approach the Watering Trough before the descent down Bradshaw's Brae, during the 1935 R.A.C. Tourist Trophy. Howe finished third, with Lewis retiring and Hall finishing second. *Photograph courtesy of Geoffrey Goddard Archive*

Below – 1935 – Ards – Howe, looking remarkably fresh, leans on his Bugatti Type 57T having finished third in the 1935 R.A.C. Tourist Trophy with, to his right, Freddie Dixon and Eddie Hall. *Photograph courtesy of Geoffrey Goddard Archive*

1936 – Ards – The Lagonda team of Howe (No.3), Fairfield (No.2) and Hon. Brian Lewis (No.1) pull away from the pits at the start of the 1936 R.A.C. Tourist Trophy. *Photograph courtesy of Arnold Davey*

Honour was regained the following year when he finished fourth. In this race he and Birkin had the fastest cars, a fact recognized by the organizers who set them some very stiff targets relative to the smaller-engined entries. Anthony Blight points out that Howe's race average in 1932 of 80.53 was only exceeded in the final T.T. at Ards in 1936. It is true, of course, that Howe achieved this speed in a supercharged car and that there was only one further year in which the organizers allowed such cars to enter. In this final outing for supercharged sports cars – 1933 – Howe had a similar result to the previous year, finishing fifth overall and second in his class.

For the 1934 race he was obliged to find an unsupercharged car and he chose one of the Talbot 105s. This was GO 54, often used as a practice car at the height of the Fox and Nichol years, though it had taken third place in the 1930 500 Miles Race, driven by John Cobb, as well as in the 1932 Le Mans (Hon. Brian Lewis/Tim Rose-Richards). By the time Howe came to drive it there had been some detuning with consequential loss of speed, but the Talbot's reputation for smooth and reliable running carried him through to a trouble-free thirteenth place.

It was the turn of Bugatti again to provide a car for Howe in 1935. Although his Type 57 and that of Hon. Brian Lewis, who had an identical model, were 'technically' privately entered, all the evidence indicates that they were works cars. Howe and Noel Rees (for Hon. Brian Lewis) had provided finance for their construction at Molsheim though the bodies were provided by the British firm, Corsica. These bodies were rather special, using electron which was a much lighter material than steel.

Even with these special bodies the two T 57s were quite heavy and their weight and size didn't make them ideal mounts for the demanding Ards circuit. Nonetheless both cars gave a good account of

1936 – Ards – Howe at speed in the Lagonda during the 1936 R.A.C. Tourist Trophy, on his way to fifth place. *Photograph courtesy of Arnold Davey*

themselves with Hon. Brian Lewis nearly equalling the lap record established by Birkin in his 8C Alfa in 1932. In the later stages of the race Lewis' clutch weakened which allowed Howe to overhaul him and finish third. The cars went straight back to Molsheim after the race, the subsequent history of Howe's chassis providing one of those puzzles for historians as two different cars ended up claiming the same chassis number!

For what turned out to be Howe's final T.T. he chose a 4½ litre Lagonda. It was one of a three car team entered by Arthur Fox, with the other two cars in the hands of Pat Fairfield and Hon. Brian Lewis. Howe and Fairfield had identical cars with four seater bodies whereas Lewis' was fitted with a two seater body. Hon. Brian Lewis was the most rapid of the three, fast enough to dispute second place with Eddie Hall in his Bentley but neither able to challenge Freddie Dixon for the lead. Lewis' challenge faded when he damaged a front wheel, compounded later on by serious oil loss. Fairfield and Howe had steady and unspectacular races running in close company and finishing fourth and fifth.

This ninth race on the Ards circuit signalled significant changes for the future of the T.T. There was a serious accident which resulted in a number of fatalities among the spectators. The R.A.C. concluded that it couldn't continue using a circuit where it was almost impossible to adequately protect spectators. Despite British sports cars filling the leading places it was clear that they were looking increasingly old-fashioned against the new French and German cars, such as Delahaye and B.M.W. For the two remaining pre-war T.T.s the scene shifted to Donington and the dominant cars were French sports cars, the Darracq in particular. If Howe contemplated an entry in 1937 it would have been put at risk by his serious accident at Brooklands in May although he did recover, against all the odds, to drive in the J.C.C. International Trophy held a week before the T.T.

Two weeks later Howe was at the wheel of a Lagonda again in the final '500' at Brooklands – though it was a race of 500 kilometres, not 500 miles like all its predecessors. Howe and his co-driver Hon. Brian Lewis used the two-seater car the latter had driven in the T.T. which had to have some new bearings fitted to remedy the oil loss at Ards. The Lagonda historian remarks on a photo taken at the beginning of the race which shows Hon. Brian Lewis being flagged away with Lord Howe "dressed as for Ascot" among various other personnel on the starting line (Arnold Davey: *Lagonda*). However he may have been dressed it certainly didn't impede his effectiveness when he was behind the steering wheel as the car finished third.

Lord Howe and the Mille Miglia: the background

Lord Howe was a great admirer of the Mille Miglia. In his account of eight European racing circuits he says that it is "perhaps in some ways the most outstanding race which takes place on the Continent…". Although he devotes more space to it than any other circuit, he concludes by admitting "I could continue a description of it for hours, but time and space would certainly not permit. The general impression left by the race is that it is very much the same in character as the great motor races of days gone by, between Paris-Vienna, Paris-Berlin, etc." (Howe: *Motor Racing* (1939)).

Although he did not compete in the race until 1933, he was involved in discussions about taking part in the previous two years. Howe had met Count Giovanni Lurani at a party held after the 1930 Double Twelve at Brooklands. They quickly established a friendship which was close and lifelong. Lurani was also very keen to take part in the Mille Miglia and, as an Italian, had the advantage of local knowledge and contacts. According to Lurani, the initial idea for the 1931 race was to enter a Bentley which he would co-drive with George Eyston. Howe was involved in this scheme but it isn't clear whether he was also going to drive another Bentley or just act as entrant and sponsor.

M.G. and the Mille Miglia: the role of Lord Howe

The collapse of Bentley Motors put paid to this idea and the focus shifted to the possibility of an M.G team. Lurani says that he took part in some discussion with Howe, Eyston, and Cecil Kimber, the managing director of M.G., in late November 1931. These discussions seem to have been rather tentative (some historians are doubtful whether they took place at all), and did not lead to a team for the 1932 race. A single M.G. did take part that year, Lord de Clifford entering his own C type, which went quite well until it retired at three-quarter distance. Howe was a spectator on this occasion and Lurani competed for the first time, co-driving a 6C Alfa with Carlo Canavesi.

Serious planning for the 1933 Mille Miglia took place in the autumn of 1932 and this time it did bear fruit with a three-car M.G. team. The result is justifiably well-known with two of the three cars not merely completing the race, but finishing first and second in their class and winning the team award. Howe's role in this outstanding achievement was crucial in three key respects – in providing the initial inspiration, in giving substantial financial support to the project and in the necessary planning and organization prior to the race. As these three aspects reflect something of Howe's general approach to motor racing it is worth saying a word or two about each one.

Howe's starting point was his strong desire to see a British car which was good enough to defeat the continental opposition. He believed that an M.G. team offered a realistic possibility of doing this, especially with the evolving K3 model. While the M.G. Company had plenty of confidence in this new car, left to itself it would not have entered a car for the 1933 Mille Miglia, never mind a team of three. John Thornley emphasizes how little had been done by the late autumn of 1932 to turn the plans for the K3 into actual cars. The K3 would undoubtedly have appeared at some stage in 1933 but, without Howe's commitment and drive, everything would have run at a slower pace. There were other obstacles to a works appearance, too. A team appearance in the Mille Miglia was a very expensive undertaking and to the ultimate 'boss' of M.G., Sir William Morris (subsequently Lord Nuffield) a good example of his belief that for manufacturers, motor sport activity "invariably led to economic disaster" (Peter Hull: *Lord Nuffield* (1993)). Others in the senior management of Morris Motors, the owners of M.G., were also unconvinced about the value of motor sport and such views eventually led to M.G.'s withdrawal from racing in June 1935.

Against this background Howe's second major contribution, a willingness to absorb a considerable share of the Mille Miglia's cost was of great importance. Howe's contribution covered entry costs, the preparatory trip in January, and various support costs during the race itself including the payment of a fee to Hugh McConnell who acted as M.G. team manager. At about this time Howe sold a valuable picture from the collection at Penn House. The picture was

Above – 1933 – Modena – Howe poses behind the team M.G. used on the Mille Miglia recce in January 1933. (l-r) Eugenio Siena, Howe, Tazio Nuvolari, Enzo Ferrari, 'Johnny' Lurani and Capt. George Eyston. *Photograph by Dott. Ferruccio Testi courtesy of Spitzley Zagari Archive*

Left – 1933 – Brescia – Howe is in characteristic pose during the preliminaries for the 1933 Mille Miglia. Standing behind him is Hugh McConnell, whilst to the right in the trilby is Mille Miglia Clerk of the Course Renzo Castagneto, with, on the extreme right, Clifton Penn-Hughes who was also competing, in a Mercedes SSK. *Photograph courtesy of Adam Ferrington Collection*

1933 – Brescia – Howe (right) and Hugh Hamilton (left) show their exhaustion at the finish of the 1933 Mille Miglia, where they finished second in class and were part of the M.G. team which won the Team Prize. To the left, behind the M.G. K3 is 'Johnny' Lurani who was teamed with George Eyston in another M.G. which finished one place ahead of Howe & Hamilton in twenty-first place overall. *Photograph courtesy of Geoffrey Goddard Archive*

by Franz Hals and it was bought by Alfred Beit and taken to the Wexford Museum in Ireland. The funds from this sale made a major contribution to the costs incurred by Howe in funding the M.G. teams in 1933 and 1934.

Howe's third important role in M.G.'s attempt on the Mille Miglia was to lead the preparatory expedition which went to Italy in January 1933. In view of the fact that the K3 was a new and untried car, and that most of the M.G. team – both drivers and mechanics – had little or no experience of the Mille Miglia, an exploratory visit was vital. Howe led the group using his 38/250 Mercedes and one of his 1750 Alfas as service cars to ferry people and equipment around. The K3 they took with them was actually the second prototype as the first car had been used in the Monte Carlo Rally. This event was hardly ideal for the new car and it finished way down the order but shortly afterwards it established fastest time in the Mont des Mules hill climb, an event that was much closer to the conditions that would be encountered in the Mille Miglia.

The testing period revealed some significant weaknesses in the K3. The front axle wasn't strong enough, the gears required different ratios, and the wheels broke up necessitating new hubs and spokes. Ettore Bugatti has usually been given the credit for spotting the problem with the front axle, but Mike Allison has challenged this, arguing that although Howe did visit Molsheim en route for Italy, the M.G.

Above – 1933 – Brooklands – (l-r) John Cobb, Howe and Sir Malcolm Campbell chat on the grid before the start of the J.C.C. International Trophy in May 1933. Howe's M.G. K3 finished fourth in the race. *Photograph courtesy of Geoffrey Goddard Archive*

Below – 1933 – Brooklands – The start of J.C.C. International Trophy. Howe is in the centre (No.15) in his M.G. K3. Other prominent cars (l-r) are (No.22) Barnes' Austin, (No.30) Elwes' M.G., (No.34) Rayson's Riley, (No.7) Hon. Brian Lewis' Alfa Romeo, (No.8) Straight's Maserati and (No.5) Fothringham's Bugatti. *Photograph by* Autocar, *courtesy of LAT Archive*

didn't go with him. Allison says it was identified by Birkin during testing, but whoever was responsible there is no doubt that it wasn't sufficiently robust and had to be re-designed. (M. Allison and P. Browning: *The Works M.G.s* (2000)).

This testing period was obviously of crucial importance in developing the car but it was also necessary for the drivers to familiarize themselves with the terrain. Although all cars in the Mille Miglia had two-man crews there was a lot of variety in how the driving was shared out among them. Howe's co-driver was H.C. Hamilton and they divided the distance on the basis of two-thirds to Howe and one-third to Hamilton. That meant each could concentrate on learning the portion where they were driving, as Howe explained: "I look upon myself as being an individual of normal intelligence in learning a circuit, and I found that, after four drives over the stretch of road which I intended to drive on during the race, I had a very fair knowledge of it; that is to say when I came to the race itself I only made a mistake at one corner in the 750 miles which I drove. I covered the other section of the course, which I did not intend to drive on, twice in practice, and therefore had a slight knowledge of that section as well..."(Howe: *Motor Racing* (1939)).

1933 – Brooklands – Howe sits on the tail of his M.G. K3, chatting to Eddie Hall, after finishing fourth in the J.C.C. International Trophy. Note the champagne glass next to his helmet. *Photograph courtesy of Geoffrey Goddard Archive*

The Mille Miglia races of 1933 and 1934

When it came to the race itself, the M.G. team cars were taken by sea from Fowey in Cornwall to Genoa – a long, complicated journey involving a boat carrying fish and china clay where the cars were lashed to the deck – and using various different railway companies in England and Italy. To further preserve the cars for the actual race all the drivers practiced on a spare car which was the second prototype that had been used during the January preparatory trip. Further problems then emerged, especially with the brakes, but H.N. Charles, the principal designer of the K3, was able to make speedy and effective modifications. McConnell, as team manager, made the final arrangements for the three refuelling stops and Howe's Mercedes was loaded up with various spares the M.G.s might need. In fact, no real demand was made upon it and, despite carrying a considerable amount of equipment it took part in the race and won its class, driven by Clifton Penn Hughes and Percy Thomas.

The M.G. strategy was for the Birkin and Rubin car to break the Maserati opposition, accepting the risk that the M.G. itself might expire in the attempt – hopefully after, rather than before, it had seen off the Maserati challenge. The other M.G.s, driven by Lurani and Eyston, and Howe and Hamilton, were to proceed more cautiously, at any rate in the early stages of the race. This strategy worked out very much as intended: Birkin/Rubin did force the leading Maserati to retire albeit at the cost of their own demise with mechanical problems. With the retirement of the leading two Maseratis, the remaining M.G.s were able to dominate their class and win the team prize.

Given this very good result, it was not surprising that a repeat M.G. entry was made for 1934. M.G.

did not rest on its 1933 laurels but made a number of changes to the K3 for its second attempt. Of particular importance was the substitution of a Marshall supercharger for the Powerplus unit used in 1933. The latter had given a lot of trouble by indirectly oiling up the plugs and the Marshall blower solved this problem, albeit with some sacrifice of power output. The K3's brakes were also improved so that they were more predictable and less prone to fade.

The M.G. drivers for 1934 were somewhat changed with only Howe and Lurani surviving from the previous year. Eddie and Joan Hall shared a car and Penn Hughes partnered Lurani; Howe teamed up with his personal mechanic, Percy Thomas. The 1934 race was marked by heavy rain to which the M.G. team reacted rather differently: Lurani and Penn Hughes proceeded with some caution but Howe was not similarly inhibited, "going at full speed and sliding in a most frightening way on the wet road" (Lurani: *Racing Round the World*). Howe was involved in a close battle with Taruffi, in the leading Maserati, on the Raticosa Pass: "Lord Howe threw himself into the battle with great temerity risking a crash at every corner" (Lurani: *ibid*).

Unfortunately this crash soon came. In a fast downward stretch near Florence the car skidded first one way and then another and went off the road, colliding with a telegraph pole which broke in half, striking Howe a blow on the head. Most fortunately neither he nor Thomas was seriously hurt, Howe's head being protected by his crash helmet. Many years later, in a parliamentary debate, he recalled that his crash helmet had saved his life on a number of occasions and this was certainly one of them. John Thornley reports that Howe temporarily lost consciousness and when he started to come round, but was not yet fully recovered said to Thomas: "'Thomas! What are we waiting for? Get on with it'" (Thornley: *Maintaining The Breed* (1956)). Shortly afterwards, when Lurani and Penn Hughes passed by, they were relieved to note there was no serious damage to the drivers but the sight of the wrecked M.G. underlined the dangerous conditions.

In fact they completed the course, finishing second in their class to Taruffi's winning Maserati. The remaining M.G., driven by the Halls, had retired with engine trouble at about half-distance. Obviously this result was something of a disappointment, especially against the benchmark of 1933. Although M.G. had improved their cars, it wasn't enough to match the Maseratis which had also made progress since the previous year, particularly in reliability.

So far as competition work was concerned, the 1934 Mille Miglia marked the end of Howe's association with M.G. (he continued to run an F Magna as a road car). His involvement with the marque was built very much around the single event of the Mille Miglia and it is doubtful whether the firm could have produced a more successful car for the 1935 race – even if Howe had been prepared to help with the funding.

A bizarre episode: a Marendaz at the 1936 French Grand Prix

Overwhelmingly Francis Howe's racing was in well-known competition cars. One clear exception was the 1936 French Grand Prix when he drove a Marendaz. Captain Donald Marendaz, whose family came from Switzerland, had been brought up in Wales and after serving in the R.F.C. during the First World War he worked in the automobile industry, initially in Coventry and subsequently in London and Maidenhead. From the mid-1920s to the mid-1930s he produced a variety of sports cars using proprietary components such as Anzani and Coventry Climax engines.

Marendaz undoubtedly made a strong impression on people. Bill Boddy says that he has been described as 'colourful' but Bill thinks 'awkward and ingenious more appropriate'. Bill's very interesting portrait of him draws on the research of Graham Skillen who tried to interview Marendaz in the early 1970s. This attempt was decisively rebuffed by Marendaz "Invitations to visit the doyen of Automobile and Aeronautical Engineers originate from Asterley Hall (Marendaz's home) and none are programmed for you" (quoted in 'Special Agenda' by Bill Boddy, *Motor Sport*, January, 2001). During the 1930s Marendaz supported Oswald Mosley which led to his internment in 1940 as a security risk. However, unlike his leader, who spent three years similarly incarcerated, Marendaz was released after a few days, apparently as a result of newspaper pressure highlighting his record in the First War.

Stirling Moss's parents, Alfred and Aileen, were closely involved with the Marendaz Company in the early 1930s, Alfred investing in it, and Aileen driving its cars in trials and rallies. They were at Montlhéry in June 1936 along with Captain Marendaz himself and Earl Howe for the French Grand Prix. It is not clear whether Marendaz or Howe had taken the initiative in arranging this entry: Boddy suggests that Howe was "somehow...persuaded" whereas Anthony

1936 – Montlhéry – Howe and his Marendaz lead Génaro Léoz in his Lagonda during the Grand Prix de l'ACF, which in 1936 was run for sports cars. Howe shared the Marendaz with Tommy Wisdom but his only race for the marque was not a success, eventually finishing in twenty-fifth place. *Photograph courtesy of Ted Walker – Ferret Fotographics*

Blight says Howe "had pressed Captain Marendaz to lend him his personal car" (Boddy *op. cit.* and Blight: *The French Sports Car Revolution*). Both mention Howe's concern to drive a British car in major events wherever possible, but as there were other British makes competing it's far from clear why he should have homed in on the Marendaz.

It had to be a sports car of some sort because the French racing authorities had decided that in 1936 its main grand prix events would be for sports cars, not single-seater racing cars. The Marendaz which Howe drove was a 15/90 model with a six cylinder two litre engine which had a top speed of about 90 mph. To begin with the car lapped consistently but somewhere on the circuit Howe struck a gate post and bent the stub-axle. Mr. and Mrs. Moss, who had travelled to the race in their own 15/90, offered its stub axle as a replacement. Locating the Moss car, which was in the public car park, and completing the repair would take a long time and Howe thought there was no point in continuing. Marendaz himself did not agree and the upshot was that he and Howe parted company so that Tommy Wisdom, the appointed co-driver, was left to complete the race. He duly did so, albeit in twenty-third and last place.

Howe had no further association with Marendaz. Alfred and Aileen Moss returned to England, whether with a stub axle that had taken part in twenty-six laps of the 1936 French Grand Prix, history does not relate. Shortly after these events the Marendaz Company collapsed and Alfred Moss re-possessed what little was left at the works, though this did include the car Howe had driven at Montlhéry.

5

The Grand Prix Years

- The background to Grand Prix racing
- Howe's choice of Grand Prix cars
- Supporting the racing cars – preparation and transport
- Howe's Grand Prix debut: Monaco, 1931
- Other initiations: Montlhéry and Nürburgring
- First steps with the Delage
- 1932: Consolidation and fresh departures
- The Type 54 Bugatti: an unsuccessful episode
- Success with the Delage
- Hill Climbing with the Type 51 Bugatti – Shelsley Walsh
- Hill Climbing with the Type 51 Bugatti in Europe – Klausenrennen
- Pleasure and pain: Pescara and Monza
- 1933: back to the Bugatti
- Retirements at Monaco, Montlhéry and Nice
- Better results with the Type 51: Pescara, Shelsley and Brighton
- The Delage redeems Howe's 1933 record on the circuits

- The beginnings of Donington
- Trying for a P3, settling for an 8CM
- Grand Prix racing with the 8CM
- The Type 51's Grand Prix swansong
- The Type 51 in British events – Brooklands, Shelsley and Donington
- Howe's voiturette racing in 1934: only a footnote
- 1935: Bugatti again for the final grand prix year
- Debut with the Type 59 at Monaco
- Two races in France: Picardie and Dieppe
- Albi: a new circuit for the Delage
- Berne: repeating the Dieppe experience?
- 500 Miles at Brooklands with the Type 59
- The Donington Grand Prix
- First visit to South Africa
- The end of the Type 59 – and of Howe's grand prix racing

Chapter 5

The Grand Prix Years

The background to Grand Prix racing

The years from 1928 to 1930 were a form of apprenticeship for Francis Howe, a period when he concentrated on sports car racing gaining experience of a variety of cars on different circuits. At the end of 1930 he decided he was ready to move up to the most sophisticated form of the sport – Grand Prix racing.

Some historians would query the use of the term 'sophisticated' to describe Grand Prix racing in the late 1920s and early 1930s. The official formulae promulgated by the A.I.A.C.R. between 1928 and 1934 found little favour and effectively many grands prix were formula libre events. Lurani says that the 1928 regulations provided no stimulus to innovation and technical progress was therefore at a standstill; in similar vein Clutton and Stanford cite the experience of the German Grand Prix of 1928 and the Pau Grand Prix of 1930: "In the first a team of 7 litre Mercedes, basically production sports cars, showed such speed that they took the first three places; while at Pau, Sir Henry Birkin, on a supercharged 4½ litre Bentley (again based closely on a production model) ran second only to a type 35C Bugatti" (Lurani: *A History of Motor Racing* (1972) and Clutton and Stanford: *The Vintage Motor Car* (1954)).

Despite the discouraging formulae new cars did eventually appear, the most important example in 1930 being the 8C 2500 Maserati. It was very successful in its first season with six grand prix victories and, as Clutton and Stanford note, it stimulated other manufacturers to produce new cars, rather than re-running old ones. The two outstanding examples in 1931 were the 8C Alfa Romeo and the T51 Bugatti. We have already encountered the 8C in the previous chapter where we noted that the Monza was the version specially developed for grand prix work.

Externally the T51 Bugatti looked very similar to the T35 model which had been so successful after its introduction in 1924. The T51's major innovation was in its 'internals' – a new engine incorporating twin overhead camshafts. At the 1931 Monaco Grand Prix it greatly impressed W.F. Bradley, the *Autocar's* reporter, who thought it was "one of the most beautiful and carefully prepared racing cars it has been my privilege to examine in a very long experience". He said that the engine developed approximately twenty per cent more power than the T35 and "is marvellously rapid in acceleration" (*Autocar*, 24th April, 1931).

Howe's choice of Grand Prix cars

Francis Howe was at Monaco with a brand new T51, the first privately-owned example T51 to leave Molsheim. It was one of two cars Howe selected for his grand prix work. The choice of a Bugatti was in no way surprising as Howe was a confirmed Bugatti enthusiast and would have been more than familiar with the T35, a proven grand prix car freely available to private customers. Rivers Fletcher says that Howe tried a T35 and was on the point of placing an order.

We don't know where he tried it, though it's most likely to have been at Brooklands with a car from Malcolm Campbell who was both an owner and distributor of T35s. At any rate the Bugatti Company, possibly Ettore himself, would have alerted Howe to the appearance of a new model which was intended to be an advance on the T35, and so it was a T51 that Howe took delivery of on 14th April 1931.

Howe's other choice was one of the 1926/7 Delage team cars that had come to the U.K. when it was bought by Malcolm Campbell. Delage history is complicated but Alan Burnard, after many years effort, succeeded in unravelling the main strands. Campbell acquired two of the ex-works cars, chassis numbers 2 and 3, the first of which he subsequently sold to W.B. Scott, with 3 going to Howe during the winter of 1930-1. In 1929/30 Campbell was increasingly pre-occupied with the Land Speed record and had not used the Delage a great deal, confining himself to short distance events at Brooklands. Howe also acquired chassis number 4 at some point in 1931/2. It has often been suggested that he bought this second car after the ex-Campbell chassis had been irretrievably damaged at Monza but this is not the case. The Monza damage occurred in September 1932 but Howe was already using the second chassis in July at Dieppe.

The 8 cylinder 1500 cc Delage cars of 1926/7 are generally acknowledged as one of the outstanding cars in the history of motor racing. The engine, in particular, has been admired as a superb piece of engineering, beautifully designed and executed. It not only looks superb but proved extremely effective, especially in 1927 when it won all the major grands prix for which it was entered. Its first season had been more difficult because the exhaust ran very close to the drivers' legs and made the cockpit far too hot. A re-design during the winter of 1926/7 switched the exhaust to the other side of the car and successfully overcame this problem, though adding to the substantial costs already incurred: Cyril Posthumus says no expense was spared in their design and construction and the four works cars cost £36,000 which makes them very expensive indeed (Posthumus in *Profile Publications* No. 18 (1966)).

Howe raced a 1500 cc Delage for five years, longer than any of his other racing cars. Although he reserved the car increasingly for voiturette events, in 1931 he wouldn't have thought of it in these exclusive terms. Given the rather confused state of grand prix racing at that time, a 1927 Delage was by no means an outdated car for front-line events. When it first appeared it was an advanced racing car and the intervening years had not been marked by major technical advance, though this situation was soon to change.

Supporting the racing cars – preparation and transport

With two racing cars added to his stable Howe needed to develop his arrangements for supporting the racing programme. Sports cars could be driven on the road to events and their preparation and tuning was normally more straightforward than with out and out racing cars. But even with his sports car programme Howe had had the services of Percy Thomas as a full-time mechanic since the beginning of 1929. Thomas had previously worked for Col. Sorel the chief English Bugatti distributor and then for Malcolm Campbell. The beginning of Howe's Grand Prix years coincided with the collapse of Bentley Motors and Sidney Maslyn who had previously worked there came to join Percy Thomas; subsequently Stan Holgate, was also recruited, prior to moving on to the Chula/Bira equipe.

Preparation facilities were created both in London and at Penn House. In London they were centered on Pitt's Head Mews which was at the rear of his London home in Curzon Street. The mews were originally used for horses and Howe's youngest daughter, Sally recalls that during her childhood (in the 1950s) the rings on the wall, to which the horses had been tethered, could still be seen. It was the horse power of the internal combustion engine that they were housing by the 1930s, indeed for some time before that. The mews were of sufficient size to house up to a dozen cars and an inspection pit and various other facilities were installed to facilitate the necessary mechanical work.

While most of the responsibility for preparation rested with his mechanics Howe wasn't above getting his hands dirty himself. We have already noted his work on the T43's back axle during the 1930 Double Twelve and at the Dieppe meeting in 1932 he excused himself from acting as a judge in a concours d'élégance because of the need to help out with preparation. When *Motor Sport* visited his garage he was helping to change the Delage's back axle ratio and adjust its tappets (neither task simple or speedy).

In 1932 Howe commissioned a purpose-built transporter for his racing cars. He asked Edmund Dangerfield, a member of the family that owned *The Motor* and *The Commercial Motor*, for suggestions

Above and opposite page – 1932 – Penn Street, Buckinghamshire – In 1932 Francis Howe had a set of photographs taken at his Buckinghamshire home, Penn House, portraying his impressive equipe of cars. From left to right can be seen his Mercedes SS 38/250, his Bugatti Type 54, his Alfa Romeo 8C 2300, his Bugatti Type 51 and his two 1½ litre Delages. Judging by the garland in front of the leftmost Delage the photograph was taken at the end of May 1932, as the garland and the racing number "1" on the Delage relate to Howe's victory in the 1932 Avusrennen. In the second photograph Howe can be seen fourth from the left, with his arms folded, with Percy Thomas, his principal mechanic, immediately to the right. *Photographs courtesy of the Howe Family*

about suitable chassis for carrying racing cars. Dangerfield provided a list from which Howe selected a Commer Invader chassis on which the Lambeth Motor Body Works built up a body and fitted it out. It incorporated a hand-operated winch for loading and unloading, a work-bench, storage facilities for a range of spares, and removable floor boards. When these were taken up the mechanics, sitting on the van's torque tube, could inspect the underside of the car – in effect a portable inspection pit! Sid Maslyn later told David Venables that the van had been extremely reliable: in eight years of continuous use it only broke down twice and on both occasions the mechanics were able to deal with the problems (David Venables: *The Racing Fifteen Hundreds* (1986)).

As was amply demonstrated by his approach to the 1933 Mille Miglia Howe attached great importance to thorough preparation. Rivers Fletcher thinks Howe was strongly influenced by his experience of naval discipline: "he was certainly strict. In his pit everything had to be 'ship-shape and Bristol fashion' and he and his car were ready right on time for scrutineering and practice; he abhorred last-minute rushes to get things ready for an event" (Rivers Fletcher: *Mostly Motor Racing*).

He was concerned that his cars should not only be right mechanically but also that they should look right. From his earliest years he adopted a distinctive colour scheme of royal blue and silver, his father's horse-racing colours. Although Francis Howe had no interest in either horse racing or horses, these family colours were maintained for the sport to which he was very firmly committed. There were various occasions where he had to defer to Britain's national racing colour of green but even here he usually managed to incorporate a blue and silver band running the length of the car on both sides. When motor racing was re-starting after the end of the war his dislike of green as the British national colour led to him suggesting it should be changed to blue.

Howe's own appearance, both in and out of the car, was distinctive too. He wore light blue silk overalls with a crash helmet painted to match; occasionally the helmet was substituted for a wind cap and the same principle applied. The famous cloth cap, worn at an acute angle, appeared when he was in the paddock – and indeed more generally. On various occasions, especially when it was wet, a large blue umbrella would accompany him to the start: there is an amusing picture of him at the 1938 Brighton Speed Trials, returning to the start in his E.R.A.,

83

1932 – Howe had a purpose-built racing transporter built for his equipe at the beginning of 1932. It consisted of a Commer Invader chassis with a body built by Lambeth Motor Body Works. In the upper photograph one of the 1½ litre Delages is seen on the ramps to the transporter. In the other two photographs amongst features visible in the interior is a fold-down bed, folded up in the middle photograph and down in the lower one. *(Upper) Photograph courtesy of David Venables. (Middle) Photograph by Sporting & General, courtesy of Mark Morris. (Lower) Photograph by Zoltan Glass, courtesy of National Media Museum/Science and Society Picture Library*

with the umbrella held aloft. Further additions to his ensemble such as a carnation and a long cigarette holder made him an unmistakable, immediately recognizable figure.

Howe's Grand Prix debut: Monaco, 1931

Howe could hardly have chosen a more demanding circuit on which to begin his grand prix career. In the account he wrote of different European circuits his discussion of Monaco emphasized the extreme physical demands it made on the driver and the natural hazards that were present at almost every point: "The race is a terrific test of a driver's physical condition; only a driver who is physically super-fit can hope to stay the course. I have taken part myself in this race on six occasions, and invariably after about 30 laps, notwithstanding the fact that I have trained most carefully for the race, I have felt so done (*sic*) that I have wondered whether it was really humanly possible to continue the race; somehow one sticks to it, and after that it seems to get somewhat easier.

The chief thing for the driver to remember... is that practically everywhere there are kerbs and if a car gets into a slide and hits a kerb sideways it is almost certain to break a wheel or to capsize, and therefore, if there seems to be any danger of hitting a kerb, it is better to steer at it and go on to it rather than slide at it sideways" (Howe: *Motor Racing*).

He also pointed to the dangers of moving off the racing line and encountering spilt oil with the likelihood of a "terrific skid", as well as the great strain on the brakes and transmission with the constant braking, gear-changing and acceleration.

Howe's T51 was distinguished from the works cars by its green paint and wire wheels. The works cars had the conventional Bugatti cast aluminum wheels though these had been slightly modified to strengthen them. It seems highly likely that Howe's choice was influenced by his concern about the vulnerability of the wheels to Monaco's kerbs. There were twenty-three starters in the race, the main absentees being the new 8C Alfas which had experienced serious tyre problems in the Mille Miglia.

The grid positions were not decided by practice times but by ballot in which Howe drew a lowly place putting him on the sixth out of eight rows. He had an early set-back when an oiled plug necessitated a pit stop but it was soon remedied. Thereafter he drove steadily moving up the field and he was in sixth place just before the sixtieth lap. Shortly afterwards an oil pipe fractured and seized the engine so his first grand prix ended in a rather spectacular skid before he came to rest. The works T51s had a most successful debut with Louis Chiron winning the race and Varzi and Bouriat third and fourth; Fagioli in the Maserati provided the most serious opposition to Molsheim, finishing as runner-up. It took Chiron nearly three and three-quarter hours to complete the hundred laps which powerfully underlines Howe's point about Monaco's great physical demands.

Other initiations: Montlhéry and Nürburgring

Howe experienced two other major European circuits for the first time in 1931 with the Bugatti. Barely a week after his Le Mans victory he was at Montlhéry for the French Grand Prix and a month later at the Nürburgring for the German Grand Prix. The French race was one of only three that conformed to the A.I.A.C.R. regulations that grands prix should last for ten hours. Not surprisingly, other races ignored this specification and it was halved in the following year. It made shared driving more or less inevitable and Howe had asked Hon. Brian Lewis to be his co-driver.

The circuit was a combination of banked track and road sections, the latter comprising by far the greater part, and the overall lap distance was seven and three-quarter miles. Sheldon and Rabagliati emphasize how bumpy the track was: "Coming off the banked turn the cars were doing over 130 mph and over the bumps threw the brave drivers well off their seats. Many overalls were torn as the drivers were tossed about the cockpits..." (Sheldon and Rabagliati: *A Record of Grand Prix and Voiturette Racing – Vol. 2*). Given what has been said about the bumps at Brooklands, Howe and Lewis would have been familiar with these conditions, but that would not have made them any more welcome.

Howe had recruited Arthur Fox of Fox and Nichol to act as his pit manager and they swapped cars immediately after Le Mans with Fox driving the winning 8C to Paris and Howe the Talbot 105 (GO

1931 – Montlhéry – On the grid for the Grand Prix de l'ACF in June 1931 Howe (No.30), in his Bugatti Type 51, may be seen to the rear, in the middle of the fifth row. Other driver/car identities are:- Row 1 No.10 Fagioli/Maserati (Maserati), No.4 Minoia/Zehender (Alfa Romeo), No.2 Scott/Armstrong-Payn (Delage). Row 2 No.12 Dunfee/Appleyard (Sunbeam). Row 3 No.22 d'Arnoux/Fourny (Bugatti), No.20 Dreyfus/Ghersi (Maserati), No.18 Campari/Borzacchini (Alfa Romeo). Row 4 No.26 Ivanowsky/Stoffel (Mercedes), No.24 Ferrant/Rigal (Peugeot). Row 5 (partly hidden) No.32 Chiron/Varzi (Bugatti), No.30 Howe/Lewis (Bugatti), No.28 Divo/Bouriat (Bugatti). *Photograph by* Autocar, *courtesy of LAT Archive*

1931 – Montlhéry – The Bugatti Type 51 of Howe and Hon. Brian Lewis leads the Ivanowsky/Stoffel Mercedes Benz SSK during the Grand Prix de l'ACF. *Photograph by* Autocar, *courtesy of LAT Archive*

54 the car he would drive three years later in the 1934 T.T.). In the race Howe completed the first stretch of driving and when Hon. Brian Lewis took over he was able to improve on Howe's lap times by about ten seconds a lap. In a letter written to Fox after Montlhéry Howe acknowledged Lewis' superior speed: "I never seemed to get anywhere near him. There must be some very definite reason for that – probably because I was making a mess of something which he was doing very much better..." (Blight: *Georges Roesch and the Invincible Talbot*). In the end their joint efforts were only able to get them to the end of the race in last place because they had a pit stop of an hour and a half to remedy a misfire. The trouble was eventually traced to a frayed high tension lead on one of the sparking plugs. Sheldon and Rabagliati note that "simple mathematics will show that, had the 90 minutes not been lost the car would have been very highly placed" (Sheldon and Rabagliati: *ibid*). Each of the leading makes had a car in the first three places: the winning Bugatti T51 was followed home by an 8C Alfa and an 8C 2500 Maserati.

These three makes renewed their contest at the German Grand Prix but Mercedes also entered a powerful team, making it a four cornered contest. Works-entered cars predominated, comprising two-thirds of those on the starting grid. For Francis Howe, one of the small handful of private entrants, it was his first experience of the Nürburgring which

1931 – Nürburgring – Zoltan Glass's three photographs capture the atmosphere of the 1931 German Grand Prix meeting. Howe chats to "W. Williams" (C.F.W. Grover-Williams), shelters from the rain with his distinctive Howe blue umbrella and is seen in the paddock at the wheel of his Bugatti Type 51. Howe finished eleventh in the race, whilst "W. Williams", in a works Bugatti Type 51, retired. *Photographs by Zoltan Glass courtesy of National Media Museum/Science and Society Picture Library*

1931 – Nürburgring – Howe and his Bugatti Type 51 pass through a typical Nürburgring landscape during the German Grand Prix in July 1931. Howe finished eleventh. *Photograph by* Autocar, *courtesy of LAT Archive*

he considered "a tremendous test of the driver's real ability; in fact, with the possible exception of the old Targa Florio circuit in Sicily, it is probably true to say...(it) is the most difficult circuit in the world" (Howe: *Motor Racing*). Among the demanding features he identified the absence of any escape roads which minimized the chances of recovering from a mistake, the fact that the road "is continually running up to the crest of a hill, over which it is not possible to see", and the variation in the weather conditions on such a long circuit. Unlike the French Grand Prix the T51 ran satisfactorily but the end result was much the same as he finished last, though rather more in touch with the rest of the field than at Montlhéry. All the finishers completed twenty-two laps, Howe's taking just over five hours compared to four and a half for the winner, Caracciola.

First steps with the Delage

If satisfaction in motor sport was only a matter of silverware, Francis Howe would have found the Delage a more rewarding car in 1931 than the Bugatti. Of course, matters are rarely that simple but, with one or two exceptions, the Delage did produce better results than the Bugatti during this first season.

He took the Delage to Brooklands in May 1931 for his first competitive outing entering it for a series of short handicap races. He won two of these events, both contested over the original Outer Circuit: the 7 lap Gold Star Handicap and the Somerset Senior Long Handicap. The handicapping was clearly of high quality as Howe's winning margins were only fractions of a second. In the Somerset race his fastest lap of 127.05 mph established a new record for Class

F, for cars between 1100 cc and 1500 cc. This time was not improved upon before Brooklands' closure in 1939, so it remains one of the circuit's all-time records.

Although the Dieppe circuit was close to the English Channel and therefore potentially attractive to British competitors Howe was the only U.K. entrant in 1931. He enjoyed the circuit and returned to it each year until 1935. It was basically a five mile triangle with a mixture of gradients, a variety of slow and fast corners, and plenty of 'natural' hazards such as high hedges and buildings very close to the road.

Louis Chiron had been entered in a works Bugatti but he did not appear and all the remaining cars were privately entered. The leading places were contested by Monza Alfas and T51 Bugattis and it was Philippe Etancelin in a blue-painted Monza who ran out the winner followed by Count Czaykowski in his T51.

Howe was next up and winner of the special award for cars of 1500 cc; his nearest rival in this special category was a T37A Bugatti which finished sixth overall, some forty miles behind him.

Two weeks prior to Dieppe, Howe had taken the Delage to Shelsley along with the 38/250 Mercedes and his Alfa 1750 GS. It was not a successful outing for the Delage with a best time of 47.8, some four and a half seconds adrift of the class winner. This indifferent time resulted from a misfiring engine and Howe's slowness off the start line. These start-line problems were to plague Howe on a number of subsequent occasions and it is interesting that W.B. Scott, another owner of the 1927 Delages, acknowledged similar difficulties. Scott attributed them to the way in which the supercharger release valve used to pop when the clutch was let in (*Motor Sport*, October, 1964). Howe tried to overcome

1931 – Shelsley Walsh – Howe chats to Percy Thomas in the Shelsley paddock at the July 1931 hillclimb meeting. Lined up behind them are his 1½ litre Delage (No.18), his Alfa Romeo 6C 1750 (No.40), and his Mercedes SS 38/250. Howe won his class in the Mercedes, finishing fifth in class in the Delage and third in the Alfa Romeo. *Photograph courtesy of Midland Automobile Club Archive*

these problems by practicing up the drive of Penn House and when it was resurfaced he banked some of the corners to simulate another track feature.

1932: Consolidation and fresh departures

Howe kept both grand prix cars for the 1932 season and returned to some of his 1931 venues. There were also some new departures. He bought a T54 Bugatti and changed the way he used the T51 and the Delage, entering the former for only two long distance races, whereas the Delage was used at AVUS, the German G.P., the Coppa Acerbo, and the Italian G.P. The last two events provided Howe with his first experience of the Pescara and Monza circuits.

In his second Monaco G.P. he finished 4th which was the best result from the six occasions he competed there. The entry was of the highest quality, dominated by the ten works-entered cars from Alfa, Bugatti and Maserati. The private entrants were also all of proven quality, Caracciola, Etancelin and Zehender with Monza Alfas and Williams, Czaykowski, Lehoux and Howe with Bugattis.

Above – 1932 – Brooklands – Howe's Bugatti Type 51 stands in the Brooklands paddock during the B.R.D.C. 500 meeting in September 1932. Howe can be seen chatting to friends to the right in the background. *Photograph courtesy of Terry Cardy Collection*

Below – 1932 – Brooklands – Howe's Bugatti Type 54 is airborne on the banking on its way to victory in the Gold Star Handicap at the BARC Whitsun Meeting in June 1932. To the right is 'Tim' Birkin's Birkin Bentley. *Photograph by Autocar, courtesy of LAT Archive*

The works-entered cars suffered badly during the race, half of them failing to finish and all but two of the remainder were afflicted with various problems. Only three cars completed one hundred laps – two of the Alfas driven by Nuvolari and Caracciola who were first and second, and Fagioli's Maserati which finished third. Howe covered ninety-eight laps for his fourth place and was the best-placed Bugatti of the eight T51s that began the race. His driving preserved the car and avoided all the many traps awaiting even the most experienced driver on the Monaco circuit. The Autocar's reporter, stationed at the hairpin opposite the gasworks, said Howe was "impenetrable under his fly screen. He is driving wonderfully well, just as fast as any of the others on the hairpin although a little slower on the hill…"

Despite this good result Howe only used the T51 for one other long distance event during 1932. This was the B.R.D.C. 500 Mile Race which took place on the Outer Circuit at Brooklands at the end of the racing season. It was a handicap race, as were the great majority of Brooklands events. Howe had competed the previous year in the T51 when he had been eliminated early on with a broken piston. He retired again in 1932 due to the back axle puncturing the fuel tank though his withdrawal came at a later stage in the race than the previous year.

The Type 54 Bugatti: an unsuccessful episode

One possible reason for Howe not making more use of the T51 in long-distance events was his purchase of a T54 in April 1932. This new model had first run towards the end of the 1931 racing season when two works cars competed in the Italian Grand Prix. W.F. Bradley claimed the T54 was built in only thirteen days and although others have doubted whether it was quite as quick as that, there's no question that it was developed very rapidly. In large part this speed was possible because the model drew on existing components, especially the T50 engine of nearly five litres. However the concoction was not successful, as Hugh Conway says: "The car was heavy and handled badly – an unhappy model which few drivers could manage and fewer had much success with" (Conway: *Grand Prix Bugatti*).

Howe only drove the car twice, and at the end of 1932 it was returned to the Bugatti depot in Brixton Road, London where it remained until it was sold in 1936 for conversion into a sports car. Howe's two events with the car were a handicap race on the Outer Circuit at Brooklands, and the French Grand Prix at Reims. In certain respects it was a suitable Outer Circuit car for the original Brooklands track placed a premium on very high speed. Howe's best lap of 128.69 was unquestionably fast, but exceeded in that particular race by both Tim Birkin and John Cobb, driving the blown Bentley and the 10 litre Delage (with laps of 134.97 and 133.16 respectively). It wasn't rapid enough to overcome his handicap and he failed to finish among the first three.

In the French G.P. Howe thought the T54 would be a suitable car for Reims because it was one of the fastest circuits then in use, with two long straights linked by a third leg of fast curves. In the race Howe, and his co-driver Hugh Hamilton, were plagued with successive mechanical and handling problems. A carburettor fault led to an early pit stop; subsequently there were difficulties with the brake gear, threatened wheel disintegration and the gearbox. The gearbox was clearly one of the model's weaknesses as it led to the retirement of two other T54s driven by Divo and Lehoux. Howe and Hamilton did struggle on to the end as the ninth and final finisher (from sixteen starters).

Howe told Rivers Fletcher that he regretted not having entered his T51. Although the race was dominated by the works P3 Alfas, the next three places were filled by T51s so it is highly likely that Howe would have been more competitive if he had taken his own tried and tested example rather than the unproven T54. The Reims experience was sufficiently discouraging for Howe to put the car on one side and he did not use it again.

Could he have avoided his involvement with this essentially unsuccessful racing car? Although hindsight judgments are easy, Howe does appear to have committed himself to the T54 without much evidence of the car's performance and little direct experience of it. As a confirmed Bugatti enthusiast who liked his T51, he probably thought the T54 would be a similar car except with considerably more power. If he had looked a little harder at its specification and tested a works example, its limitations would soon have been apparent.

Success with the Delage

Apart from a dramatic crash right at the end of the season, Howe's 1932 record with the Delage was one of consistent achievement. He finished all the events he entered, gaining one outright victory, two other firsts from winning his heat or class, and with respectable placings in all the remaining races.

Howe's first outing with the Delage was in April at Brooklands for the British Empire Trophy which, unusually, was a scratch race of two 50 mile heats and a 100 mile final. Howe won his heat for cars of up to 1500 cc and came third in the final; in the latter he was headed by two much bigger cars, Cobb's V12 Delage and Eyston's 8 litre Panhard.

His first continental event took him to the AVUS track in Berlin which he encountered for the first time. The circuit was a remarkable creation involving two parallel straights, each of about six miles, linked by two steeply banked radius curves. As one would anticipate, it was a very fast track with lap times considerably in excess of 100 mph. Howe felt that there were serious potential dangers for the very large crowd of spectators who were permitted to watch close to the track. For a driver, he emphasized the vital importance of good brakes and an exact knowledge of the braking points on the approach to the two radius curves.

Top – 1932 – Brooklands – Howe's victorious Delage 1½ litre seems dwarfed by the larger cars of John Cobb's (Delage No.47) and George Eyston (Panhard No.44) during the British Empire Trophy in April 1932. *Photograph by* Autocar, *courtesy of LAT Archive*

Left – 1932 – Brooklands – This relaxed pit scene of Howe and his 1½ litre Delage during the 1932 British Empire Trophy meeting appears as if it is during practice. *Photograph courtesy of Guy Spollon Collection*

The Grand Prix Years

1932 – AVUS – Zoltan Glass photographed extensively at AVUS and the Nürburgring in the early 1930s. These four photographs show aspects of the Avusrennen meeting in May 1932. Howe won the voiturette race in his 1½ litre Delage, his first continental race win in a voiturette. In the first photo Howe chats with Hans Stuck, who was driving a Mercedes SSKL at the meeting, in which he finished fourth. In the second and third photos he is shown posing beside the Delage in the AVUS paddock with Percy Thomas working on the car. The fourth photo shows the car being loaded into Howe's transporter after the race. *Photographs by Zoltan Glass courtesy of National Media Museum/Science and Society Picture Library*

93

1932 – AVUS – These two photographs show Howe and his 1½ litre Delage at the Avusrennen meeting. In the first photograph Howe is seen chatting on the grid with two Bugatti Type 37As behind and a D.K.W. further back. In the second photograph Howe watches as the victorious Delage is loaded into the transporter. *Photographs courtesy of David Venables*

1932 – Nürburgring – Zoltan Glass's candid photographs evoke the atmosphere of the 1932 German Grand Prix meeting. In the first three pits photographs Howe is seen 1) with Jean Bugatti, playing with a camera, 2) chatting with two female friends, one apparently with a pet dog accompanying her on the pit counter, 3) studying a part from his Delage, whilst his mechanic readies the car for the twenty-three lap voiturette race, in which Howe finished fourth. The last two *(see over page)* carefully composed photographs show Howe getting into his car, and framed in the rear view mirror of the Delage. *Photographs by Zoltan Glass courtesy of National Media Museum/Science and Society Picture Library*

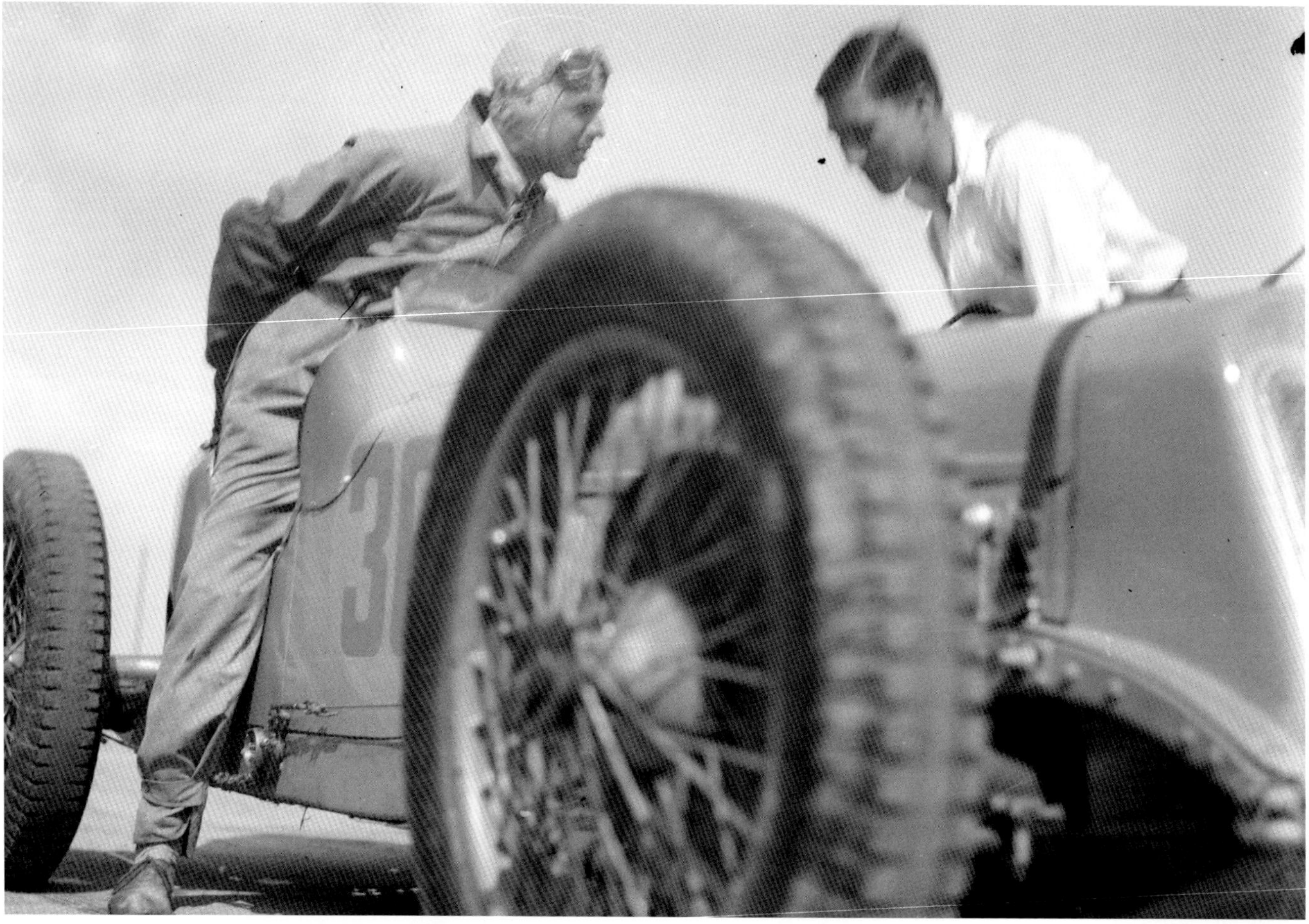

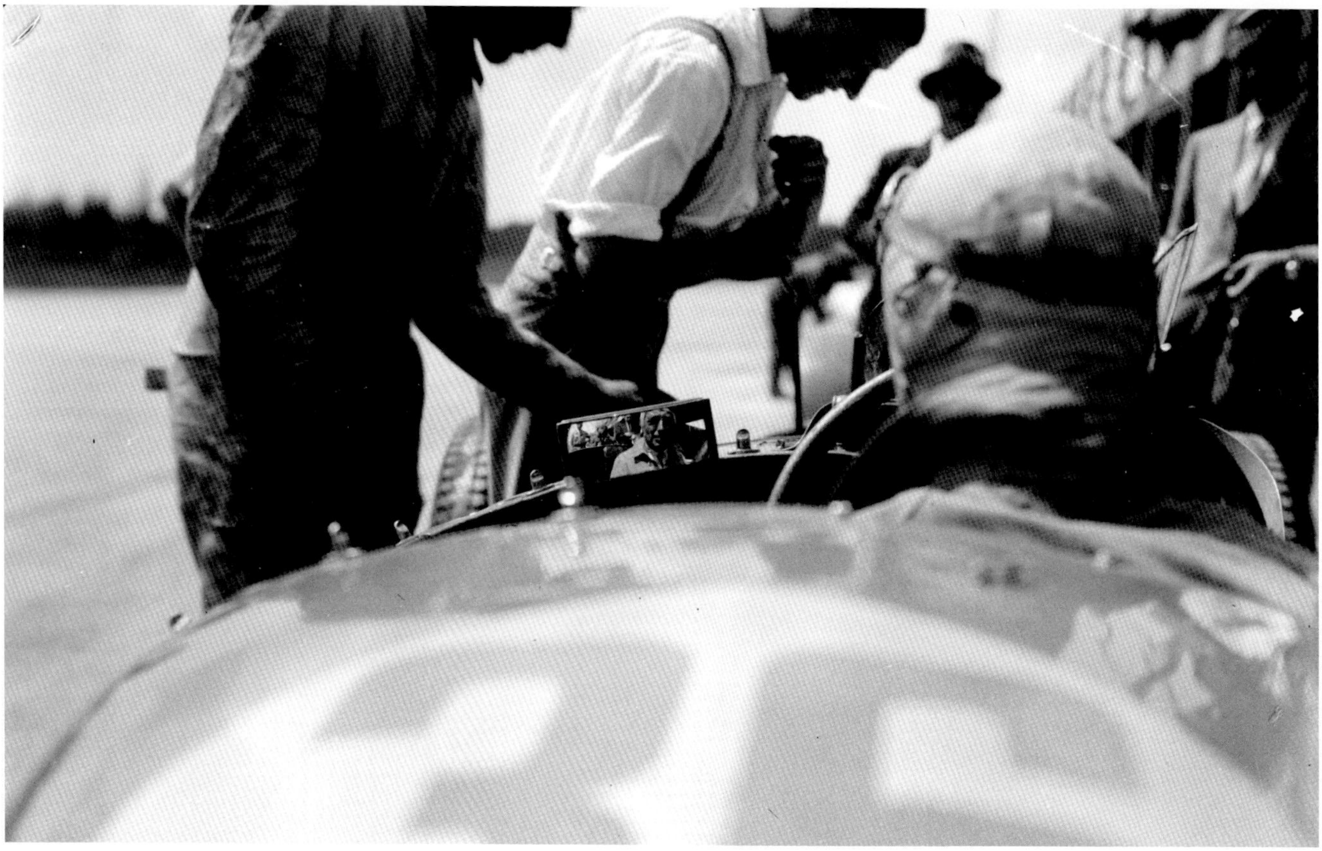

Among the seventeen cars in the 1500 cc race Bugattis, D.K.W.s and Austins were well represented. Howe's Delage proved to be easily the fastest car and he was in the lead almost from the start completing the race in what *The Autocar* described as "isolated splendour, without stopping once". His superiority can be seen from his lap times which were more than 15 mph faster than those of his nearest rivals. Although the race was quite short by the standards of the day, Howe completing the ten laps in just over an hour, it was mechanically quite demanding with the result that only five cars finished. Howe had the satisfaction of seeing the Union Jack raised on the flagpole by the start line and hearing the National Anthem played to celebrate his victory.

The remainder of Howe's races with the Delage in 1932 were full grand prix events, though in most cases there was provision for a separate award for 1500 cc cars. Two months after the AVUS meeting Howe was at the Nürburgring for the German Grand Prix. A race for 1500 cc cars was run simultaneously with the grand prix event, though the smaller-engined cars had to complete only thirty-three laps compared to thirty-five required of the grand prix competitors. Given the length of the Nürburgring, both categories of cars needed nearly five hours to complete the distance and this long race actually benefitted Lord Howe as he was in the pits for nearly twenty minutes investigating a loss of fuel pressure. He dropped to the tail of the field but was able to pull back some of the deficit and finish fourth; the gap between his Delage and the winner of the 1500 cc race corresponded almost exactly to the length of his pit stop.

Hill Climbing with the Type 51 Bugatti – Shelsley Walsh

Although Francis Howe competed in only two long distance races with the T51 in 1932 he did use it for two of the most prominent hill climbs – Shelsley Walsh and the Klausenrennen. By 1932 Howe had accumulated a considerable amount of Shelsley experience, though it was chiefly in sports cars rather than out and out racing cars.

Shelsley's first meeting in 1932 was potentially of great significance as Jean Bugatti was entered in a T53 Bugatti. Unlike the T51, which was a logical development of the T35, maintaining all its good features and supplementing them with an improved engine, the T53 was a radical departure from existing Bugatti practice. It did use that the existing 4.9 supercharged engine but the remainder of the car was highly distinct incorporating four wheel drive, IFS, and, by Bugatti standards, a rather boxy and unattractive body.

The attraction of Shelsley for this car was the possibility of lowering Hans Stuck's hill record established two years before when his time of 42.8 had cut nearly three seconds from the previous record. Jean Bugatti stayed with Francis Howe at Penn House when he came over for the Shelsley meeting bringing with him a very smart T55 sports car painted in yellow and black which he used to travel from Buckinghamshire to the hill.

A considerable amount has been written about Jean's practice session with the T53. Everyone knows that one of the climbs ended in a crash at the Kennel bend which damaged the car beyond repair for the meeting itself. For many years the notion was circulated that the crash occurred on his *second* practice climb and that on the first he had broken the hill record by a considerable – though undisclosed – margin. Only quite recently has it been clearly established that there was only one run – and that ended at the Kennel bend!

Earl Howe insisted that Jean should tell his father about the incident and accordingly he telephoned Ettore: "the resultant conversation was terrific. Holding the receiver in one hand young Bugatti gesticulated wildly with the other, while he poured a flood of voluble French into the mouthpiece, becoming more and more excited as the conversation progressed" (C.A.N. May: *Shelsley Walsh* (1946)).

Ettore's reaction is not recorded but his disappointment (this might understate his feelings!) would have been somewhat relieved by Howe's own performance with his T51 which gave him F.T.D. with a time of 44.0. It is clear from contemporary accounts that Howe's victory was something of a surprise, most probably because up until this meeting nearly all his driving had been in sports cars. The T51 gave him the opportunity of contesting the odds with the fastest racing cars and proving that he could come out on top. *The Light Car's* account is worth quoting because its editor, Eric Findon, was a very experienced Shelsley scribe and responsible for the public address commentary, relayed by the B.B.C. for the first time at this meeting: "Earl Howe in his 2.3 Bugatti made what was probably the neatest climb seen at Shelsley since von Stuck. He shot into the S bend after a wonderful getaway, braked to about 20 mph and then, accelerating amid a crash of exhaust which beat upon the ear drums screamed to the top, steady as a rock".

1932 – Shelsley Walsh – Howe's Type 51 Bugatti stands in the paddock adjacent to the Shelsley farm at the June 1932 meeting where Howe set FTD in a time of 44.0 seconds. In the background can be seen his newly-delivered, purpose-built racing transporter (see pages 81 to 84). *Photograph courtesy of Midland Automobile Club Archive*

Hill Climbing with the Type 51 Bugatti in Europe – Klausenrennen

In choosing to compete at the Klausen Pass hill climb in Switzerland Howe was opting for a very different experience from Shelsley. Klausen – an Alpine pass with grandiose scenery – was an extreme example of the European preference for long hills which climbed through thousands of feet and incorporated numerous bends, often of an acute kind. Some thirty miles from Zurich, it began in Lintal village and finished more than thirteen miles later after climbing nearly 4000 feet from start to finish. In 1932 it attracted 60,000 spectators who were not put off by having to pay up to £2 for car parking, an extremely high figure for the early 1930s.

The two largest capacity racing car classes produced the quickest climbs. Howe was in the two to three litre class in which there were nine entries. He finished third with a time of 17 minutes 21:8 seconds, headed by Stuber, also in a Bugatti (16:33:00) and Caracciola (15:50:00). Caracciola's time in a P3 Alfa comprehensively broke Louis Chiron's previous course record by over thirty seconds. Chiron himself won the class for racing cars over three litres driving a T53 Bugatti but he was nearly a minute slower than Caracciola – and slower than when he had set the course record in a T51.

The *Motor Sport* reporter, posted near the top of the hill, thought "Earl Howe handled his Bugatti with great mastery, and...seemed to cross the finishing line as fast, if not faster than the winners". If this was indeed true it means Howe lost time lower down the hill compared to Caracciola, Chiron, Stuber and Varzi (in a T54 Bugatti). Nonetheless for someone without any experience of continental hill climbs finishing with fifth best time overall was quite impressive.

Howe could not return to Klausen the following year as there was no meeting and he didn't choose to enter in 1934 which turned out to be the final Klausen meeting in the pre-1939 period. Nor does he appear to have entered for any of the other well known European hill climbs.

Pleasure and pain: Pescara and Monza

Pescara and Monza were the two Italian circuits which, like AVUS in Germany, he experienced for the first time in 1932. Before those meetings he returned to Dieppe where, as in 1931, he ran the Delage. However on this occasion he entered his second Delage, chassis number 4, which had been driven by Senechal in the 1931 French Grand Prix. Howe finished fifth overall at Dieppe and second in the 1500 cc class which was a satisfactory result though not quite as good as the 1931 outcome when he had won the small car class and was third overall.

Three weeks after Dieppe Howe was by the Adriatic coast of Italy for his debut at the Pescara circuit. He was most impressed by it – "magnificent... one of the finest and most attractive I know". Like Dieppe, it was basically a triangle in shape though three times the length of the French circuit. There were two very long straights with the connecting 'leg', in Howe's words "chiefly notable for a series of very difficult bends and corners and run (ning) through two villages". As speeds steadily mounted through the 1930s, most spectacularly with the Mercedes and Auto Union teams, chicanes were inserted in the two straights. Howe could see their logic but intensely disliked them arguing that they didn't reproduce the effect of 'natural' curves or bends and imposed a great strain on the brakes.

The Pescara race, the Coppa Acerbo, attracted a very good entry with three P3 works Alfas as well as three Monza Alfas from Scuderia Ferrari and works entries from Bugatti and Maserati. The P3s of Nuvolari and Caracciola dominated the race with Chiron in the leading Bugatti (a T51, not T54, already more or less by-passed) finishing third, ninety seconds behind Caracciola. Howe, driving the Delage, finished seventh and provided by far the closest finish as Borzacchini in one of the Monzas beat him over the line by one-tenth of a second, after two and a half hours racing!

The Monza Grand Prix followed a month later. Howe probably intended this meeting to be his final one of the season but it turned out to be 'final' for the ex-Campbell Delage in a most emphatic – and unwanted – sense. The race was run off in three heats and a repechage and it was in the latter that Howe came to grief. The starting gremlin struck with a vengeance and Howe stalled the car. He then set off behind the rest of the field and encountering two slower cars at the Lesmo bend he braked too hard and skidded off the circuit. The first tree he hit cut the front axle and the second stopped the car but at the cost of bending it so severely that the front and back nearly touched. Lurani, with whom Howe was staying during the event, says an oxyacetylene cutting kit was needed to extract the remains of the Delage from the tree. Amazingly enough, although he was badly shaken Howe escaped without either cuts or broken bones. This crash was another of the occasions where his helmet saved him from serious, possibly fatal, injury for in Lurani's words he did suffer "a terrific blow on the head". Not surprisingly in view of the car's condition, the medical crew thought Howe must have been injured and attempted to put him on a stretcher. Howe resisted, proclaiming he was perfectly all right, but the medics "were convinced that he was dying and would not let go of him" (Lurani: *Racing Round the World*). While this accident was emphatically not the end of Francis Howe, it did spell the end of the ex-Campbell Delage. The engine and some transmission parts were salvaged but 11th September 1932 marked the end of this particular car.

1933: back to the Bugatti

At the end of 1932 Howe could look back on two busy years with the Delage and the Bugatti. He had driven on many different European circuits, all of which were new to him, and he could now build on that experience. The experiment with the T54 Bugatti had been unsuccessful and it is not surprising that he returned to the T51 for 1933. In fact, the pattern of his competition year in 1933 was almost the reverse of 1932, as the Delage was only used three times, whereas the Bugatti was fully extended over five grands prix as well as at Shelsley and the Brighton speed trials. The legacy of the Monza accident meant he now had only one complete Delage and this may have inclined him to use it more sparingly than when he had a choice.

He did not buy any new racing cars for the 1933 season which wasn't surprising as there was little to choose from. In 1932 the P3 Alfa had been the outstanding grand prix car but none were available for private customers and the factory itself decided not to run the works cars or to allow Scuderia Ferrari to do so on its behalf. This decision caused considerable difficulties for Ferrari who had to rely upon their existing Monzas which did not produce results that Nuvolari, its leading driver, found satisfactory. He 'defected' to Maserati during the season and there was a considerable amount of chopping and changing among other leading drivers in the wake of his departure.

Retirements at Monaco, Montlhéry and Nice

The T51's grand prix results in 1933 were rather disappointing with three successive retirements in the first half of the season at Monaco, Montlhéry and Nice. At Monaco the former practice of allocating grid positions by ballot was abandoned in favour of practice times. Howe was on the last row but one after lapping in 2′09″ compared to the 2′2″ of Achille Varzi who was on pole position in a works T51. Howe's car lasted almost to half-distance when it had

Top – 1933 – Monte Carlo – Howe poses with Raymond Sommer in front of his Bugatti Type 51 in the pits at the Grand Prix de Monaco in April 1933. Both Howe and Sommer (driving a Maserati 8CM) retired from the race. To the right can be seen Tim Birkin's partially covered Alfa Romeo 8C 2300. Photograph by Fred Taylor, courtesy of GP Library.

Left – 1933 – Monte Carlo – Howe and "Tim" Birkin pose for the camera alongside Howe's Bugatti Type 51 before the 1933 Monaco Grand Prix. Howe retired from the race after 48 laps with a damaged rear axle, whilst Birkin, driving Bernard Rubin's Alfa-Romeo 8C 2300 also retired with differential trouble. Sadly, two months later Birkin was dead, as a result of complications following a burn sustained whilst competing in the Tripoli Grand Prix. Photograph courtesy of Geoffrey Goddard Archive

to retire with a broken back axle. At the French G.P., run at the Montlhéry circuit, Howe's retirement was not due to mechanical failure but because he was hit in the eye by a stone, thrown up by another car's wheel which struck his vizor with enough force to penetrate it. The injury was sufficiently serious to prevent him driving at Le Mans a week later. As a result of this experience he had a toughened Perspex vizor made to try and avoid any repetition of this injury. 1933 was not a good year for racing accidents as just over two months later he over-turned a K3 M.G. when practicing for the Coppa Ciano. He was doused in fuel, one of his eyes was again affected along with his wrist and thumb. His third retirement in the T51 was at Nice, a circuit at which he hadn't previously competed. According to one description it "was mostly on the promenade with a short excursion inland. It was short, slow and very hard on brakes" (Sheldon and Rabagliati). It wasn't the brakes that let Howe down but an oil pipe which broke at an early stage in the race when he had completed only fifteen of the ninety laps.

Better results with the Type 51: Pescara, Shelsley and Brighton

The only European result to redress the record of failure with the T51 was his fifth place in the Coppa Acerbo. Exactly a year after he had first raced at Pescara he returned, but on this occasion with a full grand prix car, not the Delage, as in 1932. The Bugatti produced its best result for him but it didn't run entirely trouble-free as the plugs played up. However this problem was less serious than those affecting many others for although Fagioli (Alfa) Nuvolari (Maserati), Taruffi (Maserati) and Varzi (Bugatti) finished ahead of him, there were numerous retirements.

In Britain there were better results at Shelsley and Brighton. At Shelsley Howe's best time was 43.60 which was two-fifths quicker than his FTD the previous year. However it was not good enough for FTD as both Whitney Straight and Raymond Mays were considerably faster. Straight set a new record for the hill of 41.20, driving the ex-Birkin 8C 2500

1933 – Brooklands – Tazio Nuvolari poses in the cockpit of Howe's Bugatti Type 51 during his abortive visit to the B.A.R.C. Autumn Meeting at Brooklands in October 1933. *Photograph courtesy of Terry Cardy Collection*

1933 – Brooklands – After Nuvolari's early departure from the B.A.R.C. Autumn meeting, Piero Taruffi drove Howe's Bugatti Type 51 in the Mountain Championship, finishing second. During 1933 and 1934 Howe's Bugattis carried a distinctive emblem on the side below the cockpit. The exact nature of the design is unclear, but this enlargement indicates that it featured a speeding car with mountain scenery in the background. *Photograph courtesy of Motoring Picture Library, Beaulieu*

Maserati and it broke Hans Stuck's record which had stood for three years. As Howe was running in the same class as Straight he finished second in the racing division for cars up to three litres. Howe had a close battle in both the sports car and racing categories of this class with Hon. Brian Lewis. Both had entered 8C Alfas as sports cars and Lewis headed Howe by 0.6 whereas in the racing cars the position was reversed with Howe's Bugatti defeating Lewis's Monza by the same margin.

Both Straight and Mays, who also broke Stuck's record with 42.20, used twin rear wheels. Mays had pioneered these at Shelsley in 1929 as part of the modifications made to his car which started life as a T.T. Vauxhall. As its power steadily increased there were problems with wheelspin and the car's stability. Amherst Villiers thought it was worth trying twin rears to tackle these difficulties and they did improve matters considerably. Howe had been told by Ettore and Jean Bugatti that twin rear wheels would not be helpful on the T51 but decided he wanted to see for himself. He borrowed a pair and tested them on the

# The Grand Prix Years

Outer circuit at Brooklands telling Rivers Fletcher "they were hopeless and completely spoiled the balance of the car".

The Brighton Speed Trials took place along Madeira Drive and had a long but not continuous history. They had been revived in 1932, by the Brighton and Hove Motor Club. Unfortunately the 1933 meeting was run in poor conditions with rain pouring down and a lot of water on the track. Howe's chief rival for FTD was Whitney Straight driving the same Maserati that was to set the new Shelsley record one week later. As at Shelsley, Straight ran with twin rears but the Maserati still snaked far more on leaving the line than Howe on single wheels. According to *The Autocar* Howe's runs "were a beautiful example of clean crisp driving" but they were not quite fast enough to defeat Straight who finished the kilometre two-thirds of a second ahead of Howe.

The Delage redeems Howe's 1933 record on the circuits

During 1933 the Delage was used only three times but with better results than those obtained with the T51. Two of the meetings took place in Germany within seven days of each other in the second half of May. The attempt to repeat the previous year's victory at AVUS failed, apparently due to a rebuilt engine which wasn't fully run-in; Howe had to settle for third place, headed by two T51A Bugattis who finished very close together, about four minutes in front of him.

However there was a much better result when the voiturettes moved to the Nürburgring for the Eifelrennen. The strongest opposition again came from the Bugattis of Burggaller and Veyron and it was with the former that Howe duelled for the entire race distance of 212 miles. Howe said afterwards that he thought "it was the hardest race of his career" (quoted in Venables: *The Racing Fifteen Hundreds*). In view of Howe's description of the circuit as 'the most difficult in the world' one can appreciate that to be closely pursued for over three hours would have been a very testing experience. Howe's third outing with the Delage was at Dieppe to which he was returning for his third consecutive year. The entry was dominated by Bugattis both in the under and over two litre classes and T51s finished first and second. Howe was fourth overall and second in the under two litre class. Czaykowski won the smaller or voiturette class with a 51A Bugatti, finishing a mile or so ahead of Howe.

1933 – AVUS – These photographs by Zoltan Glass capture the atmosphere of the Avusrennen meeting in May 1933. The first photograph shows Howe's Delage on the ramps – note the painting of race numbers. In the second photograph Howe poses with Ewald Kroth, a leading light in the ADAC, the organising club for the AVUS meeting. In the final photograph Howe talks to his mechanic, Thomas, on the grid before his first voiturette race of the 1933 in which he finished third. *Photographs by Zoltan Glass courtesy of National Media Museum/Science and Society Picture Library*

Top – 1933 – Dieppe – Howe congratulates Marcel Lehoux, the winner of the Grand Prix de Dieppe in July 1933. Howe finished fourth in the raced driving his 1½ litre Delage.
Photograph courtesy of Geoffrey Goddard Archive

Left – 1933 – Monza – Howe's Bugatti Type 51 is refuelled in the Monza pits. Howe raced the car in both the Gran Premio d'Italia, where he finished twelth, and in the Gran Premio di Monza where he finished fifth in his heat and retired from the final after an accident.
Photograph courtesy of the Howe Family

The beginnings of Donington

1933 was the year that the Donington circuit, near Derby opened for motor racing. It developed rapidly so that only four years later it staged the outstanding spectacle of a grand prix with full teams of Auto Union and Mercedes Benz. But its origins were modest with sports cars predominating and some rather thin entry lists at the early meetings. Some of the driving was also disconcerting leading Sammy Davis, Sports Editor of *The Autocar*, to conclude that "Now definitely something must be done to stop wild driving on this circuit. There are too many crashes..."

Davis's remarks were made in August 1933, two months before Howe's first appearance at the circuit. With his interest in developing new circuits in the U.K., especially ones that bore some similarity to continental road racing, Howe would have needed little persuasion to come to Donington. Although its track was an artificial creation it incorporated various features which were strikingly similar to those encountered on many European racing circuits where extensive use was made of ordinary roads.

Howe took part in a twenty lap 'Invitation' race in October 1933, the longest event so far staged on the circuit. Unfortunately four of the seven who had been invited failed to start so that left an all Bugatti field with Taso Mathieson and Lindsay Eccles in T35s and Howe in his T51. After eight laps Mathieson's car expired and Howe, who had led from the first lap, came home three-quarters of a minute in front of Eccles. The conditions were not very pleasant with a wet track but Howe gave a convincing demonstration of judgment and control: "he came down the twisting section to the finish faster than anyone else that day taking exactly the same path each time and

1933 – Donington – Three Bugattis comprise the whole field at the start of the twenty lap Invitation Race at the Donington Park Trophy meeting in October 1933. In the centre is Howe's Bugatti Type 51, which won the race, whilst on the left is Taso Mathieson's Type 35C (No.4) and to the right is Lindsay Eccles' Type 35B. *Photograph by* Autocar, *courtesy of LAT Archive*

1933 – Donington – Howe in his Bugatti Type 51 on his way to victory in the 1933 Donington Park Trophy at the newly-opened Donington Park circuit. *Photograph by* Autocar, *courtesy of LAT Archive*

all but, but never quite, touching the grass on the inside" (*The Autocar* 13th October, 1933). Howe returned to race at Donington for the next five years and was therefore one of the few leading drivers who experienced the three different tracks. By the time Donington opened for its second season it had been slightly extended and late in 1937 a further longer extension was made for the T.T.

Trying for a P3, settling for an 8CM

In the latter part of the 1933 season Scuderia Ferrari finally succeeded in persuading the Alfa Company to release some of the P3s. Their reappearance on the tracks further convinced anyone who wasn't already persuaded that the P3 was the outstanding grand prix car. Howe decided he should buy one and paid a deposit during the autumn of 1933. At this time it appears a production batch of two dozen cars was envisaged but before the end of the year Howe's deposit had been returned with a letter from the directors "saying that the single-seater cars were only to be supplied to Italian drivers residing in their own country" (*Motor Sport*, January, 1934).

If there was to be no P3 the 8CM Maserati was the obvious alternative. By contrast with Alfa, the Maserati company had no inhibitions about selling cars to whoever wanted them. It had a straightforward commercial orientation and was clearly not subject to any overall direction from the Italian state about who could and couldn't have its cars. Howe had seen the 8CM on various occasions during 1933 and although it produced its best results when Nuvolari drove it, Goffredo Zehender had demonstrated it was possible to do quite well with a privately-owned example.

The 8CM was a single-seater unlike its predecessor, the 8C 2500 which was a two-seater, albeit a largely nominal one. Both cars were powered by a straight eight, twin overhead camshaft engine with a Roots type supercharger positioned at the front of the engine. In the 8CM's case there was a bore of 69 mm and a stroke of 100 mm which gave a capacity of 2992 cc, slightly bigger than the 26M's. The four-speed gearbox used some FIAT proprietary components and the brakes were hydraulic, the latter an unusual feature in the early 'thirties but increasingly common later in the decade. The original chassis frame was very narrow but it had to be widened in 1934 to comply with new A.I.A.C.R. regulations.

While Howe has not left any direct impressions of the 8CM he would probably have agreed with the general view, summed up more than fifty years later, by Doug Nye: "Objectively (its) career is characterized by early notoriety for having more power than road holding in 1933, replaced by the reputation for having too little of either in 1934" (*Classic and Sports Car*, June, 1987). The second owner of Howe's car, T.P. Cholmondeley Tapper, was very clear about its handling difficulties: "I began to appreciate the universal complaints concerning the road holding of the Maserati for I would be fighting away with all my energy, while the car jumped about on its almost rigid suspension like a cat on hot bricks" (T.P. Cholmondeley Tapper: *Amateur Racing Driver*). He says that Maserati itself accepted there were problems with the chassis and that later 8CMs had stiffened frames; he also notes that Whitney Straight had two of his cars modified – at Thomson and Taylor's, under the direction of Reid Railton – to improve their road holding and increase their power.

Howe used the Maserati for five continental grands prix and one long-distance British event. After running at the Swiss Grand Prix in late August 1934, he did not compete in the car again, lending it to Hon. Brian Lewis on two occasions in 1935, and then storing in Italy until sold to Cholmondeley Tapper in 1936. Howe didn't rely on it exclusively for his grand prix work, for three grands prix he used the T51 and the Bugatti was also used for a number of U.K. events – at Brooklands, Donington and Shelsley. 1934 was, in fact, the busiest of all Howe's racing seasons – between early April, when he started his season at Monaco, and early October when he concluded it at Donington, he competed in nineteen different events.

Grand Prix racing with the 8CM

Whatever the limitations of the Maserati's road-holding it had a good reputation for reliability though it did seem vulnerable to fuel tank problems. This weakness probably arose because the tank was bolted direct to the frame and any chassis flexing strained it. A modified and strengthened tank was one of the modifications Straight made to his 8CMs. The fuel tank played up on Howe's first appearance with the car during practice at Monaco in May 1934. He was able to capitalize on his naval connections by using artificers from *H.M.S. Delhi*, a cruiser anchored in the bay, to make repairs. These were effective but in the race itself he had constant problems with the engine not running cleanly and made many pit stops to change the plugs and adjust the carburettor. He was the final finisher, but he had fallen a long way behind, completing only eighty-five of the one hundred laps. He had a recurrence of the fuel tank problem in the Coppa Acerbo in August which led to his retirement.

Better results came at AVUS where he finished fourth, and at Dieppe where he was third both in his heat and in the final. The entry at AVUS included full teams from Auto Union and Mercedes Benz though the latter withdrew because of fuel pump problems. Eleven cars eventually came to the line and the Scuderia Ferrari P3s dominated the race, finishing first and second. Momberger's Auto Union was third, followed by Howe and Nuvolari (driving a P3 with his left leg in plaster!). At Dieppe Chiron and Lehoux drove works Alfas and Zehender a works 8CM, with the remaining runners all being private entries. It was a good day for the 8CMs as Etancelin

1934 – Monte Carlo – Howe in his newly-acquired Maserati 8CM during the 1934 Monaco Grand Prix on his way to finishing in 10th place. *Photograph courtesy of Adam Ferrington Collection*

won his heat and the final in his own car, Zehender was second in his heat (he had to drop out of the final after only one lap) and Howe picked up two third places. Howe finished ahead of Tim Rose-Richards (in a T51), fairly comfortably in the heat but there was a much closer contest in the final with Clifton Penn Hughes' Monza Alfa, making it a three-way scrap.

The only circuit to which Howe took the 8CM where he hadn't previously raced was the new Bremgarten circuit at Berne in Switzerland. Howe described the circuit as "a road, more or less circular in character, most of it through a wood...There is a stretch of about one mile past the pits and grandstand which is surfaced with very good pave and the rest of the circuit has a rather fine tarmac surface".

The Grand Prix Years

Above – 1934 – Brooklands – Howe pushes his Maserati 8CM through the Brooklands paddock prior to the 1934 British Empire Trophy. Howe hit a bank during the race and the resultant damage lead to his retirement. *Photograph courtesy of the Brooklands Society*

Below – 1934 – Brooklands – On the grid for the J.C.C. International Trophy Howe's Bugatti Type 51 (No.2) can be seen on the extreme right of the second row. He finished fifth in the race. The first row consists of (l-r) Brackenbury (M.G.), Esson-Scott (Bugatti Type 51), Eccles (Bugatti Type 35C), Handley (M.G.), Horton (M.G.), Hamilton (M.G.), Lewis (Maserati 8C-3000) and Straight (Maserati 8CM). *Photograph by Autocar, courtesy of LAT Archive*

109

1934 – AVUS – Howe prepares to climb into his Maserati 8CM in the pits at the Avusrennen meeting in May 1934, at which Howe finished fourth. *Photograph courtesy of Adam Ferrington Collection*

Prince Bira, who first drove on the circuit the following year, told his cousin that "he found the circuit fast but dangerous. Although there were only two real corners, there was, so to speak, no straight at all. The course was rich with mild corners which had to be negotiated quite fast" (Prince Chula: *Wheels at Speed*). Howe identified one of these fast corners between the pits and the grandstand as particularly difficult, needing exact judgement and with any error likely to lead to a serious accident.

The entry for this first grand prix attracted all the main teams – Auto Union, Mercedes Benz, Scuderia Ferrari and a single works T59 Bugatti for Rene Dreyfus. In addition to Howe's car other 8CMs were in the hands of Nuvolari, Hugh Hamilton (a Whitney Straight entered car) and Hans Ruesch. Howe's car ran the full distance but was outclassed finishing ninth, five laps behind Stuck and Momberger in the winning Auto Unions. It was on the final lap of this race that Hugh Hamilton went off the road and was killed. He had been Howe's co-driver in the 1933 Mille Miglia as well as at Reims in 1932 where they had struggled to keep the troublesome T54 Bugatti in the French G.P. Like Howe himself, Hamilton was one of a small group of British drivers who had built up considerable experience of continental motor racing. He was a driver of real promise and his death was a considerable loss.

The Grand Prix Years

1934 – Brooklands – This group of three informal photographs shows Howe chatting (l-r on first photo) to John Cobb, Prince Bertil of Sweden, Lindsay Eccles and Whitney Straight at the 1934 British Empire Trophy meeting at Brooklands. *Photographs courtesy of Geoffrey Goddard Archive*

111

Above – 1934 – Brooklands – Howe's Maserati 8CM passes under the bridge, crowded with spectators, during the British Empire Trophy in June 1934. The white Type 35 Bugatti of John Houldsworth (No.39) can be seen at the edge of the banking, Houldsworth ultimately succumbing to the injuries he sustained in the accident. *Photograph by* Autocar, *courtesy of LAT Archive*

Below – 1934 – Dieppe – Howe rounds the Virage du Maison Blanche in his Maserati during the Grand Prix de Dieppe held in July 1934. He is followed by Clemente Biondetti's older Maserati 26M. Howe finished third in both his heat and in the Final. In the background the distinctive petrol pumps dispense Esso and Standard brands whilst the road sign indicates a distance of 163.7 km to Paris. *Photograph courtesy of Motoring Picture Library, Beaulieu*

1934 – Dieppe – In these two photographs Howe in his Maserati 8CM is seen in the distinctive road circuit scenery on the St. Aubin to Maison Blanche section of the Dieppe circuit, during the 1934 Grand Prix de Dieppe. In the second photograph he is following Clemente Biondetti's older Maserati. *Photographs by* Autocar, *courtesy of LAT Archive*

The Type 51's Grand Prix swansong

1934 was the fourth season for Howe's T51. Over the preceding three years he had driven it with varying frequency – in 1931 it had given him his first experience of grand prix racing at Monaco, Montlhéry and Nürburgring but he used it much more sparingly the following year. 1933 turned out to be the car's busiest season with five grands prix as well as some shorter events. By 1934 the T51 was no longer a leading grand prix car, having been overtaken by both the P3 Alfas and the 8CM Maseratis. Nevertheless Howe chose to enter the Bugatti, rather than the 8CM, for the races at Reims, Vichy and the Italian Grand Prix at Monza. The Reims race was run over the very fast Reims circuit for which the 8CM would seem a much more suitable car than the Bugatti. Though there was one other privately-owned T51 the rest of the entry was Alfa or Maseratis. Howe finished five laps behind the winner but he wasn't the last finisher quite apart from the fact that more than half those who started the race failed to complete it.

At the Vichy race the Bugatti should have felt among more familiar company as there were six other T51s. This circuit, north of Clermont Ferrand, was twisty and Howe may have thought the 8CM's brakes were vulnerable – as indeed they proved to be for Etancelin's Maserati, costing him the race. Howe finished fourth in his heat, three minutes behind the winner, Whitney Straight. In the final he was the last finisher, two laps behind Trossi and Straight who finished first and second.

The Vichy race's heats and final amounted to about two and a half hours racing. By comparison, the Italian G.P. was something of a blockbuster: a single race demanding nearly five hours at the wheel to complete more than a hundred laps of the Monza circuit. The previous year there had been a classic Italian Grand Prix but it was succeeded, later in the day, by a separate Monza G.P., an extremely grim affair in which Campari, Borzacchini and Czaykowski all lost their lives. Unsurprisingly the Monza authorities had produced a new circuit but it was "very hard on the drivers and only four were able to go through without relief" (Sheldon and Rabagliati). Francis Howe was one of this quartet and undoubtedly showed great determination and application in staying the distance. He was the final finisher, twelve laps behind the winning Mercedes shared between Caracciola and Fagioli. Although a works T59 Bugatti had been entered for Antonio Brivio, its supercharger failed on the first lap. It could be said, therefore, that Howe kept the Bugatti flag flying but it really only underlined how Bugatti was struggling, not merely in relation to its Italian rivals, but even more so against the new German cars.

The Type 51 in British events – Brooklands, Shelsley and Donington

The T51 displayed the same reliability in its 1934 U.K. events as in its grand prix appearances and the less competitive British fields generated better results. Howe had only competed once at Brooklands in 1933 but in 1934 he came to the Weybridge track on four different occasions. One of these was the only time he raced the 8CM in a U.K. event, the British Empire Trophy. It wasn't a very successful appearance as he spun backwards through the straw bales at the 'Railway Snake' and retired. However all three meetings with the Bugatti were more rewarding. In April he finished fifth in the J.C.C. International Trophy and also shared the team prize with Rose Richards and Esson-Scott. As with most Brooklands events, the International Trophy was a handicap race but the J.C.C. had devised a new system of running the cars through bends of varying severity at the Fork and it made the race much more understandable to spectators. Howe had already experienced this system as it had been used for the first time the previous year when he drove a K3 M.G. into fourth place.

Three weeks after the International Trophy he won the Gold Star handicap in the T51. This race was run on the Outer Circuit where Howe took "a most interesting course off the Member's banking pulling down early to avoid the famous bump and sometimes passing slower cars on the inside" (W. Boddy: *The Story of Brooklands*, Vol. 3). His race average of 125.71 exceeded his previous fastest lap and he set a new fastest lap for Class D cars of 129.70. However, unlike his Class F record with the Delage, set in 1931, this one did not go into the permanent record book as it was bettered in 1938 by Chris Staniland in the Multi-Union.

At Shelsley Howe was consistent, both times being within 0.4 of each other and the faster one equalling his own previous best of 43.6. Nonetheless it was nowhere near fast enough for overall FTD which fell to Whitney Straight driving the best – known of his 8CMs – 3011 – with a new record of 40.0. He also had to cede the claim to the fastest Bugatti ascent of Shelsley to Thomas Fothringham who climbed in 43.0 He probably had most satisfaction at this meeting from taking the 38/250 Mercedes to the top in

1934 – Brooklands – Howe somewhat reluctantly poses at the wheel of his Type 51 Bugatti in the Brooklands paddock during the B.A.R.C. Whitsun meeting in May 1934. Howe won the Gold Star Handicap. The motif mentioned on page 102 can be seen on the side of the Bugatti's cockpit. *Photograph courtesy of Geoffrey Goddard Archive*

46.20 which was the best time he attained with this car at Shelsley.

Howe's final racing appearances with the T51 were in early October: at the Donington Park Trophy and in the Mountain Championship at Brooklands. At Donington, as in 1933, the race was run over twenty laps and it was somewhat better supported with ten cars facing the starter. Whitney Straight dominated the race, leading from start to finish. Howe was initially third and although he then slipped down the field a little he regained his third place by the chequered flag finishing two and a half seconds behind Clifton Penn Hughes' Monza Alfa which was runner-up. Another third place came in the ten lap Mountain Championship where Howe finished about one hundred yards behind Raymond Mays who, in turn, was about double that distance behind the winner, Whitney Straight again.

Above – 1934 – Shelsley Walsh – Howe powers his Bugatti Type 51 up the hill at the June 1934 meeting. He finished third in Class in the Bugatti. *Photograph by* Autocar, *courtesy of LAT Archive*

Below – 1934 – Donington – At the start of the Donington Park Trophy in October 1934 Howe in his Bugatti Type 51 (No.21) can be seen following the leader, Whitney Straight in his Maserati 8CM. The other cars on the grid are:- (l-r) Penn-Hughes (Alfa Romeo 2300), Gunter (No.32 Riley), Martin (No.26 Bugatti T35B), Dixon (No.23 Riley), Austin Dobson (Alfa Romeo 2300), Staniland (No.25 Bugatti T51) and Shuttleworth (No.27 Bugatti T51). *Photograph by* Autocar, *courtesy of LAT Archive*

Howe's voiturette racing in 1934: only a footnote

Howe concentrated his efforts in 1934 on the Maserati and the Bugatti. The Delage was only used twice, in voiturette races, at the Prix de Berne and in the Nuffield Trophy at Donington. There were separate voiturette races at AVUS and Pescara to which he took the Maserati and he did enter the Delage at AVUS but non-started. He didn't enter it for the voiturette race at Pescara.

Neither of the races in which the Delage did take part was entirely satisfactory. When it made its first appearance of the season, at Berne in August, it had been fitted with an E.N.V. pre-selector gearbox. Howe had first encountered this type of gearbox on the K3 M.G.s and it's clear he was sufficiently impressed to conclude that the Delage ought to have one. It gave him a wider choice of gears but added to the car's weight and was one of the features Ramponi subsequently removed when Howe sold it to Dick Seaman.

At Berne the engine did not run smoothly and the Delage wasn't able to compete effectively against the Bugattis or the M.G.s – the latter giving away some 400 cc to the Delage. The Donington race was for the newly instituted Nuffield Trophy, donated by William Morris, Viscount Nuffield, who also made a substantial contribution to the prize money. The race was for cars up to 1500 cc and run on handicap which continued to prevail until it was changed to a scratch race in 1939. As at Berne, the Delage was not running at its best: an eye witness said "To me the Delage was terribly disappointing, long flames from the car's exhaust, especially on Coppice corner, alarming the spectators..." (Norman Smith: *Case History*). Howe seems to have had an unhappy race in another way as he thought the flag marshals weren't doing their job properly in ensuring that slower cars gave way to faster ones. All that said, he finished fourth with Raymond Mays, Dick Seaman and Kenneth Evans ahead of him.

Mays was driving the original E.R.A., R1A and the Nuffield Trophy was its first long-distance victory. Howe had already seen this new car running at Brooklands and Dieppe and would have noted its speed and acceleration. The Nuffield Trophy win was significant because it demonstrated these qualities could be sustained in a long race. When Sammy Davis had attended Howe's pre-Mille Miglia lunch earlier in the year, Howe had said "Give me a British car good enough to have a chance, and I'll drive it, but if you can't produce it then I'll drive a continental car. I am not going to be robbed of my sport because you won't build a racing car" (*The Autocar*, 23rd February, 1934). After Donington Howe could see there was now a real possibility of Britain building a viable racing car but it was another twelve months before he finally threw in his lot with E.R.A.

1935: Bugatti again for the final grand prix year

For his grand prix races in 1935 Francis Howe chose a T59 Bugatti. This car has always had high marks for aesthetic appeal but much lower ones for its racing record. It appeared just at the moment when grand prix design moved on to an entirely new plane with the advent of Auto Union and Mercedes. If there is a case for characterizing some changes in racing car design as 'revolutionary' rather than 'evolutionary', developments in the mid-1930s would be a prime example.

Francis Howe had seen the new German cars in action during 1934 at AVUS, Berne and Monza and would have been fully aware of the enormous technical advance they embodied. However, they were exclusively works cars so there was no possibility of buying one as a replacement for the 8CM. The Maserati itself had been a second – best choice after the attempt to buy a P3 had been rebuffed. It had not proved entirely congenial and he doesn't appear to have considered replacing it with another, updated, car from Bologna, such as the 6C-34.

With his attachment to Bugatti he was a fairly obvious customer for the T59s once Ettore Bugatti had decided to sell some of them. Anthony Blight sees Howe not just as a customer but the T59s' chief salesman. Blight says that Ettore "nursed a strong streak of snobbery which frequently prevented him discussing matters of mere trade with anyone much inferior to a reigning monarch". In these terms Howe was, of course, 'inferior' but much less so than many others!

Blight contends that when Howe paid a visit to Molsheim and was told that there were T59s for sale "he promised to pass the word discreetly among his British racing colleagues" and subsequently Blight refers to Howe as having "helped to procure" the T59s' English owners (Anthony Blight: *The French Sports Car Revolution*). There may be something in this, but Blight has almost certainly over-estimated Howe's role. Neither Charlie Martin nor Lindsay Eccles makes any reference to Howe in their accounts of how they came to acquire their T59s.

What is certainly not denied by all the English

1935 – Monte Carlo – Amongst the group of drivers being addressed by Clerk of the Course Charles Faroux on the grid before the 1935 Grand Prix de Monaco are (l-r) Philippe Etancelin, Raymond Sommer, Tazio Nuvolari, René Dreyfus, Giuseppe Farina, Rudolf Caracciola, Francis Howe, Luigi Fagioli (hands on hips) and Goffredo Zehender. *Photograph by* Autocar, *courtesy of LAT Archive*

owners is that the T59s were somewhat troublesome and consequently expensive to race. Hon. Brian Lewis, who drove the car bought by Noel Rees, said that "it would not hold the road at all until we had added two cwt. of lead in its tail" (in Foreword to Anthony Blight: *Georges Roesch and the Invincible Talbot*); Charlie Martin was a little more generous (at least on the car's road-holding) "She was a magnificent car to handle and a joy to drive when she was running properly, but she gave me endless trouble and cost me a small fortune in repairs..." (*Bugantics*, September, 1937)

How did Francis Howe's experience compare? So far as basic reliability is concerned, his car was rather better than the other three. He did have brake problems both at Monaco and Dieppe and in 1936 one of the tyres threw a tread at Brooklands. He also suffered a cracked cylinder head when practicing at Reims but there is no record of the transmission problems and sundry engine 'explosions' experienced by both Martin and Eccles. And, contrary to Blight's notion that the T59s were especially suitable for the British racing environment – "where there were no Grands Prix or weight limits" – Howe ran his car overwhelmingly in European events which were lengthy races most likely to reveal weaknesses in both engine and transmission.

Debut with the Type 59 at Monaco

The first of these European races was at Monaco, an especially demanding test given the strains this circuit imposed on both cars and drivers. Although Auto Union did not enter, believing that its cars were not suited to the circuit, Mercedes sent a full team and among the Scuderia Ferrari P3 Alfas were two cars with enlarged engines – 3.2 rather than 2.9. Howe was on the last but one row of the grid with a best practice time of 2 minutes 4 seconds which was more than six and a half seconds behind Fagioli's Mercedes, on pole position. In the race itself Howe ran much as the practice time indicated, i.e. among the back-markers until brake problems intervened. The T59's brakes began to operate unevenly with the off-side front pulling much harder than the others. At the chicane the unbalanced front-brake "pulled him head-on into the strongest part of the sand-bagged fence. The impact was violent, and the front springs badly bent. A very disappointed man, Lord Howe sat on a nearby wall drinking a glass of wine handed to him by a sympathetic spectator" (*The Autocar*, April, 1935).

Two races in France: Picardie and Dieppe

Howe's second grand prix with the T59 was at Picardie and was a much more modest affair than the Monaco race. There was no German representation as the AVUS race took place on the same week-end, and Ferrari was also absent. In addition to Howe's car there were two other works T59s for Benoist and Wimille, though the latter did not materialize. The main rivals to the Bugatti were Raymond Sommer's P3 Alfa and various 8CM Maseratis. Benoist and Howe dominated the race which took over three hours to complete and shared the fastest lap. Although both Bugattis needed attention to their brakes it is worth noting that mechanical attrition was much greater among the Maseratis, all of which failed to finish.

Howe had plenty of experience at Dieppe having competed there every year since 1931. Mostly he had driven the Delage but in 1934 he had used the Maserati to finish third in both his heat and the final. In 1935 he decided on a two-pronged attack bringing the Delage for the voiturette race and the

1935 – Péronne – This sequence of photographs on this and the two following pages well illustrates the atmosphere of the Grand Prix de Picardie, in which Howe finished second in May 1935. In the first photograph Howe, leaning on his Bugatti Type 59, speaks to Thomas on the grid. Robert Benoist's Works Bugatti Type 59 can be seen to the left. In the second photo *(see over page)* Benoist lead's Howe at the start of the race, followed by Brunet's Maserati 8CM (No.4). In the third photo Howe's Bugatti is refuelled in the pits. The fourth and fifth photographs show the distinctive nature of the triangular Péronne circuit. *Photographs by* Autocar, *courtesy of LAT Archive*

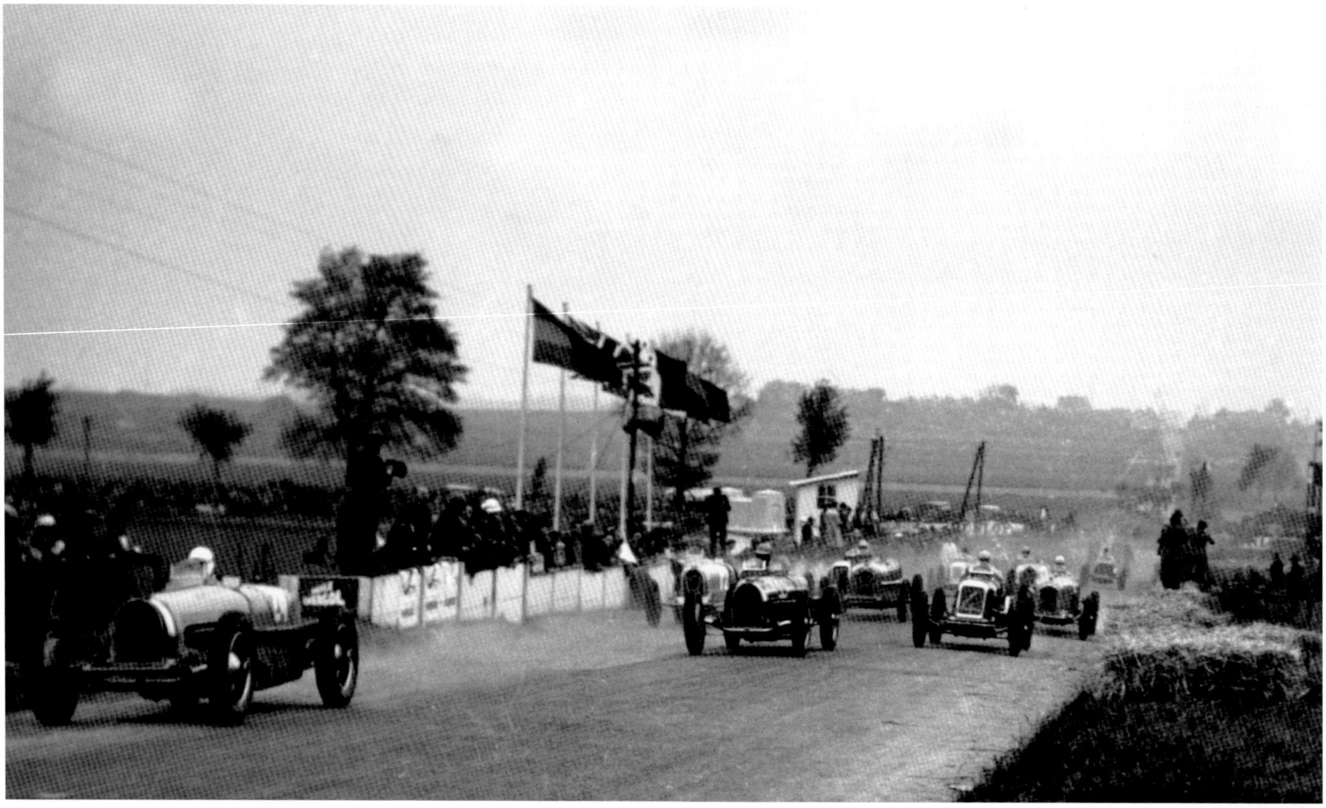

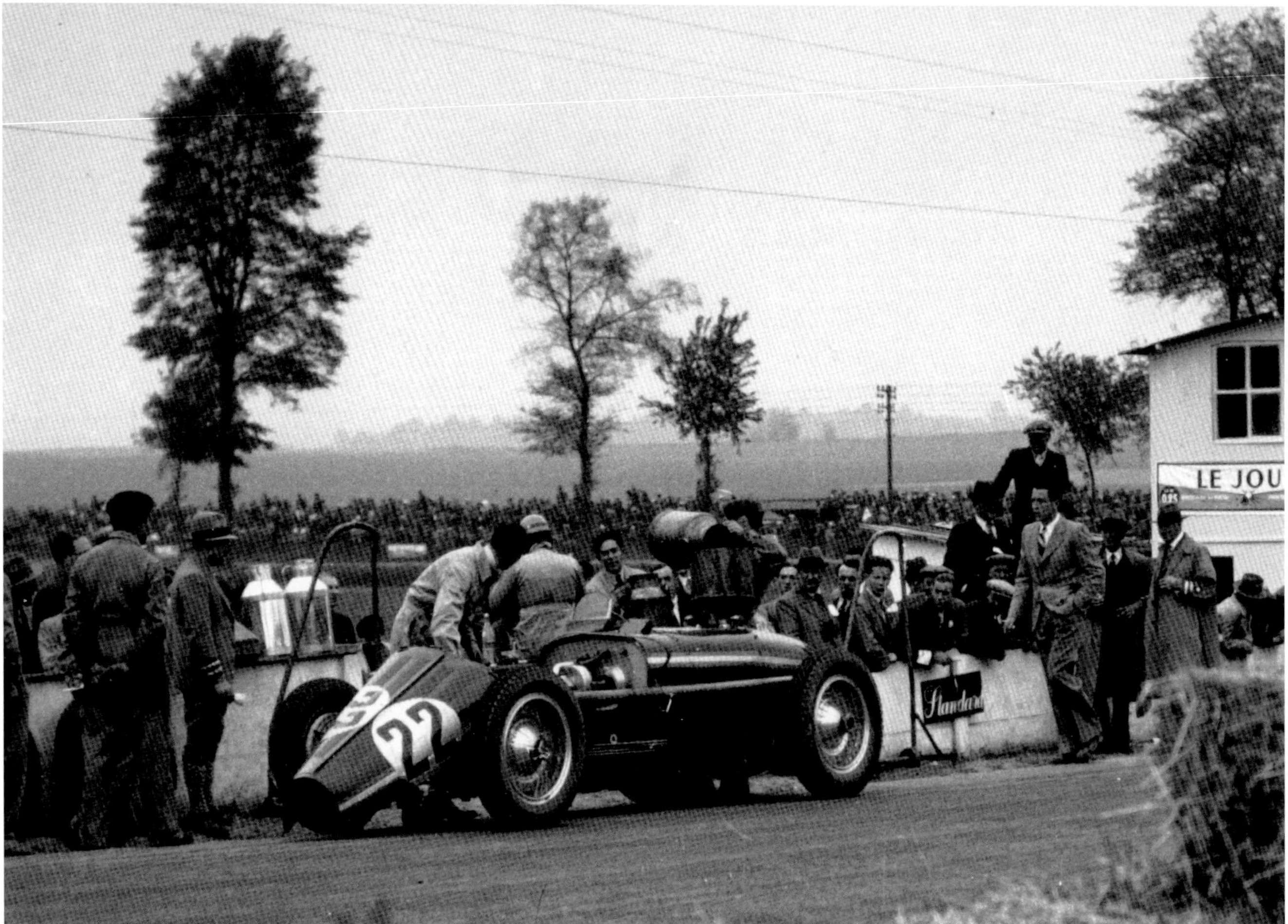
LE JOU
22
Standard

T59 for the grand prix. It was the voiturette race that turned out to be the more significant of the two events as it marked the debut of Prince Bira driving his E.R.A., *Romulus*. The car was a twenty-first birthday present from his cousin, Prince Chula and Bira made a big impression by finishing second in the race. Howe was initially among the leading cars but the Delage's brakes played up forcing his retirement. It was the second occasion when Howe was able to observe E.R.A.s in a long distance race and although two retired (Seaman and Mays) the other three finished first, second and fourth.

In the 'senior' race, which took place the day after the voiturette event, the two Scuderia P3s, driven by Dreyfus and Chiron, had little difficulty in maintaining the leading positions. Jean-Pierre Wimille in a works T59 was third, but all the remaining Bugattis fell on hard times. Benoist retired early with the second works car and was soon followed by Charles Martin and Lindsay Eccles. Unlike the other Bugattis, Howe did finish the race but en route had to make a number of pit stops to adjust his brakes and consequently he fell a long way behind. He also overshot a corner and stalled the engine. Due to trouble with the side-mounted crank handle he had to push the car to a slope and then bump start it.

1935 – Péronne – Howe and his Bugatti Type 59 pass the ACPA memorial to Guy Bouriat and Louis Trintignant during the 1935 Grand Prix de Picardie. Both Bouriat and Trintignant (the brother of 1950s Grand Prix driver Maurice Trintignant) had been killed during the 1933 Grand Prix and the impressive memorial seen in the photograph was erected at the Mons-en-Chausée corner just before the pits in their memory. *Photograph courtesy of Guy Spollon Collection*

1935 – Dieppe – Howe poses beside his Bugatti Type 59 on the grid before the start of the 1935 Grand Prix de Dieppe, in which he finished twelth. Howe started from the outside of the third row of the grid. Richard Shuttleworth's Alfa Romeo Tipo B (No.18) can be seen behind him. *Photograph by George Monkhouse courtesy of Spitzley Archive*

Albi: a new circuit for the Delage

The Albi race was formally titled 'Grand Prix d'Albigeois' but in 1935 the organizers chose to make it a voiturette event, not a full grand prix. The race consisted of two heats with all contestants taking part in both and a final overall classification from combining the two results. This format was unusual at the time but subsequently copied by other races

The entry lacked any E.R.A.s, chiefly because the Nuffield Trophy race was taking place in England on the preceding day. David Venables says the entry had "the appearance of a race from a bygone era" and the outcome, a victory for Pierre Veyron in his T51A Bugatti, was the final time Bugatti received the chequered flag in a voiturette race. The circuit was a typical French triangle of about five miles with a mixture of varying gradients, corners of differing severity and stretches of open country alternating with villages where the buildings were very close to the road. Slightly less familiar was an unguarded level crossing bisecting one of the straights. Cholmondeley Tapper, who was competing at the circuit for the first time, described this feature as "somewhat disconcerting" and noted that "it was as well to keep one's eyes on it as trains were liable to appear without warning" (Tapper: *Amateur Racing Driver*).

The race was not entirely satisfactory for Howe as he had recorded the best practice time but in the first heat the Delage was not working properly and the best he could manage was fifth. It went better in the second heat but he was still headed by Pierre Veyron. His two heat times were good enough to place him second overall, helped by a number of drivers who failed to finish in the second heat.

Berne: repeating the Dieppe experience?

At the end of August Howe went to the Bremgarten circuit which had been launched the previous year with both a voiturette race and a full grand prix. The same pattern was followed in 1935 and Howe chose to enter both races, as he had done at Dieppe. Unlike Dieppe the Swiss grand prix attracted entries from both German teams together with three Scuderia Ferrari P3s, all of which had 3.2 litre engines. Not surprisingly cars from these three teams filled the first seven places followed by Farina (Maserati 8C-34), Sommer in his privately entered Alfa P3 and Howe. Howe had stalled on the line but this wasn't a very serious handicap in a race lasting three and a half hours. Although he was ten laps behind Caracciola's winning Mercedes, the T59 had not given any trouble – it was simply not competitive with the German cars.

Before he came to the line for the grand prix in the afternoon he had driven in the Prix de Berne in the morning. As at Dieppe his Delage was disputing the odds with the E.R.A.s of Mays, Seaman and Bira. Again, as at Dieppe, Mays led initially only to run into mechanical difficulties, but unlike the French event Dick Seaman maintained perfect tune and came home the winner. Bira was second again with Howe, enjoying a much better race than at Dieppe, finishing third one minute behind Bira. It was the last race for Howe and the Delage, though he would certainly not have been aware of it at the time. Jock

1935 – Bremgarten – Howe's two cars, the Bugatti Type 59 and the 1½ litre Delage, are shown in the pits at the 1935 Swiss Grand Prix meeting in August 1935. He finished third in the Preis von Bern voiturette race in the Delage and tenth in the Grand Prix in the Bugatti. In addition Hon. Brian Lewis drove Howe's Maserati 8CM in the Grand Prix, retiring on lap three. *Photographs courtesy of Reggie Tongue Collection / David Morris.*

1935 – Bremgarten – Howe stands beside his Bugatti Type 59, with his mechanic holding his helmet, stands on the grid of the Swiss Grand Prix in August 1935. He finished tenth. *Photograph Courtesy of Guy Spollon Collection*

Finlayson, Dick Seaman's mechanic in 1935, subsequently told Chula that Berne was the first occasion when the idea was floated that Dick should buy Howe's car to compete with in 1936 (Chula: *Dick Seaman* (Foulis, 1941)).

500 Miles at Brooklands with the Type 59

The B.R.D.C.'s 500 Miles race was one of Brooklands' most prestigious events. Prior to 1935 Howe had competed a number of times, his best outing being the 1931 race in which he finished fourth in the special single-seater Talbot. In 1935 it looks, at first glance, as though he entered his T59 but it was clear to contemporary reporters that the car was not in standard form and subsequent investigation has further modified the picture.

At the time of the race it appeared that the T59 had been fitted with a T57 block but subsequent research argues it was a full T59 engine albeit without a supercharger and with only one carburettor. It has also become clear that the chassis was neither Howe's nor Noel Rees' (for whom Hon. Brian Lewis, Howe's co-driver, usually drove). The chassis came

1935 – Brooklands – Howe and Hon. Brian Lewis celebrate their third place in the B.R.D.C. 500 in September 1935. The distinctive ribbed tail of the Bugatti Type 59 can be clearly seen in the foreground. *Photograph courtesy of Geoffrey Goddard Archive*

1935 – Brooklands – Howe leaps from the cockpit of his Bugatti Type 59, which he shared with Hon. Brian Lewis, during the B.R.D.C. 500 in September 1935. Howe and Lewis (who can be seen on the right leaning down from the pit counter) finished third. *Photograph courtesy of Simon Lewis*

from Molsheim and returned there after the race. According to Percy Thomas, Howe had unsuccessfully tried to persuade the factory that his T57 T.T. car should be entered for the '500'. The works preferred to send a T59 "fitted according to some factory notebooks with a 'Tubular inlet manifold to T.T. specification'" (Y. Kaltenbach: Brooklands Society *Gazette*, Summer 1997).

The rationale for this one-off T59 was to assemble a car specially suited to the demands of the 500 miles race. The result seems to have vindicated the underlying calculations as Howe and Lewis finished third, only eight seconds behind Percy Maclure and Bill von der Becke in a Riley who, in turn, took just over seven minutes longer to complete the 500 miles than the winners, John Cobb and Tim Rose-Richards in the Napier Railton. The result could have been even more satisfactory if the Bugatti hadn't had to make one or two unscheduled pit stops to deal with an over-pressurised fuel tank which flooded some of the plugs.

The Donington Grand Prix

1935 was Donington's third year as a racing circuit and, like the two previous years, the season concluded with a major race. However the event was a significant step-up from those of 1933 and 1934 as it was a full grand prix race contested over 125 laps of the two and a half mile circuit, which resulted in a

1935 – Donington – Howe (No.1) in his Bugatti Type 59 can be seen in the middle of the second row of the start of the Donington Grand Prix in October 1935, in which he finished second. The first row consists of (l-r) Sommer (Alfa Romeo Tipo B), Giuseppe Farina (Maserati V8 RI) and Percy Maclure (Riley). Flanking Howe on the second row are (left) Richard Shuttleworth (Alfa Romeo Tipo B) and (right) Buddy Featherstonhaugh (Maserati 8CM). *Photograph by* Autocar, *courtesy of LAT Archive*

race ten times longer than in 1934. Donington had already put on longer-distance events, particularly the two Nuffield trophy races, the second of which run earlier in 1935, had been won by Pat Fairfield. He was one of those competing in the Donington Grand Prix co-driving Lindsay Eccles' T59. Charlie Martin had also entered his T59 and other grand prix cars included P3 Alfas driven by Richard Shuttleworth and Raymond Sommer. There was a variety of Maseratis, the fastest potentially being a 4.5 litre V8 model for Farina. A number of Rileys also featured and one E.R.A., Prince Bira in *Romulus*

(R2B). In practice Farina duly demonstrated he was far ahead of the rest of the field with a lap five and a half seconds faster than his nearest rival. Howe had a good practice session ending up on the second row of the grid with fourth best time.

Farina had no difficulty in dominating the race itself for the first forty laps but a broken half shaft eliminated him shortly afterwards. Howe had been running in the first half dozen cars up to that point and at fifty laps he was third behind Martin who was about a minute and a half in arrears of Sommer's blue-painted P3 which had taken over the lead after

Farina's retirement. Pit stops led to some changes among the leaders, and Sommer then fell victim to the same problem as Farina – a broken half shaft. Martin then led the race followed by Everitt (Type 34 Maserati), Shuttleworth and Howe. Martin had the misfortune to spin at Macleans in the closing stages of the races, stalling the Bugatti in the process. By the time he got going again Shuttleworth and Howe had gone by and although Howe made up some distance on Shuttleworth he finally finished forty-five seconds behind him. Nonetheless to finish less than a minute in arrears in a race lasting nearly five hours was not a bad achievement.

First visit to South Africa

At the end of 1935 Howe set sail for South Africa aboard the *Warwick Castle*. Along with a number of other British drivers he was off to compete in the second South African Grand Prix. The previous year's race had been won by Whitney Straight driving the 8CM Maserati (3011) for the last time, providing a fitting climax to a most successful racing career. That race had taken place on 27th December but the 1936 race was scheduled for New Year's Day which subsequently became the race's fixed date. In 1937 two further races were instituted thus effectively creating a mini-season. Such an arrangement had an obvious attraction to those who could afford the time and expense of travelling 4000 miles to extend the season – or make an early start on the next one, depending upon how one looked at it!

The South African Grand Prix was run on the Prince George circuit in East London. It was one of the longest circuits used in the 1930s with an original distance of over fifteen miles. For the 1936 race it had been reined in a little but still measured more than eleven miles to the lap. The track had been made up from pre-existing rough roads which had been given a proper macadamized surface. While it was not an intrinsically difficult circuit, in certain parts it was subject to high levels of wind blowing across it and these conditions did create a significant hazard. Raymond Mays, who went out for the 1937/8 season, described this danger as a "weird kind of whirlwind which, quite unpredictably, would tear across the high coastal road". Mays himself experienced this force in his E.R.A. – "an irresistible blast of air picked it up boldly and threw it clear across the road" – and although he came to no harm he felt it was "possibly the narrowest escape of my whole racing career" (Mays: *Split Seconds*).

In order to create some viable competition among an extremely varied entry – ranging from more or less contemporary grand prix cars to local home-grown specials – the South African races were handicap affairs, except for the final two pre-war events in 1939. Richard Shuttleworth in a P3 and Jean-Pierre Wimille, in a T59, were on scratch in the 1936 race with Howe in his T59 starting two minutes ahead of them. The two scratch cars were in a strong position as the race progressed but some thirty miles short of the finish Shuttleworth had a major accident and was taken off to hospital in East London. A local driver, Mario Mazzacurati, won the race in a Maserati. Wimille was second and Pat Fairfield (E.R.A., R4A) was third. Howe didn't finish the race, having experienced a 180 degree spin at about the same time that Shuttleworth crashed.

According to Kevin Desmond, Howe played an important part in securing medical attention for the seriously injured Shuttleworth. Desmond says Howe sent an aeroplane from Johannesburg to fly Shuttleworth back so that he could receive specialist care. Initially he wasn't considered fit to fly but received some attention from the Johannesburg specialist; subsequently two further doctors came down to accompany Shuttleworth on the plane (K. Desmond: *Richard Shuttleworth*). Cholmondeley Tapper doesn't mention Howe's name in connection with Shuttleworth but otherwise his account agrees with Desmond's. Tapper thinks that the strong wind was the main factor in Shuttleworth's accident because the Alfa had gone off the track at precisely the point where there was a gap in a line of houses through which the full force of the wind could have struck the car. Whether Howe had had a similar experience in the Bugatti we don't know but with the evidence of what had happened to Shuttleworth it wouldn't be surprising if he decided the risks were too great to be worth continuing. It's also possible that when he spun the Bugatti the engine stalled and he couldn't re-start it.

The end of the Type 59 – and of Howe's grand prix racing

Howe only drove the T59 on two further occasions. The car returned from South Africa for its final U.K. appearance in his hands at Brooklands in June 1936. He took it back to South Africa for the 1936/7 season where he drove it for the last time on New Year's Day 1937 in the South African Grand Prix. Given that both the Brooklands and South African races were handicap events, not orthodox grand prix races, Donington in October 1935 marked the real end of Howe's grand prix racing.

By the end of the 1935 season it was abundantly clear that the two German teams had decisively re-shaped grand prix racing. With the exception of Nuvolari's spectacular win in the German Grand Prix, Mercedes-Benz or Auto Union had won all the remaining races and occupied most of the other leading places as well. Other teams, and especially independents such as Howe, looked increasingly marginalized and it is unsurprising that 1935 was the last year in which he attempted to participate in the grand prix world. No doubt he regretted the end of his grand prix years but such feelings would have been counter-balanced to some extent by the prospect of new opportunities opening up in voiturette racing.

6

The Voiturette Years

- The transition from Grand Prix Racing to Voiturette Racing
- Changing the Delage for an E.R.A.
- The problems of the E.R.A. Works Cars in 1936
- Howe's first steps with E.R.A. – not the best steps
- Better results with R8B
- The J.C.C. 200: an outstanding drive
- A visit to the New World: The Vanderbilt Cup
- Returning to South Africa
- The accident at Brooklands
- Picking up the threads: two races at Donington
- A third visit to South Africa
- 1938: the final full season
- Four disappointments
- A different kind of racing: R8C at Shelsley and Brighton
- R8C redeemed: improved results at Berne and Brooklands
- 1939: the final race
- New departures?

Chapter 6

The Voiturette Years

The transition from Grand Prix Racing to Voiturette Racing

Howe's decision to give up grand prix events and concentrate on the voiturette class was in many respects bowing to the inevitable. Nonetheless, however 'sensible' or 'realistic' it appears, it meant a considerable change in the kind of racing he pursued for the remainder of his career. Obviously it was not a complete change because he had been competing in voiturette events since 1931. But, as we have seen, such events had only been a minor element in his racing programme both in 1934 and 1935, with most of his time and effort devoted to the 8CM Maserati and the T59 Bugatti. Apart from the occasional sports car race, such as the T.T. and the rather curious episode with the Marendaz, all his racing would now be in the voiturette class. How distinctive was this kind of racing in the mid-1930s?

In the first place although voiturette cars were manufactured in a number of different countries the political overtones were less evident than at the grand prix level. The previous chapter noted how Maserati operated at a much greater distance from the Italian state than Alfa-Romeo. This greater detachment allowed Maserati to sell their cars to anyone who could afford them, unlike the situation at Alfa, as Howe himself had found out in 1934. An independent, therefore, could acquire the latest Maserati and be highly competitive with any works-backed entries. In England E.R.A. was in a very similar position, indeed in 1936 private owners generally achieved better results than those obtained by the works cars. The most striking case of an independent not merely rivalling works cars but roundly defeating them, was Dick Seaman with Howe's former Delage. When Chula and Bira acquired this car in 1937 their intention was that after further modification it would continue to defeat the fastest E.R.A.s and Maseratis. Although this hope was not fulfilled it was not an unreasonable aspiration and the Chula/Bira E.R.A.s continued to offer a major challenge to any works entries.

A second key question concerns the drivers of voiturette cars. Were they people like Howe with grand prix experience or, alternatively, drivers hoping to win their spurs and 'graduate' to a grand prix team? In the twenty-first century we are familiar with a motor sport hierarchy headed by Formula One and underpinned by a variety of other formulae. Very few drivers end up in F1 without an apprenticeship elsewhere, though the speed with which the rise occurs differs a good deal. Although motor sport in the 1930s was a fraction of its contemporary size, the notion of a hierarchy, with grand prix racing at the top, still made sense. Dick Seaman was probably the most obvious British example of a driver whose voiturette career made him a credible candidate for a grand prix drive with both Auto Union and Mercedes-Benz. Among Italian drivers Giuseppe Farina would be a similar example. But many other drivers confined themselves to voiturette racing, not able or not wishing to transfer to grand prix work. Howe, in fact, seems rather atypical for there are few other examples of drivers who drove at both grand prix and voiturette level, as he did between 1931-5, or who then gave up the 'senior' level in favour of the 'junior'.

A third important aspect of voiturette racing involves the circuits that were used. Although there were some, especially in Italy, which only featured in the voiturette calendar, the major 1500 cc races were contested on the same circuits used by the grand prix cars. In some cases such as the Prix de Berne in Switzerland and the Coppa Acerbo in Italy the 'junior' and 'senior' races were run on succeeding days, or even on the same day, as part of the overall fixture. In 1936 Howe had some marginal advantage from this situation because he was familiar with all the European circuits on which he competed; only the Isle of Man was new to him. Obviously in succeeding years this benefit counted for less.

Changing the Delage for an E.R.A.

Howe's familiarity with voiturette racing had all been gained with the 1927 Delages, but it was with an E.R.A. that he launched himself on this final phase of his driving career. The change of car was part of the 'new opportunities' referred to at the end of the previous chapter. Howe had competed alongside E.R.A. at Donington in 1934 and on a number of occasions during 1935 – at Dieppe, Berne and Donington. Although he didn't compete at the Eifelrennen he would have certainly known about Raymond Mays' victory and of the resultant publicity and prestige that flowed from it. By the autumn of 1935 he was sufficiently convinced of the E.R.A.'s merits to order a car for himself. His desire to drive a British car was long-established and his activities with Talbot and M.G., though satisfactory at the time, hadn't provided a firm basis for an extended racing programme.

The other part of this equation was Dick Seaman's desire to buy Howe's Delage. When this idea was first put to Seaman he wasn't convinced the car would be sufficiently competitive even with all Ramponi's planned modifications. When Dick did come round to agree with the plan he found that to begin with Howe wasn't keen to sell. Howe, too, then had second thoughts and agreed that Seaman could buy the car. In November 1935 the Delage, together with its substantial stock of spares, left Howe's premises in Mayfair and moved to Seaman's workshop in Knightsbridge.

Howe's initial reluctance to part with the Delage might have been a bargaining ploy (he did obtain a good price for it), but also probably reflected his view that there was still some competitive life left in the car. While this view might have made sense in the autumn of 1935 the car in its original, unmodified, form would have struggled against the E.R.A.s and Maseratis in 1936. Consequently even if Howe had retained the Delage it's very likely that he would have turned to E.R.A. before long.

The problems of the E.R.A. Works Cars in 1936

The period between the end of the 1935 season and the beginning of the new season in 1936 was an exceptionally busy one for the E.R.A. company. In addition to Howe's car it had orders from Prince Chula, Dr. Dudley Benjafield, Arthur Dobson, Denis Scribbans, Peter Whitehead, and Reggie Tongue. There were also the 1936 works cars to prepare and their racing programme to plan. While the works cars were not entirely new, Mays and Peter Berthon (one of the original E.R.A. designers) were committed to using the Zoller supercharger to replace the Roots-type unit originally developed for the car by Tom Murray Jamieson.

This commitment created various difficulties. In the first place the Zoller did produce a lot more top-end power, but it was a much trickier unit than Murray Jamieson's and needed a great deal of attention to get the best from it. In the second place time taken attending to the Zoller meant less for other aspects of preparation. Some historians have passed harsh judgements on this aspect of the works cars. David Venables, for example, says "The preparation of the works E.R.A.s during 1936 was very poor" (Venables: *The Racing Fifteen-Hundreds*). A third difficulty was that Humphrey Cook, who financed the E.R.A. company, was increasingly worried about the poor results during 1936. He was more and more sceptical about the Zoller whereas Mays and Berthon felt exactly the opposite, more and more convinced of its merits. A difference of this kind, about a fundamental aspect of the car's design, was far from ideal.

This background to Howe's first season with E.R.A. is of some relevance, though its precise importance is more difficult to assess. Throughout 1936 Howe was entered by H.W. Cook or E.R.A. Limited and therefore, in a formal sense, he was part of the works team. For a few races in 1936 the car was painted in the appropriate E.R.A. works green, but when the official works colour changed to black, at the Prix de Berne in July, R8B changed to Howe's own colours of blue and silver. R8B had the standard Jamieson supercharger throughout 1936 and 1937, so one major source of difficulty, the powerful but fragile Zoller, was not a problem for Howe's car. Of course, as we have noted above, time taken to deal with the Zoller meant less time for everything else and Howe's car might have suffered in this way. Exactly how responsibilities for its preparation were split between Howe's own mechanics and those employed by Bourne is not known, but it certainly was the case that Sid Maslyn continued to be a part of Howe's equipe, as did his personal transporter, described at the beginning of the previous chapter.

Howe's first steps with E.R.A. – not the best steps

It is obvious that the resources of the E.R.A. company were severely over-stretched in the first few months of 1936 and not all the new cars were ready for the start of the season. Howe's R8B was one of those that were not quite finished and so he was invited to share Dr. Benjafield's car, R6B, in the British Empire Trophy. This car ran quite well finishing in eighth place; it would have been higher up the order but for an engine stall at Starkey's which required the mechanics to go out and re-start it.

By the time of the Monaco voiturette race – the Coupe de Prince Rainier – Howe's car had been delivered and he was entered as part of the official works team. He had the advantage of knowing the circuit, unlike most of the other drivers, and his language facility was also in demand as he translated the chief official's French instructions into English for his fellow British drivers. His circuit knowledge must have helped to put him on the front row of the grid and after an excellent start he led the race in the opening laps but this situation didn't last for long as plug trouble then intervened and he had to come into the pits to renew them. Although this change of plugs improved matters the car still did not run entirely cleanly and it was impossible to retrieve the

1936 – Donington – For his first appearance in an E.R.A., at the British Empire Trophy in April 1936, Howe drove Dr. Dudley Benjafield's E.R.A. R6B. Here he leads A.P. 'Ginger' Hamilton's Alfa Romeo Monza. Howe finished 8th. *Photograph by* Autocar, *courtesy of LAT Archive*

Above – 1936 – Monte Carlo – Howe and his E.R.A. R8B are followed by Omobono Tenni's Maserati 4CM around the Gazomètre hairpin during the Coupe Prince Rainier de Monaco voiturette race, which supported the 1936 Monaco Grand Prix. Howe finished fifth in the race. *Photograph courtesy of Guy Spollon Collection*

Below – 1936 – Douglas, Isle of Man – Howe stands, cigarette in hand, in front of the E.R.A. of Raymond Mays in the pits during the 1936 R.A.C. Light Car Race meeting. Mays can be seen leaning on his car, chatting to Madge Cook, whilst Humphrey Cook can be seen on the left of the photograph, in raincoat and trilby hat. Howe retired from the race on lap twenty-three with a split fuel tank. *Photograph courtesy of Adam Ferrington Collection*

1936 – Brooklands – Howe relaxes during the B.A.R.C. Whitsun Meeting in June 1936. He drove his Bugatti Type 59 in three races at the meeting, finishing third in the First Long Handicap breaking the Class C Lap Record. *Photograph by* Autocar, *courtesy of LAT Archive*

1936 – Nürburgring – A beautiful George Monkhouse photograph of Howe and his E.R.A. R8B during the Eifelrennen voiturette race in June 1936, in which Howe finished eighth. *Photograph by George Monkhouse, courtesy of Spitzley Archive*

time he had lost. The race was won by Bira driving his original E.R.A., *Romulus*, the first of many victories for this combination.

Matters did not improve at the next few meetings, indeed they got worse. In both the International Trophy race at Brooklands and in the R.A.C.'s Light Car Race held in the Isle of Man, Howe had to retire. At Brooklands he hardly got going at all, an oil pipe fracturing within the first ten minutes of the race. In the Isle of Man which turned out to be the first big victory for Dick Seaman and the Delage, his prospects seemed much brighter. Howe's car was used for practice by Marcel Lehoux, another of the works drivers. Under the race rules the qualifying times were attached to the car, not the driver. Lehoux had practised so effectively that R8B was on pole position. Howe made the best possible use of this advantage and led the field in the opening laps. He was then overtaken by Seaman but could have remained among the leading cars if the engine had not lost its edge. The problem was an over-pressurised fuel tank and when the tank finally split he couldn't go on.

At the Eifelrennen he was dogged by plug trouble and could not finish higher than eighth. Similar plug problems intervened in the Nuffield Trophy race at Donington, held three weeks after the Eifelrennen, but as in Germany he did finish the race, in sixth place. At Albi he set the fastest lap in practice but gearbox problems put him out in the race itself at an early stage.

Better results with R8B

However the season was not unrelieved gloom, better results came at Picardy and Berne and especially in the last U.K. event of the season in which he drove the E.R.A., the J.C.C. 200.

The Grand Prix de Picardie at Péronne, which took place two weeks before the Nuffield Trophy, consisted of two heats and a final and Howe was second in his heat and third in the final. There was a high quality entry with Mays, Lehoux, Howe and

1936 – Donington – Two photographs from the 1936 Nuffield Trophy meeting at Donington. In the first, Howe, helmet in hand, chats on the grid to Raymond Mays in front of E.R.A. R8B, whilst in the second he climbs into his E.R.A. Teddy Rayson's Maserati 4CM can be seen to the left, with Rayson, in white overalls and body belt standing beside the car. Arthur Dobson's white E.R.A. R7B is visible on the row behind. Howe finished sixth in the race. *Photographs courtesy of Guy Spollon Collection*

Above – 1936 – Peronne – Howe's Commer Invader transporter with trailer is seen in Northern France on its way to the 1936 Grand Prix de Picardie. *Photograph courtesy of Adam Ferrington Collection*

Fairfield driving works E.R.A.s, plus Reggie Tongue and Arthur Dobson in their own cars, Count Trossi and Gino Rovere in works Maseratis, and Dick Seaman in his Delage. Seaman won Howe's heat and this was another occasion where Mays demonstrated tremendous speed in his Zoller–blown car, but the recurrent unreliability too, so he failed to finish. In the final Howe benefited from retirements by both Seaman and Trossi to finish third to Bira and Fairfield.

The Prix de Berne entry was similar to that at Péronne insofar as it largely consisted of works-entered and privately-entered E.R.A.s, Maseratis – though there were no works cars – and Seaman's Delage. Seaman dominated the race and scored his third successive victory on the Bremgarten circuit.

Embiricos and Reggie Tongue's E.R.A.s were second and third with Howe, after a poor start, moving up the field to finish fourth a lap behind the leaders.

The J.C.C. 200: An outstanding drive

The J.C.C. race was unquestionably Howe's best result in circuit racing in 1936 and indeed one of the very best in his whole competition career. The Junior Car Club had run a series of 200 mile races at Brooklands from 1921 to 1928 and the 1936 race was a revival of this event, but staged at Donington. The J.C.C. had also decided that it would be a scratch event, although not confined to 1500 cc cars. In fact most of the cars were in the voiturette category and certainly they dominated the race,

1936 – Donington – Dick Seaman and Howe enjoy a celebratory drink after finishing first and second respectively in the 1936 J.C.C. 200 race at Donington. To the left of the cockpit of Seaman's Delage 1½ litre is Seaman's chief mechanic Guilio Ramponi.
Photograph by Autocar, *courtesy of LAT Archive*

the only car outside that class to make any impression was Howe's former 8CM Maserati driven by Cholmondeley Tapper.

During practice Pat Fairfield (E.R.A.) set a new lap record and together with Douglas Briault (E.R.A.), Peter Whitehead (E.R.A.) and Dick Seaman (Delage) occupied the front row of the grid. By the second lap Seaman was in the lead and four laps later Howe had worked himself up into second place ahead of all the other E.R.A.s. On lap 13 Howe overtook Seaman and he led the race for the next forty-seven laps. On lap 50 he had to come in to refuel and Seaman took over the lead which he kept until the chequered flag, finishing fifty-one seconds ahead of Howe. Seaman knew that had enough fuel to carry him through the race whereas Howe would have to stop and refuel at some point. Consequently he made sure he didn't let Howe build up too great a lead and, when the latter was re-fuelling, Seaman speeded up to give himself a comfortable margin. Seaman told John Dugdale, who was an *Autocar* staff journalist, that the J.C.C. race was "probably the one he had enjoyed the most that year, as it was essentially one of tactics" (*Autocar*, 9th October, 1936).

All the reports confirm that Howe drove right at the top of his form. Rivers Fletcher was a spectator and wrote, fifty years later, about Howe's performance: "The Old Man drove like a demon, right on the limit all the time, but never put a foot wrong. I watched him coming into the Hairpin on several laps, locking over to the right very early on and scrubbing off the speed, and opening up the throttle half way round the corner, sliding in a four wheel drift to the outside of the corner nearly on the grass,

The Voiturette Years

before straightening out and shooting under the bridge. I thought his cornering was better and faster than any other driver on that day" (Rivers Fletcher: *Mostly Motor Racing*).

A visit to the New World: The Vanderbilt Cup

A most unusual event took place on October 12th 1936 when the Vanderbilt Cup race was staged at the Roosevelt Raceway, on Long Island, New York. It was an interesting mixture of two distinct motor racing cultures. It brought together American and European racing cars on an American circuit, but one designed to be much closer to a European-style circuit than to an American one. Chris Nixon suggests that the Roosevelt Raceway bore a striking resemblance to a modern, i.e. late twentieth century, track as it featured run-off areas, steel guard rails and warning lights (Chris Nixon: *Racing the Silver Arrows* (1986)). Its artificiality proved somewhat disconcerting to those accustomed to European road racing: Dick Seaman, for example, found the absence of landmarks for braking a problem and he felt that it bore little resemblance to true road-racing, "it was just a track with bends in it" (Prince Chula: *Dick Seaman, Racing Motorist* (1943)).

In addition to the substantial sums spent constructing the track, there was very generous prize money, with the winner receiving the contemporary equivalent of over half a million dollars. Forty-five cars were entered, with a considerable European presence which included three works Alfas, three V8 Maseratis, two T59 Bugattis (though only one actually started) and three E.R.A.s. Howe and Fairfield

1936 – Roosevelt Raceway, New York – Howe gives the photographer a sideways look in the paddock at the 1936 Vanderbilt Cup in October 1936, where Howe was racing his E.R.A. The unknown American photographer relates the circumstances of taking the photograph as follows: "I asked Howe if I might take a picture of him. He said 'I can't stop you'. With this left-handed acquiescence I backed up a shot. I think he tried to blow enough smoke to lay down a screen, but I must have beaten him to it!" *Photograph courtesy of Richard Crump*

were entered by Humphrey Cook and R1A, entered by Major Sidney Cotton, was in the hands of Hon. Brian Lewis. It was a 300 mile race and as the lap speed wasn't all that high it took the winner four and half hours to complete the 75 laps. The E.R.A.s were the smallest capacity cars in the race but managed to finish fifth (Fairfield), thirteenth (Howe), and fifteenth (Lewis).

Howe subsequently told *The Autocar* that while he was "most impressed with American enthusiasm", there was too much about the race that derived from dirt-track racing. In particular he didn't like the uneven surface – in some parts it was softer than expected, but in others much harder. This combination led to some of it breaking up and the creation of pot-holes. Like most of the European drivers Howe thought the circuit had too many corners, which limited speed and risked oiling-up the plugs. The American organisers responded to these criticisms and smoothed out many of the corners by the time of the 1937 event. Shortly before that race, which was held in July rather than October, Howe wrote to Dick Seaman (who was going to the race for the first time) giving him advice about the race and about dealing with the organisers.

Returning to South Africa

Howe's second visit to South Africa was for the first 'mini-season', as two other races had been added to the South African G.P. There were to take place at two new circuits, one at Cape Town measuring just under five miles to the lap, and the other at Johannesburg over a shorter distance of two and a quarter miles.

These 1937 races are the best known of the pre-war seasons in South Africa because the Auto Union team decided to enter two of the three races. Its main motive was commercial, a belief that a convincing demonstration by Auto Union would help boost sales of the D.K.W. car in South Africa. It was apparently successful and Howe frequently alluded to it in future years when he was endeavouring to make the case that motor sport provided a basis for technological advance and commercial success.

Although Auto Union knew the races would be run on handicap it didn't know the actual timings until shortly before the first race. When they were disclosed it considered the odds had been stacked very heavily against it, making victory virtually impossible. So far as the South African G.P. was concerned its fears were more or less correct. Despite a stunning drive by Bernd Rosemeyer, who had emerged in the second half of 1936 as the outstanding Auto Union driver, he couldn't finish higher than fifth. Howe, driving the T59 for the last time, set off sixteen and a half minutes ahead of Rosemeyer and finished in sixth place. The race was won by Pat Fairfield in the E.R.A., R4A, who had been given just under half an hour's advantage over Rosemeyer. In the Grosvenor G.P. Howe drove R8B for the first time on South African soil and had a good race actually leading the Auto Unions until they caught him two laps before the end of the race. In this race Howe was slightly faster than Fairfield and if R8B hadn't had to make a late stop for plugs Howe might just have held on to his first place. The third race, the Rand Grand Prix was a somewhat tamer affair as the two Auto Unions did not enter and some of the other cars that had featured in the first two races had fallen by the wayside. Fairfield and Howe finished first and second.

Overall Howe had had a rewarding time in these three South African races. He had finished on all three occasions, well up the order with the E.R.A. and with a respectable sixth place in the T59. The Bugatti did not return with him to the U.K. as it was sold to a garage in Durban. Howe had only used it once in 1936 during the British racing season for some short handicap events at Brooklands. Suitable long-distance events for the T59 were now rare and so he chose to concentrate solely on the E.R.A. and voiturette events.

The accident at Brooklands

During the winter of 1936/7 two of the works E.R.A.s, originally built as B types, were modified to C type specification and re-labelled R4C and R12C. Mays and Berthon had persuaded Humphrey Cook that the Zoller blower could be reliable providing certain other components were modified. The need for these changes arose from the substantial increase in power the Zoller produced which put a strain on certain aspects of the original E.R.A. design. The C type was a response to these problems and incorporated strengthened connecting rods, independent front suspension (IFS), hydraulic brakes and an enlarged fuel tank. Howe's car, although it continued to run as part of the official works entry, did not receive these modifications for a further twelve months. The only modification made to R8B for the new season was to substitute De Ram shock absorbers for the original Hartfords. The Chula/Bira equipe made this change to *Romulus* at the same time. These

1937 – Brooklands – May 1937 start of the Campbell Trophy with Howe in E.R.A. R8B (No.8) third from left. Other cars prominently visible (l-r) are:- No.7 Walker (E.R.A. R10B), No.27 Bira (Maserati 8CM), the eventual winner, No.3 Arthur Dobson (E.R.A. R7B), No.9 Mays (E.R.A. R4B), No.15 Rayson (Maserati 4CM), No.24 Staniland (Alfa Romeo Tipo B), No.21 Powys Lybbe (Alfa Romeo 2300), No.29 Austin Dobson (Alfa Romeo Bi-motore), No.6 Scribbans (E.R.A. R9B), No.25 Brackenbury (Alfa Romeo Tipo B) and Connell (E.R.A. R6B. *Photograph by* Autocar, *courtesy of LAT Archive*

dampers were expensive and more complicated than the Hartfords (though the latter need regular adjustment) but their attraction was increased stability which was an important consideration as pre-war tracks lacked the smooth surface taken for granted on contemporary circuits.

Howe's first British event in 1937 was the Campbell Trophy race at Brooklands. The race was celebrating the creation of a new track at Brooklands – the Campbell circuit – which was designed to offer an experience a little closer to road racing. For the first twenty-four laps Howe showed similar form to his J.C.C. 200 drive as he duelled closely with Bira, at the wheel of the 8CM Maserati. *The Autocar* reported that "For six successive laps the front hub caps of both cars passed within four inches of the Vickers Bridge parapet". On the twenty-fifth lap it appears that the very fine judgement needed to clear the parapet failed and Howe struck the earth bank surrounding it. R8B's right-side wheels went up in the air and the front of the car struck the palisade over the parapet. It was then thrown across the road with its left wheels now high in the air. Howe was flung out of the car but prompt action by officials ensured that both he and the E.R.A. were quickly moved away from the risk of being struck by other cars. Initially Howe seemed to be mainly suffering from shock but subsequent examination at Weybridge Cottage Hospital diagnosed injuries to his arm, shoulder and ribs as well as a head wound.

There was considerable anxiety about his condition. Humphrey Cook and his wife gave a party in London after the race and there was much concern among their guests especially as Raymond Mays, who had been to the hospital, reported that he was in a serious state. Bulletins about his condition appeared for some days after the accident in *The Times* and, most fortunately they were able to report some improvement. Howe himself wrote to *The Autocar* in the middle of June, some six weeks after the accident, reporting that he was able to drive again and that "if my luck holds in about six or eight weeks I shall be able to get going again" (*The Autocar*, 18th June, 1937).

1937 – Brooklands – The aftermath of Howe's crash in E.R.A. R8B in the Campbell Trophy. The damaged car can be seen being pushed to the side of the track, whilst Howe lies injured on the infield on the extreme left. His injuries necessitated a four month lay-off from racing, missing the bulk of the 1937 season. Dennis Scribbans' E.R.A. R9B can be seen passing the scene to the right.
Photograph by Autocar, *courtesy of LAT Archive*

Picking up the threads: Two races at Donington

What he meant, of course, by 'get going again' was that he would be able to resume motor racing. By the second week in July he had recovered sufficiently to drive down to Brooklands and act as an Observer precisely at the point where he had had his own accident. He was back behind the wheel of the E.R.A., more or less exactly as he had hoped, on the 28th August for the J.C.C. 200 Mile Race at Donington. By quarter distance he was in fourth place but in the next part of the race matters began to deteriorate and by half distance he was having trouble with his brakes and had to stop at the pits for adjustment. Whatever was done was not successful as shortly afterwards he failed to slow at Starkey's, went off onto the grass and spun round through 180 degrees throwing turf in all directions. His brakes had failed and that was the end of his race.

Howe returned to Donington in early October for the Donington Grand Prix. He was very much among the 'also-rans' for this was the event at which full teams from Mercedes and Auto Union appeared for the first time in Britain. Naturally they dominated the race; the British entered cars could not possibly compete effectively with them and really constituted a separate race of their own. As such, Howe drove very well completing seventy-seven laps in just over three hours, finishing seventh overall, one lap behind Bira in the 8CM Maserati who was sixth and the first non-German car to finish.

Although it took some time to emerge there was an interesting controversy about whether the E.R.A.s should have taken part in the Donington G.P. In an *Autocar* editorial it was suggested that "It was a mistaken policy for E.R.A.s to have run against German cars of three times their engine size...Spectators did not appreciate the difference between these small

Above – 1937 – Donington – Howe poses with his repaired R8B in the Donington paddock before his return to racing in the 1937 J.C.C. 200. E.R.A. mechanic Ken Richardson can be seen to Howe's left with his arms folded. *Photograph courtesy of Adam Ferrington Collection*

Below – 1937 – Donington – The drivers are briefed by Clerk of the Course John Morgan on the grid for the J.C.C. 200. Chief Track Marshal Charles Follett can be seen on the extreme left. Howe is to the immediate right of Morgan, followed by Austin Dobson, Reggie Tongue, Johnnie Wakefield, (?), Kenneth Evans, Bira (with his back to the camera) Robin Hanson, Raymond Mays, Arthur Dobson, Peter Whitehead (partially hidden by Dobson), Charlie Brackenbury and Percy Maclure (putting on his gloves). *Photograph by* Autocar, *courtesy of LAT Archive*

home-built English cars and the G.P. machines of the vast State-encouraged German organisations". A feature article by Charles Houghton widened the issue to make a general case that grand prix racing was not the best way to develop production cars and that the main reason the German teams engaged in it was "national propaganda...These machines are being run principally in order to raise the prestige of Germany all over the world".

Howe responded in another feature article the following week. He entirely rejected the idea that

Top – 1937- Donington – Howe poses with two of his fellow E.R.A. drivers, Raymond Mays and Arthur Dobson on the grid at the J.C.C. 200 meeting. Behind the group is Mays' E.R.A. R4C. Howe eventually retired with brake trouble. *Photograph courtesy of GP Library*

Left – 1937 – Donington – Howe and R8B on the Donington straight before his retirement from the J.C.C. 200 in August 1937. *Photograph by* Autocar, *courtesy of LAT Archive*

Above – 1937 – Donington – Howe, sporting a jacket, presumably over his racing overalls, drives E.R.A. R8B onto the grid for the Donington Grand Prix in October 1937. Howe finished the race in seventh, but unclassified, three laps behind Rosemeyer's Auto Union.. In the background an Auto Union mechanic drives Rosemeyer's soon-to-be-victorious car (No.5) with Arthur Dobson's E.R.A. R7B (No.19) and Robin Hanson's Maserati 6CM (No.15) also prominent. *Photograph courtesy of John Maitland Collection*

Right – 1937 – Donington Park – Howe greets Rudolf Caracciola on the grid of the Donington Grand Prix. Caracciola and his Mercedes W125 were placed third in the race, whilst Howe was not classified, three laps behind the all-conquering Silver Arrows. At the rear of the grid is Percy Maclure's Riley (No.20). *Photograph by* Autocar*, courtesy of LAT Archive*

there was little or no connection between technical development in racing cars and ordinary cars: "there is hardly a single feature of the modern production car which does not owe its development very largely directly, or indirectly, to racing". He also contended that the German racing success had "undoubtedly...a great effect upon the sales of German motor cars". He didn't share the *Autocar's* concern – that Donington spectators wouldn't realise the difference in size between the German cars and the E.R.A.s. If there was anything in it then it was the job of the race commentators (via the public address) and of journalists to make these differences clear.

A third visit to South Africa

Howe must have looked forward to his races in South Africa as his accident had severely truncated his 1937 season in Britain and Europe. The opening race was not altogether encouraging: in the Rand Grand Prix which was run nine days before Christmas he finished ninth, having suffered intermittent mis-firing, and he was the last classified finisher as the remaining four behind him were flagged off. This was the race in which Raymond Mays was hoping to score some vital points to defeat Bira in the 1937 Gold Star competition. Unfortunately for him he didn't finish high enough up the order to produce sufficient points to overhaul Bira.

Mays was experiencing the South African season for the first time and it left him with two outstanding impressions – "the fantastic hospitality of our hosts" and the "glories and hazards of the Prince George circuit". His very uncomfortable experience on that circuit during the South African Grand Prix has already been referred to but he was still on course to finish strongly until fuel starvation intervened and dropped him down to seventh. Howe again finished ninth in this race. His third race was much more satisfactory bringing him his first victory with R8B. This was the Grosvenor Grand Prix run on 15th January over the 4.6 mile circuit in Cape Town with an entry of two dozen from which twenty cars actually appeared on the grid. Raymond Mays was again a very strong contender but troubled by a faulty scavenge pump so the focus of attention shifted to a close struggle between Howe and Piero Taruffi who was driving a Maserati 6CM. During the final ten laps they both caught and passed the leading 1100 cc Riley and although Taruffi then began to gain a little on Howe, R8B passed the chequered flag twenty seconds ahead of the Italian combination. Their race averages – Howe, 74.72 and Taruffi, 74.55 – indicate how close the competition was

1938 – Cape Town – Howe's E.R.A. R8B leads Taruffi's Maserati 6CM on his way to victory in the Grosvenor Grand Prix.
Photograph by Cays Photo Agency, courtesy of Guy Spollon Collection

1938 – Cape Town – Howe is shown with the trophy he won for winning the Grosvenor Grand Prix in his E.R.A. This was E.R.A. R8B's last appearance before being converted to "C" specification upon its return to Europe. The race was the third of the series of races run in South Africa during December 1937 and January 1938. Howe is shown in the centre with (l-r) Bill Everitt (fourth in Howe's Maserati 6CM), Piero Taruffi (second – Maserati 6CM), Luigi Villoresi (third) and Johnny Lurani (third sharing his Maserati 4CM with Villoresi). *Photograph by Cape Times, courtesy of Guy Spollon Collection*

1938: the final full season

When Howe returned to the U.K. R8B was taken to Bourne and converted to C type specification, emerging as R8C. Although it was a 'standard' C type, meaning that the key features of Porsche IFS, Zoller supercharger, strengthened connecting rods and hydraulic brakes were all incorporated, the modification to the chassis wasn't undertaken in the same way as the conversion of R4B and R12B in 1936/7. Simultaneously with the changes to Howe's car, Raymond Mays' R4C was being converted to D type specification and this change required a new chassis. The chassis of R4C was therefore surplus to requirements and it made good sense to use it as the basis for reconstructing Howe's car, especially as converting the two B types in 1936/7 had involved a fairly laborious process of cutting off the chassis just beyond the steering box and welding on a new section to carry the IFS. If a car is defined by its chassis then there was a case for Howe's car being known as R4C, not R8C, but perhaps an R4C and an R4D would have led to considerable confusion. The car was re-sprayed in the green colour the works cars had re-adopted and then again, later in the season, when the works colour was changed it was repainted in a blue/grey mixture.

Four disappointments

Howe's 1938 season shows some significant shifts from his activities in 1936. In 1938 most of his races were in Britain with only two foreign outings, to Picardie and the Prix de Berne, whereas in 1936 half his events were at home and half abroad. In 1938 he also returned to an earlier interest in sprints and hill climbs, entering for Shelsley and Brighton.

The works cars had been much more reliable in 1937 and vindicated the faith Mays and Berthon had in the Zoller supercharger, especially when it was harnessed to the other C type modifications. Although Howe did experience supercharger problems in the final at Picardie (after finishing second in his heat) which led to his retirement, it was other difficulties that got him off to a rather disappointing start with R8C.

His season began in early April with the British Empire Trophy at Donington, followed a month later by the J.C.C. International Trophy at Brooklands. At Donington he set a very good time in practice and in the opening stages was among the leading cars, actually in first place for a brief while but almost immediately he came in to change a plug and subsequently retired with a collapsed valve after less than a quarter of the race had run. A similar pattern prevailed in the International Trophy: after maintaining third place at quarter-distance he began to slow and came into the pits complaining of a slipping transmission. After refuelling he carried on until half-distance but told his pit when he came in again that the situation was hopeless and he retired.

The Picardie race, which took place in the middle

1938 – Donington – Howe's E.R.A. R8C, newly converted to "C" specification, leads the Maserati 6CMs of Luigi Villoresi and Johnny Wakefield during the British Empire Trophy in April 1938. Howe eventually retired from the race with valve trouble.
Photograph by Light Car, *courtesy of Guy Spollon Collection*

1938 – Brooklands – Two views of Howe's pit stop in his E.R.A. during the J.C.C. International Trophy in May 1937. Howe eventually retired with gearbox trouble. *Photographs by* Autocar, *courtesy of LAT Archive*

of June, has already been mentioned. His fourth successive circuit failure was in the Nuffield Trophy race at Donington. Before the race began Howe unveiled the memorial designed and executed by Bira to Pat Fairfield who had been killed at Le Mans in June 1937. According to Sammy Davis, Howe "said exactly the right thing, and said it in exactly the right way" (*The Autocar* 15th July, 1938). It was a Bira's day as a driver too, as he drove to a convincing victory in the ex-works E.R.A., R12C. Howe had no similar good fortune, R8C completing only 5 laps before engine problems forced him to stop out on the circuit and return to the pits on foot.

A different kind of racing: R8C at Shelsley and Brighton

Interspersed with these failures on the track Howe had two successful outings to Shelsley and Brighton. He was familiar with both events, but hadn't previously driven the E.R.A. at either. Since his last Shelsley appearance, in June 1934, Raymond Mays with the E.R.A. had established a dominating presence, though it had been disturbed in September 1937 by Fane setting a new record of 38.77 with a twin-blown, single-seater Frazer Nash. Mays hadn't been present at that meeting and there was keen interest in seeing how the battle between them would be resolved at the opening meeting in 1938.

As sometimes happens, expectations were slightly disappointed because Fane's car had mechanical problems on the second run. The first runs had seen Mays and Fane set identical times, but well outside the latter's record. Mays improved considerably on his second run but not quite enough to overtake Fane's record. Howe proved to be the fastest of a number of other E.R.A.s with a best time of 41.25. This time was good enough for fourth FTD; the third spot, following Mays and Fane, was taken by Bert Hadley in one of the very rapid Austin single-seaters. Howe's car had its normal 1½ litre engine so it was unlikely to be as quick as Mays with a two-litre, but Charlie Martin, at the meeting when Fane broke the record, had climbed in 39.67 demonstrating that it

1938 – Shelsley Walsh – Howe gives his characteristic quizzical look at the camera whilst waiting with his E.R.A. in the Shelsley paddock during the May 1938 meeting. *Photograph courtesy of John Pearson*

The Voiturette Years

Above – 1938 – Shelsley Walsh – E.R.A. R8C with Howe at the wheel waits to come forward to the line at Shelsley in May 1938, where he set fourth fastest time overall (41.25 sec) and finished second in class. Behind Howe can be seen Ian Connell in E.R.A. R6B, followed by AFP Fane in his Frazer-Nash B.M.W. *Photograph courtesy of Midland Automobile Club Archive*

Below – 1938 – Shelsley Walsh – Howe powers R8C up the Shelsley hill at the May 1938 meeting where he set fourth fastest time of the day. *Photograph by* Autocar, *courtesy of LAT Archive*

153

1938 – Brighton – Howe and E.R.A. R8C leave the line at the Brighton Speed Trials in July 1938, followed by Charles Mortimer's Alta. Howe set a time of 23.83 on this run, but later set a time of 22.94 – the second fastest time of the day. Photograph courtesy of Guy Spollon Collection

was possible for someone other than Mays to record a sub-forty seconds climb in an E.R.A..

At the Brighton Speed trials Howe ran in two classes, the first for racing cars up to 1½ litres and the second for cars up to 3000 cc. He won the 1500 cc class and set a new class record with a time of 23.83 which placed him comfortably ahead of two Altas driven by Charles Mortimer and Hugh Hunter who both needed more than 26 seconds to complete the kilometre. In the bigger capacity class he was up against an Alta again, but this time a two litre car driven by Geoffrey Taylor. R8C improved to 22.94, but the Alta succeeded in clipping half a second off that, establishing a new overall course record with a time of 22.45.

R8C redeemed: improved results at Berne and Brooklands

The 1938 season concluded on a more satisfactory note than it had begun. Unlike the early and mid-season events which had been dominated by problems and retirements, Howe not only completed the distance, but finished in the first four in three successive races. At the Prix de Berne, held in late August, he finished second in his heat and fourth in the final. However, though R8C did remain intact it was not running perfectly and some of the contemporary reports suggest its engine still didn't sound quite right a week later when it ran in the J.C.C. International trophy at Brooklands. This race witnessed a large number

1938 – Bremgarten – Howe and Raymond Mays are seen in discussion with an official from the Automobile Club de Suisse organising club, in the pits at the 1938 Swiss Grand Prix meeting. Howe drove his E.R.A. in the voiturette race, the Preis von Bern, finishing second in his heat and fourth in the final. Photograph courtesy of Adam Ferrington Collection

1938 – Brooklands – Howe, glass in hand, congratulates Johnnie Wakefield, the winner of the J.C.C. 200, in August 1938. Howe had finished third in E.R.A. R8C. To Howe's left is John Morgan, Clerk of the Course and Secretary of the Junior Car Club. Photograph by Autocar, courtesy of LAT Archive

Above – 1938 – Brooklands – Raymond Mays in E.R.A. R4D leads Howe in E.R.A. R8C during the B.R.D.C. Road Race. *Photograph by George Monkhouse, courtesy of Spitzley Archive*

Below – 1938 – Brooklands – Howe in typical racing pose during the B.R.D.C. Road Race held on Brooklands' Campbell Circuit in September 1938. Howe finished fourth in the race. *Photograph by George Monkhouse, courtesy of Spitzley Archive*

1939 – Brooklands – The Junior Car Club International Trophy in May 1939 was Francis Howe's last race. Here he is seen on the extreme right of the group of drivers being briefed on the grid by the Clerk of the Course before the race. Other drivers prominent in the group are (l-r) Arthur Dobson, Percy Maclure (white overalls), Reggie Tongue, Kenneth Evans (white overalls and cap), Robin Hanson, Frank Ashby (glasses), Johnnie Wakefield, Raymond Mays (behind Wakefield in helmet), Ian Nickols, Norman Wilson (between the scrutineer and the Clerk of the Course) and Peter Whitehead. Maclure's Riley (No.28) can be seen on the extreme left behind the drivers' group. *Photograph by* Autocar, *courtesy of LAT Archive*

of retirements, more than half the starters failing to complete the race so that those that did survive, such as Howe, obviously benefited. Only the winner, Johnnie Wakefield in E.R.A. R14B and Bira, runner-up in the 8CM Maserati, completed the full 88 laps, with Howe two laps behind in third place.

Howe's final British circuit race in 1938 was also at Brooklands – the B.R.D.C. Road Race. Here again more than half of those who started failed to finish. Although Howe wasn't among the leaders to begin with, he worked his way up the field and was holding third place prior to his pit stop. This took some time as the petrol filter needed cleaning and Hon. Peter Aitken took over the third spot which Howe wasn't able to retrieve before the race ended.

If Howe hoped that his South African visit would maintain R8C's late-season improvement he would have been somewhat disappointed for the outcome wasn't very satisfactory. The South African 'season', in fact, consisted of only two races and by contrast with the previous three years they were both straightforward scratch events. The 6CM Maserati won both races with Luigi Villoresi victorious in the South African Grand Prix and Franco Cortese in the

1939 – Brooklands – Howe climbs into E.R.A. R8C for the final time, on the grid of the J.C.C. International Trophy. By this time his car was being run by E.R.A. works mechanics, rather than by his private equipe, and a works mechanic is visible to the right of the car. Billy Cotton's E.R.A. R1B (No.15) can be seen to the left along with an Alfa Romeo 2900 (chassis number 412022) which seems to have been acting as course car at this meeting. *Photograph by* Autocar, *courtesy of LAT Archive*

Grosvenor Grand Prix. Howe finished fifth in the South African Grand Prix having initially been further up the field but he was dogged by the old plug problem and lost time when he had to stop to rectify it. The Grosvenor race was very punishing with only four of the twelve starters finishing. Howe was among the retirements, half-way through the race, with a broken gearbox.

1939: The final race

Howe's 1939 British racing season began at Brooklands in the second week of May, five days after his 55th birthday. He was there for the International Trophy which had attracted a good entry, albeit with little of the 'international' about it other than Prince Bira who was driving with a Siamese licence rather than his previous British one. The race should have seen the debut of the E type E.R.A. but it was withdrawn; Reggie Tongue's 4CL Maserati, on the other hand, did make its first appearance and was prominent in the race finally finishing third to Bira (8CM Maserati), and Leslie Brooke, driving his own Riley-powered special.

E.R.A.s were numerous among the runners but did not distinguish themselves in the results, Howe's R8C being one of six Bourne cars that failed to finish. Howe was caught out by the rain which fell in copious quantities before the race had reached its half-way point. He was holding fourth place when he mistook the track limits which had been obscured by large amounts of standing water. He skidded into a concrete wall and though suffering no personal injury the E.R.A. was not so fortunate, suffering some front-end damage.

New departures?

The 1939 International Trophy was the end of Howe's competition career but almost certainly it was not intended to be. David Venables does claim that he had decided to retire in 1939 but this seems very unlikely as he had embarked on a most interesting development of his E.R.A..

The details were made public in August, barely a month before the war started and brought all motor sport to an end. What was revealed was a new engine for R8C designed by J.L. Jameson, of Jameson Aero Engines of Ewell, Surrey. A hurried reading of this name might suggest some affinity with Tom Murray Jamieson, especially as Jameson was also responsible for the design and manufacture of a supercharger. But in fact both the initials and the surname are different and the only connection is that both have an involvement with E.R.A.

Jameson had been experimenting with two stroke engines since the early 1930s. Before he designed Howe's unit he had produced two such examples, in 1933 and 1936. He was by no means the first person to be attracted to the theoretical advantages of the two stroke principle in preference to the prevailing four stroke practice. With two stroke action each time the piston descends it is doing useful work and in its simplest form there is no need for valve gear as the piston itself times the incoming and outgoing gases by uncovering ports during its travel. However to set against these advantages there were off-setting difficulties – extracting the exhaust gases from the cylinder before a new charge arrived, the need for broad ports at the base of the cylinder which complicated lubrication and a tendency to over-heat the pistons.

In the light of his experience with his earlier engines Jameson decided that R8C's should incorporate two independently operated valves on either side of the cylinder block. The supercharger (one of Jameson's own) was fed by two carburettors and very highly pressurised at 30 lbs. His 1933 engine, when it had actually been run, had fallen well short of its projected output and the supercharger's high boost was one way of trying to bridge this gap. The engine incorporated a five bearing crankshaft with balance weights drilled so that oil would flow direct to the main bearing and through the hollow crank to the big ends. Oil was also passed up the connecting rods past the roller small end bearings and out to the inner face of the pistons to cool them. At the rear of the crankshaft there was a small flywheel which was intended to take the clutch as an ordinary, i.e. non-pre-selector, gearbox was fitted.

After the damage sustained in the International Trophy had been rectified by Thomson and Taylor, the experimental engine was installed. Weguelin reports that it completed a few experimental laps at Brooklands but its subsequent fate remains a mystery. The facts so far as they can be established are that when the war began R8C was at Brooklands with Thomson and Taylor. It almost certainly remained there throughout the war, though without its Zoller blower, which had been taken to Pitt's Head Mews by Sid Maslyn for some repair work. Sid left for war service before finishing this work and almost immediately the mews was taken over by the fire brigade. Various parts of the Zoller got scattered about the garage but Maslyn was able to collect them altogether again at the end of the war (Weguelin: *History of E.R.A.*).

Towards the end of 1945 *Motor Sport* interviewed Howe and asked him about his future plans. He refused to commit himself but did say that he still had the E.R.A.. Shortly afterwards the car was sold to Reg Parnell with the standard E.R.A. engine and Zoller supercharger installed. Whether Howe was seriously contemplating driving competitively again, or simply taking his time to come to the conclusion that the E.R.A. would have to be sold, it obviously made sense to assemble R8C with a tried and tested engine and supercharger, not an experimental one. Motor racing faced all kinds of difficulties in the immediate post-war world and an experimental engine would have compounded the problems. It seems most likely that the Jameson engine went back to its designer's premises in Ewell, Surrey, but it has not been possible to discover the post-war fate of either Jameson or his company.

7

Motor Racing Man – Organising The Sport

- B.R.D.C. President, 1929-1964
- Francis Howe's achievement as B.R.D.C. President
- Francis Howe as a 'circuit entrepreneur'
- Proposed racing circuits: the Wash and the South Downs
- The End of Brooklands
- An attempt to revive racing at Donington, 1945-1947
- Road Racing in the Peak District?
- Five attempts – and five inevitable failures?
- Second best as circuit entrepreneur: the creation of airfield circuits
- Francis Howe and the running of race meetings
- The death of Francis Howe
- Obituary – *The Times* 27th July 1964

Chapter 7

Motor Racing Man – Organising The Sport

While everyone interested in motor racing knows that it needs organising it's not an aspect of the sport that has aroused much sustained interest or curiosity. It's the cars and drivers who have always been centre stage with the tracks or circuits attracting some interest but the organisational structure more or less taken for granted except when something goes wrong when it usually comes into the firing line. At the highest level of the sport – grand prix racing – the decisions of its controlling body sometimes arouse interest, particularly when it is considering the Formula One regulations.

Racing drivers are more aware of the importance of organisers because they determine the basic structure of the sport at all its levels – from world championship grand prix events to local club meetings. Prince Bira, one of Francis Howe's fellow-competitors during the voiturette years, said he thought that three – quarters of the success of a race-meeting was due to the organisers (Prince Bira: *Bits and Pieces*). For the most part organisers organise and drivers drive though it's quite common for the latter to move over to the organisational side of the sport when they cease to race.

Francis Howe was therefore unusual not only in *combining* driving and organisational work but also because his organisational roles were among the most important in key motor sport bodies such as the B.R.D.C., R.A.C. and F.I.A. He was elected B.R.D.C. president in 1929 and held that office until his death; he became chairman of the R.A.C.'s Competitions Committee in 1935 and immediately after the war one of the U.K.'s representatives on the F.I.A. At that stage his driving years had come to an end but he was still seen very frequently at the circuits acting as a steward. Francis was also something of a 'circuit entrepreneur' constantly on the look-out for new motor sport venues and in the immediate post-1945 period he resolutely campaigned for the army to leave Donington so that motor racing could resume.

In the discussion that follows each of these areas of activity will be discussed beginning with his role in the B.R.D.C..

B.R.D.C. President, 1929-1964

Francis was not involved in the various discussions that led to the formation of the British Racing Drivers Club (B.R.D.C.) but he was one of the first to be elected a member once it was established.

The B.R.D.C. came about through two rather different ideas – one was about social activity, the other about the need for some kind of drivers' 'trade union'. Dr Dudley Benjafield had organised a number of dinners to bring his motor racing friends together. It was felt that these should be put on a slightly more formal basis in the form of a club so that their cost would not fall exclusively on Benjafield. More or less at the same time A.V. Ebblewhite, the well-known Brooklands time-keeper, suggested that racing drivers needed an organisation to pursue certain shared interests. Benjafield himself recalled that shortly before the B.R.D.C. came into existence Colonel

Lindsay Lloyd, who was Clerk of the Course at Brooklands, had attended one of his dinners and that this was the first occasion that a group of drivers had met an official in that way. After some discussions these two ideas – of a social club and a representative association – were brought together in the British Racing Drivers' Club which was formally established in April 1928 (S.C.H. Davis in *B.R.D.C. Silver Jubilee Book*, 1952; Dudley Benjafield: *The British Racing Driver's Club, 1927-1952*, B.R.D.C. Archive).

The following month Francis Howe, still then Viscount Curzon, was elected a member having been proposed by A.G. Miller and seconded by Kenelm Lee Guinness. He made rapid progress within the new Club being chosen for committee membership in June and to preside as chairman at the first annual dinner in November. Finally, less than a year after being elected a member, he became President at the A.G.M. in January 1929. This was a contested election – Ebblewhite and Guinness were also presidential candidates. Once in office he faced no further electoral challenge, successive AGMs recording his re-election 'with acclamation'.

Although the B.R.D.C.'s social function was an important element in its activity it recognised almost immediately that its initial idea of combining dinner and committee meetings wasn't practicable. Either the business wouldn't be transacted or the dinner would be spoilt – probably both! Its business and social activity was accordingly divided. For the latter it had an annual dinner – a large-scale, set-piece occasion together with special lunches and dinners to honour particular achievements such as new land speed records. Its 'business' was conducted through monthly meetings of its main committee with various sub-committees for more detailed work assisted by a small paid staff for detailed planning and administration.

Even though it was operating on a fairly modest scale it soon became apparent that its finances would not be viable if it relied solely on membership subscriptions. Accordingly it decided to organise a long-distance event at Brooklands, the 500 Mile Race,

1928 – Ambassadors Club, London – Howe makes the inaugural presentation of the B.R.D.C. Championship Plaque to Kaye Don as "premier British motorist" on 24th November, 1928. During 1928 Don's successes included victory in the R.A.C. Tourist Trophy at Ards and setting a Brooklands Outer Circuit flying start lap record at 131.76 mph. At this point Howe was still known as Viscount Curzon, and, despite having only started racing that year this presentation shows he was already seen as an influential personality in the world of British motor racing. Photograph by Planet News, courtesy of Getty Images

which was run for the first time in October 1929 and this principle was extended further in 1932 with the British Empire Trophy initially at Brooklands and then, from 1936, at Donington.

Howe was a very active President. In the 1930s only a handful of those who served on the B.R.D.C.'s main committee were as regular in their attendance as he was; in some years he was present at every meeting held. This pattern resumed once the Club revived in 1945-6, only falling away a little in the mid and late 1950s. And it was not just the main committee where he was busy, he was often appointed to sub-committees, such as those organising the 500 Miles race and the annual dinner-dance. These committees frequently generated ideas which individual members agreed to follow-up and here again Francis undertook a considerable amount of work. For example to ensure a good entry for the B.R.D.C.'s own races it wanted to offer substantial prize money and awards. That meant approaching individuals or organisations who would be willing to give money or trophies and Howe frequently volunteered to sound out those who might oblige. There were interesting one-off tasks as well where Howe was the key intermediary:

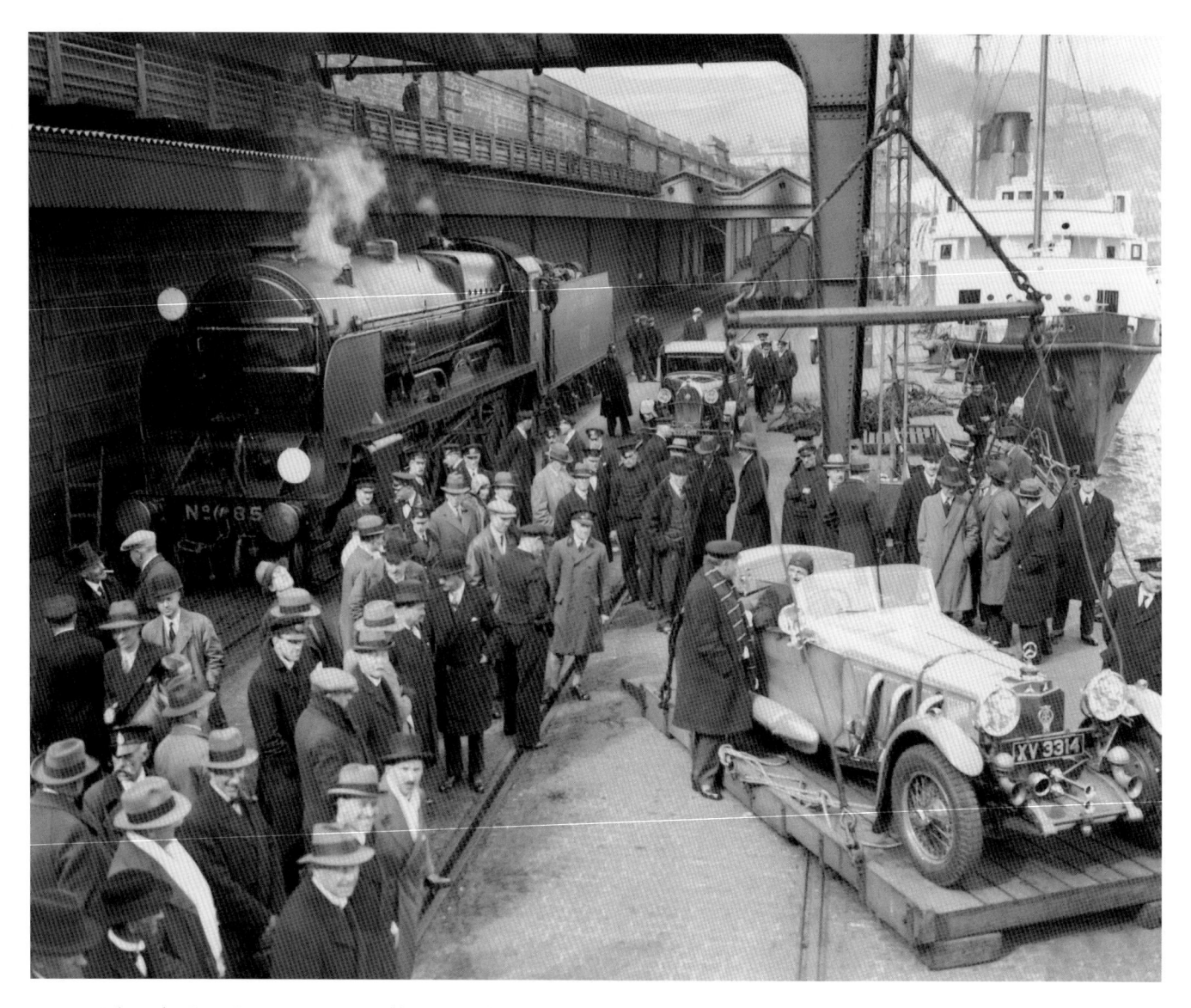

1931 – Admiralty Pier, Dover – Howe and his Mercedes-Benz SS 36/220 are about to be loaded onto the Southern Railway's cross-channel steamer *"Autocarrier"* on 30th March 1931 as guest of honour on the ship's maiden voyage from Dover to Calais. Clear evidence that, by 1931, Howe was seen as a significant personality in the motoring world. The *"Autocarrier"* was the first purpose-built car ferry in Britain, capable of carrying 26 cars and 307 passengers. *Photograph by WG Phillips, courtesy of Getty Images*

George V's son, Prince George subsequently created Duke of Kent, was a motor racing enthusiast and had attended the original Benjafield dinners. In 1932 the B.R.D.C. wanted to make him President-in-Chief and it was Howe who made the contacts and established his willingness to accept the post.

During the war the B.R.D.C., to all intents and purposes, closed down although a core of members continued to pay a subscription. In the immediate post-war period the absence of a viable British racing circuit was a major problem for everyone involved in motor sport. It affected the B.R.D.C. because its members had nowhere to race in their own country and because it created a significant problem for the Club's finances. Fortunately in 1947 it was able to revive the British Empire Trophy at a circuit in the Isle of Man and the profit from this event enabled the Club to rebuild its finances. The following year Silverstone was used for the first time when the R.A.C. organised the British Grand Prix at this former airfield. In 1949 the B.R.D.C. began to operate the circuit and that initiated an involvement that has continued to exercise a major influence on the Club ever since. Effectively the last decade and a half of Francis Howe's Presidency – through the 1950s and into the early 1960s – was dominated by the implications of running, and then owning, the Northamptonshire circuit.

Francis Howe's achievement as B.R.D.C. President

Francis Howe placed a high value on his B.R.D.C. role: at the first post-war AGM in March 1946 he said it was a "very great honour to be President... an Office which he put above all others he held" (B.R.D.C. Minutes, 13th March, 1946). As we have seen he undoubtedly devoted much time and effort to B.R.D.C. concerns and this commitment did not falter when he ceased to be a driver himself. In considering the impact of all this work there are really two basic questions – firstly what did the B.R.D.C. achieve in its first thirty years and secondly what part did Francis Howe play in those achievements?

As an organisation the B.R.D.C. quickly established itself as the leading association of active racing drivers. That meant its representations to race organisers had an obvious credibility and equally that the Royal Automobile Club (R.A.C.), as motor sport's governing body, should consult it on various matters. In the mid-1930s the R.A.C. resisted the B.R.D.C.'s claim that it should have a representative on the R.A.C.'s Competitions Committee but in the late 1940s it elected Desmond Scannell, the B.R.D.C.'s secretary, as a member. The Club used its influence with race organisers principally to discuss safety improvements and starting money.

It had some success with both these matters. In the pre-war period Brooklands was the focus of much of its activity on safety issues. But there were also some concerns about the Ards circuit which were pressed on the R.A.C. as the organiser of the T.T. races. Starting money, or the more euphemistic version which was assistance with expenses, was a matter raised repeatedly with the Brooklands authorities because the B.R.D.C. wanted to attract continental drivers to its events. Brooklands usually resisted this kind of subsidy so the B.R.D.C. emerged, at best, with half a loaf. In the immediate post-war years with finance tight for many British drivers starting money was an important element in deciding whether to enter European races and an area in which Desmond Scannell was particularly skilful (S.C.H. Davis: *op.cit.*)

The safety agenda changed as well after 1945 with the emphasis now on the former airfield circuits which came into widespread use. They provoked a variety of complaints, for example that their surfaces were unduly rough or inconsistent, that there were

1933 – Hastings – Both Howe and his son, Viscount Curzon, were participants in the R.A.C. Rally. Howe competed in 1932, driving a Humber Snipe whilst Viscount Curzon competed in 1933 and 1935. Here, in the 1933 event, Curzon, driving an Alvis Speed 20, starts the Stop and Restart test at Hastings, where the rally finished. *Photograph courtesy of Motoring Picture Library, Beaulieu*

too many loose stones, or that they were excessively slippery (B.R.D.C. minutes: 5th September and 5th November, 1951). Continental circuits didn't escape criticism either: during 1947 there were complaints about the conditions at the Swiss Grand Prix and at Chimay.

1934 – Brooklands – Howe unveils the commemorative plaque on the Brooklands clubhouse to the late Sir Henry 'Tim' Birkin, who had died a year earlier. Howe had co-driven his Alfa Romeo 8C 2300 with Birkin on three occasions, including their victory in the 1931 24 Heures du Mans.
Photograph by Autocar, *courtesy of LAT Archive*

1936 East London – Howe, dressed more casually than at European racing circuits, signs an autograph at the South African Grand Prix meeting at East London in January 1936.
Photograph courtesy of Guy Spollon Collection

1937 – Crystal Palace – For unexplained reasons Howe never competed at Crystal Palace. However he was Senior Steward at the Coronation Trophy meeting. Here in April 1937 he can be seen with the first four finishers in the Trophy race; (l-r) Robin Hanson (Maserati – third), Arthur Dobson (E.R.A. – second), Pat Fairfield (E.R.A. – first) and Percy Maclure (Riley – fourth). In the background can be seen Dr. Dudley Benjafield (to the left of Hanson), Ken Richardson (between Hanson and Dobson) and Peter Berthon (between Dobson and Howe). *Photograph courtesy of Guy Spollon Collection*

1938 – Crystal Palace – Howe congratulates Bira, the winner of the 1938 Coronation Trophy race, in April 1938. *Photograph by Sport & General, courtesy Adam Ferrington Collection*

1939 – London – Dick Seaman was killed at Spa in June 1939 driving his Mercedes-Benz. Here, at Seaman's funeral in London, Howe can be seen outside All Saints Church in Ennismore Gardens, with representatives of the Mercedes and Auto Union teams: (l-r) Rudolf Hasse (glasses), Hermann Lang, Alfred Neubauer (partially hidden), Manfred von Brauchitsch (head bowed), Karl Feuereissen and Rudolf Caracciola. *Photograph by* Autocar, *courtesy of LAT Archive*

More generally the B.R.D.C. promoted the cause of motor sport and record breaking. Its own races added to the number of events organised in the U.K. and in recruiting Prince George as its President-in-Chief it added to the publicity the sport received and probably to its legitimacy. Similar results flowed from the various celebrations it organised when Segrave, Campbell, Eyston and Cobb broke the land-speed record.

Did Francis Howe lead 'from the front', actively shaping the B.R.D.C.'s agenda or did he wait for a consensus, or at least a majority view, to emerge? The latter seems more plausible, even though we have only the written record as evidence which has obvious limitations. We know that Francis had clear views on a wide range of topics but the B.R.D.C.'s agenda seems to reflect what most of the committee wished to discuss and its decisions what the majority wanted to do. For the most part it seems that Francis agreed with both; there is the occasional indication of a distinctive 'Howe issue' as in December 1930 when he suggested it was desirable to raise a British team for the Mille Miglia but this failed to find support: "It was generally felt that the expenses incurred would prevent a team being got together" (B.R.D.C. Minutes, 1st December, 1930). As Chapter Four has recounted Francis persisted with the idea and successfully carried it through two years later but then the 'expenses incurred' came directly out of his pocket not the B.R.D.C.'s. The B.R.D.C. also became entangled in Francis' attempt to change British racing green to blue but as soon as he sensed there was significant opposition he backed away. The B.R.D.C.'s attitude towards crash hats was a more typical example of Francis and the Committee being on the same wavelength. Francis favoured crash helmets and thought his own life had been saved on a number of occasions by using them but he considered that compulsion could only be effective if it came from the F.I.A. and was universally enforced throughout motor sport. The B.R.D.C. 'recommended' their use to drivers in its 1931 500 miles race and six years later declared itself in favour 'in principle', but thought that effective implementation had to come from an International rule not a 'purely National ruling' (B.R.D.C. Minutes, 20th July, 1937).

Francis Howe as a 'circuit entrepreneur'

As we have seen, some time before Francis began his own racing career he was spectating at major continental events such as the Mille Miglia. He knew that the kind of motor racing in many European countries was very different from what was possible in the U.K. and he was keen to bridge the very obvious gap between the two. In the pre-war period he was associated with two schemes to develop new racing circuits, one around the Wash in eastern England and the other on the South Downs in Sussex. He gave enthusiastic support to the Donington circuit when motor racing began there in 1933 and raced his T51 Bugatti in the final event of its opening year. He also presided at the ceremony which initiated car racing at the Crystal Palace in May 1937. Immediately after the war he chaired meetings protesting at the sale of Brooklands and he campaigned for Donington to be restored for motor racing. In the mid-1950s he was involved in a scheme to have a road racing circuit in the Peak district.

Proposed racing circuits: the Wash and the South Downs

In May 1931 Francis chaired a public meeting at which ambitious plans were announced for what *The Times* called 'Speedways on the Wash': the proposal was to reclaim sixteen square miles of marshland which would be used to construct a racing track as well as a speedway area for motor boats and an airfield. The area would stretch from Clayhole to Gibraltar Point on the Lincolnshire coast and the fifteen mile race track, two hundred yards in width, would have facilities for 200,000 spectators. The management group responsible for the proposal was called the Automobile Racing Association and among motor sport figures involved, in addition to Francis, were Woolf Barnato, Lord March (subsequently, as the Duke of Richmond and Gordon, the founder of Goodwood) and Malcolm Campbell (*The Times*, 13th May, 1931; *Classic Cars*, June 2001)

Francis boldly proclaimed the virtues of the projected development: 'it would have no equal and no serious competitor in the world'; and in very similar terms he claimed that a version of the track intended specifically for the T.T. would also 'be one of the foremost tracks in the world'. He made his familiar case about the importance of adequate test facilities for car makers and the way in which motor sport influenced the design of ordinary cars, 'every type of car in the country has been developed as the result of racing'(*The Times, ibid.*)

Despite the optimism of the project's general manager who said the scheme 'would be offered to the country at no cost' and that there would be 'no need for a public issue' nothing more was heard of it. A serious economic and political crisis erupted in Britain only three months later which led to a National government and economic retrenchment which scarcely provided a propitious climate for a project of this kind.

The South Downs proposal did make rather more progress than the Wash project but ultimately, in the same way, didn't lead anywhere. In fact it was really a case of two-bites at the cherry as the proposal surfaced in 1927 and again in 1933-4. Any proposal to build a racing circuit on the South Downs was always likely to face problems. There were two main ones in 1933/4, a lack of agreement among the effected local authorities and resistance among major conservation and preservation groups. In purely numerical terms most of the local authorities were opposed to a circuit but one of the biggest, Brighton Corporation was a prominent supporter. It owned a considerable amount of land within the area that had been designated for the circuit but it needed planning approval from a neighbouring authority which was not forthcoming.

One of the major county councils involved – East Sussex – was not only opposed but sufficiently alarmed to mount a Private parliamentary Bill to ward off the proposal. When this Bill was introduced in the House of Lords major spokesmen for preservation and conservation such as Lord Zetland (Chairman of the National Trust), Lord Buxton and Lord Ponsonby supported the Bill and made their opposition to a race track quite clear. Francis Howe made only a brief contribution to the debate but he also spoke outside the House in support of the proposal. He attempted to mollify the opposition by emphasising that only a small amount of land would be required (and that the track would be entirely different from the concrete 'bowl' of Brooklands) with a very small number of permanent buildings. He said that the Downs was scarcely virgin land citing places such as Peacehaven and Saltdean and he pointed to various other structures that had been put up for Brighton's race course and for a golf course. This latter argument cut no ice with those opposed to a circuit; one of the local conservation lobby groups said it had been founded precisely as a reaction to the creation of places such as Peacehaven and, with a rhetorical flourish, asked Francis: 'And, in any case, Sir, how long have two blacks made a white?' (House of Lords, *Debates*, May, 1934; *The Times*, 1st– 5th December, 1933).

The End of Brooklands

On August 9th, 1939 Brooklands held its final meeting before the Second World War and, as it turned out, its last-ever meeting. Apart from the First World War it had been in continuous use as a racing circuit since 1907 and inevitably was the focus of strong feelings about its importance. However many, including Francis Howe, also acknowledged its limitations: 'The Brooklands track was rather out of date. It was constructed of old concrete which required renewal and that would have cost a great deal of money' (Lords, *Debates*, 15th July, 1946). Francis put more emphasis on all the testing at Brooklands and in those terms he said the track 'was a tremendous loss...because it was the custom for tyre firms, accessory firms and car firms to take this track for days on end and to send out cars to keep up sustained high speeds hour after hour' (*ibid.*).

Although those remarks were made when he was arguing the case for Donington as a test venue (which is discussed in the following section), they are consistent with what he said on other occasions. His reservations about Brooklands, particularly about its suitability as a post-war racing circuit, did not stop him chairing a protest meeting about its sale which took place on 2nd January, 1946. The meeting registered an almost unanimous condemnation of the sale but it did nothing to stop the train of events; indeed only five days later the key decision was made by the Brooklands shareholders to sell the controlling company to Vickers. One of those shareholders was Sir Malcolm Campbell who had been an important figure in introducing Francis to competition work in 1928 and whose land speed records in the early 1930s had been celebrated by the B.R.D.C.'s special lunches or dinners over which Francis had invariably presided. It would be interesting to know whether Francis attempted to persuade Campbell against the sale or whether their previous friendship was put under strain. Campbell did not survive for long in the post war period, dying at the end of 1948.

An attempt to revive racing at Donington, 1945-1947

By 1939 there were three British racing circuits – Brooklands, Crystal Palace and Donington. Of these Francis clearly favoured Donington: as we have seen although he backed the protest about the sale of Brooklands he readily acknowledged its limitations. Equally he said publicly that Crystal Palace compared to Donington was 'unimportant' (House of Lords *Debates* 15th July, 1946).

In May 1945 the Donington circuit was still intact but in need of extensive repair. The more serious problem was that it had been requisitioned for military use and the grounds were occupied by hundreds, or on some estimates thousands, of army Lorries. In November 1945 Howe headed a deputation which went to the War Ministry seeking to persuade it to remove the lorries and allow the resumption of motor sport. There was some interest from the Ministry especially in arguments about the need for tracks which could carry out stringent testing of components. Accordingly the Ministry suggested a 'dual-user' arrangement might be possible which would allow the army to continue using the site but also rehabilitate the track so that it could be used for testing work. Francis Howe was invited to submit such a scheme which he duly did in January 1946. The War Ministry – both politicians and civil servants – had doubts about Howe's scheme but that issue was overtaken by the involvement of another government department, the Board of Trade.

Francis and his allies had approached the Board hoping that it might be an additional ally in the case for Donington as a British test track. Unfortunately the opposite turned out to be the case. The Board of Trade's custom on motor industry matters was to consult with the Society of Motor Manufacturers and Traders (S.M.M.T.). It soon emerged that there was no agreement among the big car manufacturers about the idea of Donington as a test track, some like Standard were in favour, and others such as Austin were against it. Further, more specialised, investigation by the Motor Industry Research Association (M.I.R.A.) produced the same result.

Once it was clear that there were divided counsels in the motor industry the revival of Donington was effectively dead. The military authorities did not want to release it and the only real hope of forcing them to do so lay in the idea that it could become the home of M.I.R.A. and its test track. Even if that had gone ahead it is far from obvious that it could have accommodated motor sport. When Francis raised the whole issue in a Lords debate in July 1946 some of the ambiguities of the campaign were exposed. Lord Brabazon was refreshingly frank in his approach when he described the proposal that Donington should become a testing ground as 'cowardly' language. He argued that Brooklands and Donington had been created as racing circuits and that was what they should remain. It wasn't for those who wanted to use them in that way to justify themselves; on the contrary it was for the government that had taken them over to explain why it wouldn't return them.

Apart from Francis, Lord Brabazon, and the government's spokesman, there were only two other speakers both of whom stressed the testing rather than the racing role of Donington. Francis didn't wholly give up on the Donington cause: in November 1947 he asked the War minister whether a date could be given for de-requisition. No hope was held out by the minister who stressed that it was 'the Army's best and main vehicle reserve depot in the United Kingdom' (Lords *Debates*, 26th November, 1947).

It was another nine years before the Army finally left and not until the 1970s that Tom Wheatcroft was able to buy the estate and re-start racing. However, at least the circuit *was* eventually rehabilitated after some thirty years or more of 'lost' racing. When Francis was 'fighting the good fight' in 1946-7 the only likely alternative to exclusive use by the military would have been for some kind of testing facilities to run alongside continuing military occupation, the so-called dual-user scheme. It's very unlikely that such an outcome could also have incorporated a motor racing circuit and once a testing regime had been established it would have almost certainly ruled out the possibility of Donington's revival for motor sport.

Road Racing in the Peak District?

Although there was to be no revival of Donington until the late 1970s, in 1955 the county of Derbyshire was the site for another substantial proposal to create a road racing circuit. The idea of a circuit in the Derbyshire Dales had some similarities with the South Downs scheme, but equally there were important differences. A major difference compared to the South Downs was that the latter's track would have been specially constructed whereas in the Peak District it would have used existing roads.

The use of public roads for motor racing was forbidden under the 1930 Road Traffic Act and in February 1955, when the House of Lords was discussing what ultimately became the Transport Act of 1956, Lord Brabazon sought to alter this by proposing an amendment allowing for road closure. Effectively this made public what had been previously been proceeding privately over some months and unsurprisingly provoked a considerable amount of political lobbying – chiefly hostile to the idea.

The Derbyshire County Council proposal was to combine sections of the A515 the B5055 and some unclassified roads to form a circuit situated a few miles south of Buxton and just to the west of Bakewell. It would be about twelve miles long and, as Francis Howe admitted, to make it suitable for racing would "require the expenditure of large sums of money" (Lords, *Debates*, 22nd February, 1955). Francis had clearly been involved in the planning of this circuit, as had the R.A.C., together with other bodies such as the Automobile Association and the Royal Scottish Automobile Club. The proposal was familiar in Whitehall too: "the Minister and his Department know all about it, and his officials have seen it...The site has been inspected" (*ibid.*).

Although Francis did not actually name the site he gave a strong hint by saying "It is up in the Midlands", and the precise details were soon made known which allowed those opposed to it to mobilise. In the February debate the minister had made clear the government's opposition to Brabazon's amendment arguing that the right way to proceed was via a Private Bill (another parallel with the South Downs) which would allow for a full examination of the case for road closure and the development of a circuit. Brabazon agreed to withdraw his amendment having successfully extracted a commitment from the government that it would not automatically oppose any Private Bill if and when one was introduced.

Four months later Lord Lucas initiated a debate just in advance of Derbyshire County Council's decision on whether to promote a Private Bill. Opponents of the circuit occupied most of the debating time, Francis being the only speaker to support the idea. The opponents were trying to persuade the government to declare its opposition to any Private Bill sanctioning motor sport and if they had succeeded that would have more or less doomed any Bill in advance. The government rejected this option and re-iterated its view that a Private Bill, allowing for a full examination of the case, was the right way to settle the matter. However the critics got what they wanted because Derbyshire decided not to go ahead. Quite apart from the particular arguments over the site, the Le Mans disaster – involving over eighty deaths – had happened only a few weeks before. Francis Howe claimed that the disaster "required certain prerequisites to bring it about and the chances against those same circumstances all being present again are literally millions to one" – but the tragedy hardly provided a propitious climate in which to argue for a major motor sport development in Britain (Lords, *Debates*, 19th July, 1955).

Five attempts – and five inevitable failures?

These five attempts, either to initiate motor racing or to re-start it, were all failures. In retrospect none of them seems to have had much chance of success. The two 're-starts' – Brooklands and Donington – might have seemed a better bet than the new proposals but in both cases the odds against their revival were overwhelming. The three 'green-field' projects – the Wash, the South Downs and the Peak district – all faced substantial obstacles, in the case of the latter two touching sensitive conservation/preservation nerves. Any proposal for a new motor racing circuit is likely to involve changing the landscape and erecting new buildings and, once completed, considerable noise and large crowds none of which is easily compatible with 'areas of outstanding natural beauty'.

Apart from the public meeting called to protest at the sale of Brooklands, the other campaigns were all examples of 'insider' politics which means they were created by a handful of people and organisations whose aim was to persuade other influential and powerful individuals or groups. The broader public was not targeted and therefore the apparatus of mass campaigns such as petitions, advertising, rallies and demonstrations was excluded. The emphasis on insider strategy reflected the thinking of people such as Francis Howe and Lord Brabazon who recognized that motor sport was a minority interest among both elite and mass opinion. Thus any appeal to the general public was unlikely to evoke much response; so far as elite opinion was concerned it was necessary to use arguments that had some purchase. One example was Francis' contention that there was a close link between motor sport and the technical progress of the ordinary car. Politicians and civil servants might be indifferent or even hostile to motor sport but if it was helping to maintain the competitiveness of a key British industry then its claims could not be so easily dismissed.

When the Peak District proposal came forward in the mid-1950s motor sport was better established than it had been when the Wash scheme was floated nearly twenty-five years before. But that cut both ways: by 1955 a number of new circuits had been established and those arguing for the Peak District had to have convincing answers to two questions – why another circuit and why there? Francis, of course, was quite clear about his answers: the Derbyshire dales would provide a proper road racing circuit not merely different from Goodwood and Silverstone but *superior* to them. It was the chance to create a British circuit which could be the equal of the best road circuits in Europe which served as Francis' 'gold standard' throughout his life.

Second best as circuit entrepreneur: the creation of airfield circuits

The obvious problem about the 'gold standard' in the immediate post-war period was its complete inapplicability. Donington was the only British circuit that came anywhere near satisfying it and as we have seen Francis' revival efforts came to nothing. As the two other pre-war circuits, Brooklands and Crystal Palace, could not be used the British mainland was without a circuit venue of any kind. Francis knew that not only was it very frustrating for drivers and spectators (potentially greatly expanded with so many learning to drive during the war) but it was also damaging to the B.R.D.C.'s finances if it couldn't earn money through race organisation. As noted above, the Club was able to negotiate with the Isle of Man authorities to run the B.E.T. in August 1947 but this still left the U.K. mainland without a circuit.

To many the obvious answer was to utilise the airfields built during the war most of which were no longer needed. However the shift from available 'in principle' to available 'in practice' was a much more complicated matter. Gransden Lodge was one such airfield situated a few miles west of Cambridge and the Cambridge University Automobile Club (C.U.A.C.) used it for a semi-clandestine meeting in 1946. A much larger-scale meeting followed in July 1947 jointly organised by C.U.A.C. and the Vintage Sports Car Club (V.S.C.C.). The latter's *Bulletin* subsequently related the myriad complexities of securing the necessary permissions and agreements – involving various government departments, the Gransden land-owners, the R.A.C. and, of course, the two clubs organising the meeting.

The V.S.C.C. had also used a section of an airfield at Elstree for some speed trials in April 1946. A moving spirit in bringing these about was Rivers Fletcher and they were a step towards his goal of a full-blown circuit revival. The first stage in this campaign was the Cockfosters Rally in July 1945 which Rivers organised following a discussion with Francis Howe. Francis, while entirely enthusiastic about the idea of racing cars in action again, cautioned Rivers that a demonstration rather than an actual race was the best choice. Francis worked with Rivers on the detailed organisation of the Cockfosters event (held on roads laid down for a housing estate) and formally opened proceedings with his Bugatti 57S Atalante (Rivers Fletcher: *More Motor Racing*, Foulis (1991)).

Once Cockfosters had proved a success Rivers used it as a platform to push the case for mobilising airfields for fully competitive events and he was successful with the Elstree meeting, though this was a sprint meeting not a full circuit event. It's clear that during 1946/7 different organisations and individuals were at work on the issue of airfield use. Francis Howe told the B.R.D.C. Committee in August 1946 that the Air Ministry had received no less than fifteen applications from clubs for the use of airfields. The B.R.D.C. Secretary, Desmond Scannell, had been invited by the Air Ministry to inspect three sites although when he visited two of them he found they had already been ploughed up. The third was Castle Donington – doubtless an unintentional irony or maybe a way of drawing the fire from the campaign to retrieve the 'proper' Donington? (B.R.D.C. Minutes, August 1946) The idea was that if one or more of the sites were deemed suitable the R.A.C. would then allocate them among different clubs.

Nothing concrete emerged from this process and although the B.R.D.C. had pencilled in two dates for September 1946, one for an international and one for a national event, no suitable circuit emerged and neither proceeded (B.R.D.C. Minutes August and October 1946). Obviously the C.U.A.C./V.S.C.C. meeting at Gransden represented a little progress but it wasn't until April 1948 that Francis Howe reported inspecting a site in the Midlands described as 'very suitable for racing'. Silverstone had finally emerged officially – some enthusiasts had already identified it as a suitable circuit and put in some unofficial 'practice'.

Francis' inspection of Silverstone took place at a "slow dignified pace which was said to make him look like an ambulant cigar. Having discerned its hidden promise, he persuaded the R.A.C. to purchase a short lease from the Air Ministry to put on the first grand prix in Britain since the war" (Piers Brendon: *The Motoring Century*, Bloomsbury (1997)). The B.R.D.C. did not make extravagant claims about Silverstone: in his Annual Report in March 1949 Desmond Scannell said "whilst by no means ideal...(it) provides a valuable stop gap either until Donington becomes available or some other circuit is built to replace it" (B.R.D.C. Minutes, March 1949). However the 'stop gap' soon became a permanent part of the B.R.D.C.'s structure; Donington disappeared for nearly thirty years and for the immediate future the only 'new' circuits were adapted airfields.

Francis Howe was much in evidence when Silverstone's inaugural meeting – the R.A.C. British Grand Prix – was held in October 1948. He climbed on to a chair and brought down the starting flag. In 1950, when Silverstone was the venue for the Grand Prix d'Europe and the inaugural round of the newly – instituted World Drivers' Championship he escorted the Royal Family and introduced them to the drivers. And, it was under his chairmanship that the B.R.D.C. assumed responsibility for the circuit and its surrounding land. But airfield circuits were always a second best: in 1946 he argued that "aerodromes are not really satisfactory for use from a racing point of view ; they are bound to be flat and very uninteresting...better than nothing at all, but that is about all that can be said..." and nine years later, with Silverstone now well-established, his tone was little different: "Silverstone, Aintree and other tracks of a similar character are, on the whole, rather flat, and in places extremely wide; and they introduce a lot of artificial conditions" (Lords, *Debates*, 15th July, 1946 and 19th July, 1955).

Francis Howe and the running of race meetings

Quite apart from holding senior positions in clubs such as the B.R.D.C. and the R.A.C. with their demands for regular committee work Francis often acted as a race steward, particularly in the post Second World War period when he had retired from driving. In addition he regularly acted as steward for the Commission Sportive Internationale de la F.I.A. (C.S.I.), the sporting arm of the world governing body of motor racing. No doubt like many former drivers he could enjoy the racing at

Top right – 1949 – Silverstone – Howe, sporting his CSI Steward's armband, talks to Sir Miles Thomas at the trackside at the R.A.C. British Grand Prix in May 1949. Sir Miles Thomas was by that time Chairman of B.O.A.C., having previously headed Morris Motors, under Lord Nuffield, from 1940 to 1949. *Photograph by Sporting and General, courtesy of Guy Spollon Collection*

Below – 1947 – St. Helier, Jersey – Howe, by now known affectionately as 'The Old Man', watches practice for the Jersey International Road Race In May 1947 from a privileged position. The race was the first major post-war race to be held on British territory, with Howe acting as R.A.C. Steward for the meeting. Nello Pagani in his Scuderia Milan Maserati 4CL is seen rounding Le Marquand's corner. *Photograph courtesy of Adam Ferrington Collection*

Motor Racing Man – Organising The Sport

Above – 1949 – Rest and Be Thankful, Ayrshire – Howe, complete with trade-mark cap, cigarette holder and carnation, applauds Raymond Mays as he receives the "Motor World" Challenge Cup for Fastest Time of the Day in his E.R.A. R4D at the Rest and Be Thankful hillclimb in July 1949. To the right, with his back to the camera can be seen Ken Hutchison who won the trophy for the best time by a Royal Scottish Automobile Club member. *Photograph by MR Kenneth, courtesy of Roger Clark.*

Right – 1950 – Silverstone – During practice for the R.A.C. British Grand Prix in May 1950 Howe chats to members of the all-conquering Alfa Romeo team (l-r) Gianbattista Guidotti (team manager), Juan Manuel Fangio, and Luigi Fagioli. Note the contrast in Howe's dress to the next photograph, (see over page) taken the following day. *Photograph courtesy of GP Library*

1950 – Silverstone – Francis Howe, as President of the British Racing Drivers Club and an R.A.C. Steward, escorts Queen Elizabeth, with Princess Elizabeth behind her, during the King and Queen's visit to the R.A.C. British Grand Prix on 14th May 1950. To date, this is the only occasion when a reigning British monarch has attended Britain's premier motor race. *Photograph by Planet News, courtesy of Getty Images*

Right – 1957 – Aintree – Mrs. Mirabel Topham, owner of Aintree racecourse, who had been instrumental in bringing motor racing to the track, congratulates Stirling Moss on his victory in the 1957 R.A.C. British Grand Prix. Howe, one of the race stewards, can be seen looking on. *Photograph by* Autocar, *courtesy of LAT Archive*

Below – 1958 – Silverstone – Howe, now bespectacled, looks on as John Eason-Gibson of the R.A.C. congratulates Walt Hansgen, winner of the sports car race at the 1958 R.A.C. British Grand Prix meeting. On the extreme right of the photograph is Max Aitken of the Daily Express newspaper. *Photograph courtesy of GP Library*

1959 – R.A.C. Club, London – Howe, on behalf of the Royal Automobile Club, presents the Seagrave Trophy for "outstanding achievement in transport by land, sea or air" to Donald Campbell, for his achievement in breaking the world water speed record on Coniston Water at 248 mph in November 1958. *Photograph courtesy of the Howe Family*

second hand, keeping an eye on the way the sport was developing and meeting up with many old friends. But if he was acting as a steward he had responsibilities which meant he was not free to wander about and mix as an ordinary spectator is able to. All in all, Francis's presence as a senior steward at race meetings throughout the post war years gave him an ideal involvement in the sport in the period after his retirement from racing.

The death of Francis Howe

Francis Howe died at his family home, Penn House in Buckinghamshire, on 26th July 1964, just under three months after his eightieth birthday, His obituary in the following day's *Times* covered approximately fifteen column inches and more than adequately summarised the achievements of this remarkable man.

Earl Howe

Obituary – *The Times* 27th July 1964

Earl Howe, P.C., C.B.E., a former Member of Parliament for South Battersea and Conservative whip, died at his home in Buckinghamshire yesterday at the age of 80. He will also be particularly remembered for his enthusiasm for motor racing, a sport which ideally suited his robust personality.

As a driver, Earl Howe brought skill, courage, and enthusiasm to the sport he loved: in later years as an elder statesman he showed calm wisdom that few men could equal when dealing with the many and diverse problems that continually occur in every branch of motor sport. He was a great man and a fine sportsman whose loss is irreplaceable. Perhaps he will best be remembered for his valuable contributions to the sport of motor racing as chairman of the R.A.C. Competitions Committee and with affection as chairman of the British Racing Drivers Club. This club, which originated in 1927, is unique. It came into being during a series of private dinner parties given by Dr. J.D. Benjafield, one of the original Bentley drivers, when notable British drivers met over his table to discuss their sport. On December 21, 1928 Earl Howe was asked to become chairman of the British Racing Drivers Club, an office he held until his death.

Earliest ambition

Francis Richard Henry Penn Curzon, P.C., C.B.E., fifth Earl Howe of Langar in the County of Nottingham, Viscount Curzon, Baron Curzon and Baron Howe, all in the peerage of the United Kingdom, was born May 1, 1884, the only son of the fourth Earl Howe. His earliest ambition centred in the Royal Navy, but lack of robust health, hardly credible to those who knew him in later life, sent him to Eton and Christ Church, Oxford. He joined the Sussex division of the R.N.V.R. (which for many years he was to command) in 1904; and in 1914, as Commander Viscount Curzon, was given the Howe battalion of the Royal Naval Division with which he fought at Antwerp. He left this force to serve in the Queen Elizabeth throughout the Dardanelles campaign and to the end of the war.

The peacetime Navy did not appeal to Viscount Curzon; in 1918 he won South Battersea as a Conservative and until his succession to the earldom in 1929, was a vigorous, hardworking and (till he became a Whip in 1924) hard hitting member of Parliament. In 1924 he was made C.B.E. and in 1929 a Privy Councillor. In 1927 he succeeded Lord Jessel as London Whip in the Conservative Office. He later became the chairman of the Central Council of the party for 1932 and 1933.

He became keenly interested in motoring while in France during the summer of 1898, and after the First World War owned many fast cars. As Viscount Curzon he had several times been fined for speeding and it was at the suggestion of a magistrate that he took up motor racing in 1928 at the age of 44, in a Type 43 supercharged Bugatti. Viscount Curzon's first motor race was the Essex Club's six hours sports car race at Brooklands in May, 1928.

In 1929 as Earl Howe, in the Double 12-hour race for sports cars at Brooklands, he again ran his Bugatti, which proved rather temperamental, and after working on the car for a long time himself, was forced to retire, Shortly afterwards he bought a supercharged 2.3 litre Grand Prix Bugatti, the first of several Grand Prix machines which were to gain him wins in Brooklands handicap races. He was especially fond of Bugatti. Indeed his fastest car was a 3.3 litre Grand Prix machine of this make that was always regarded as extremely tricky to drive, but on several occasions during 1936 he lapped at more than 135 mph and became one of the few holders of the coveted 130 mph Brooklands badge.

A lucky escape

After the Delage Grand Prix team gave up racing in 1927, Lord Howe bought two of the cars, later embarking on several seasons of Continental racing with some degree of success until he crashed badly at the Monza track in Italy during 1932; his single-seater Delage coming to rest against a tree, Lord Howe receiving few injuries and being lucky to escape with his life.

His worst crash occurred in 1937 when his E.R.A. struck a parapet at Vickers Bridge Corner, Brooklands, in the very first long distance race for Grand Prix cars over the then new Campbell semi-road circuit. The E.R.A. rolled at speed, flinging out Lord Howe, who suffered a broken wrist, a broken rib, and a smashed shoulder. In typical fashion, two months later he was back at the track, acting as an observer at the very corner where he had crashed.

Howe crowded many activities, adventures and friendships into his life. Much time was given to the painstaking tuition of novices in motor racing; many drivers of a later generation owe him gratitude for sound advice and practical demonstration, and he edited the *Lonsdale Library* volume on motor racing. Howe was also interested in the training of police drivers and in testing for driving licences. He often spoke wisely and informatively in the House of Lords debates on road safety, constituting himself the defender of the skilled motorist against the advocates of extreme restrictions.

He married first in 1907 Mary, daughter of Colonel the Hon. Montagu Curzon, and they had one son and one daughter. That marriage was dissolved in 1937 and in that year he married Joyce Mary McLean, daughter of C.M. Jack, of Johannesburg, by whom he had one daughter. The marriage was dissolved in 1943, the year before his marriage to Mrs. Sybil Boyter Johnson Shafto, daughter of Captain Francis Johnson. They had one daughter. The earldom now passes to his son, Viscount Curzon.

The Times – *27th July 1964*

Appendices

APPENDIX ONE – Francis Howe – Racing Appearances – 1928 to 1939
APPENDIX TWO – Lord Howe's Cars
APPENDIX THREE – Lord Howe's Armbands

Appendix One

Francis Howe – Racing Appearances – 1928 to 1939

Notes : – Entries in italics are cars entered by Lord Howe but driven by other drivers. Competition Numbers are known for the majority of Lord Howe's racing appearances. However where the number is not known this is indicated by a "?"

Date	Venue	Event	No.	Car	Co-Driver/(Driver)	Result	Remarks
1928							
May 12, 1928	Brooklands	Essex 6 Hour Race	16	Bugatti Type 43 43188 (YT 8241)		Retired – 16 Laps	Magneto
June 09, 1928	Brooklands	150 mile Fuel Consumption Race (Surbiton M.C.)	?	Bugatti Type 43 43188 (YT 8241)		2nd	
August 18, 1928	Ards	R.A.C. Tourist Trophy	50	Bugatti Type 43 43188 (YT 8241)	with Percy Thomas	Retired	Leaking Fuel Tank
1929							
May 10-11, 1929	Brooklands	J.C.C. Double Twelve	14	Bugatti Type 43 43188 (YT 8241)	with Leslie Callingham	Classified	Engine Problem – In Pits when Race Finished
May 18, 1929	Southport	100 Mile Race	6	Bugatti Type 43 43188 (YT 8241)		6th	
June 15-16, 1929	Le Mans	24 Heures du Mans	11	Bentley 4 1/2 Litre	with Bernard Rubin	Retired	Broken Magneto Drive – Entered by Bentley Motors
July 05, 1929	Brighton – Wilson Avenue	Speed Trials	?	Bugatti Type 43 43188 (YT 8241)		2nd in Sports over 1500cc s/c Class	47.4
August 10, 1929	Craigantlet	U.A.C. Hillclimb	?	Bugatti Type 43 43188 (YT 8241)		2nd	1.39.0
August 10, 1929	Craigantlet	U.A.C. Hillclimb	20	Mercedes SS 36/220 (XV 3314)		F.T.D.	1.38.8
August 10, 1929	*Craigantlet*	*U.A.C. Hillclimb*	*8*	*Alfa Romeo 6C 1750*	*Leslie Callingham*	*1st in Class*	
August 17, 1929	Ards	R.A.C. Tourist Trophy	52	Bugatti Type 43 43188 (YT 8241)		Unplaced	Flagged off after 24 Laps out of 30
August 17, 1929	*Ards*	*R.A.C. Tourist Trophy*	*43*	*Alfa Romeo 6C 1750*	*Leslie Callingham*	*18th*	
September 14, 1929	Shelsley Walsh	M.A.C. Hillclimb	1	Alfa Romeo 6C 1750		1st in 4 1/2 to 2 litre Sports Class	53.2, 54.0
September 14, 1929	Shelsley Walsh	M.A.C. Hillclimb	17	Bugatti Type 43 43188 (YT 8241)		1st in 2 to 3 litre Sports Class	53.8, 52.2
September 14, 1929	Shelsley Walsh	M.A.C. Hillclimb	50	Mercedes SS 38/250 (UW 302)		1st in Over 3 Litre Sports Class	48.0, 47.6
October 12, 1929	Brooklands	B.R.D.C. 500	17	Lea Francis	with Sir Ronald Gunter	9th (Won Vacuum Cup)	Entered by Sir Waldrond Sinclair
1930							
March 22, 1930	Brooklands	B.A.R.C. Opening Meeting – First Mountain Handicap	1	Bugatti Type 43 43188 (YT 8241)		1st	
May 9-10, 1930	Brooklands	J.C.C. Double Twelve	25	Bugatti Type 43 43188 (YT 8241)	with Malcolm Campbell	22nd Overall, 1st in 3 litre Class	
June 21-22, 1930	Le Mans	24 Heures du Mans	23	Alfa Romeo 6C 1750 0312917 (UV 5647)	with Leslie Callingham	5th Overall, 4th Index of Performance	
July 01, 1930	Brighton – Wilson Avenue	Speed Trials	2	Mercedes SS 36/220 (XV 3314)		1st in Class	
July 19, 1930	Phoenix Park	Irish Grand Prix	2	Mercedes SS 38/250 (UW 302)		4th Overall, 3rd in Eireann Cup	Entered by Capt. Malcolm Campbell
August 16, 1930	Craigantlet	U.A.C. Hillclimb	?	Mercedes SS 38/250 (UW 302)		1st	1.38.4

Appendix One

Date	Venue	Event	No.	Car	Co-Driver/ (Driver)	Result	Remarks
August 23, 1930	Ards	R.A.C. Tourist Trophy	41	Mercedes SS 38/250 (UW 302)		18th, 2nd in Class	Entered by Capt. Malcolm Campbell
September 06, 1930	Brooklands	Brighton & Hove M.C. High Speed Trial	?	Mercedes SS 38/250 (UW 302)		First Class Award – Class 4	
September 06, 1930	*Brooklands*	*Brighton & Hove M.C. High Speed Trial*	*?*	*Alfa Romeo 6C 1750 0312917 (UV 5647)*	*Leslie Callingham*	*1st in up to 2 litre Class*	
September 13, 1930	Shelsley Walsh	M.A.C. Hillclimb	1	Mercedes SS 38/250 (UW 302)		7th Overall, 1st in Racing & Sports over 4500cc Class	53.2, 53.8
September 13, 1930	Shelsley Walsh	M.A.C. Hillclimb	3	Bugatti Type 43 43188 (YT 8241)		1st in Sports Car Class	57.6, 55.6
September 20, 1930	Brooklands	B.A.R.C. September Meeting – Middlesex T.T. Handicap	1	Mercedes SS 38/250 (UW 302)		3rd	
September 20, 1930	Brooklands	B.A.R.C. September Meeting – September Mountain Speed Handicap	3	Mercedes SS 38/250 (UW 302)		Unplaced	
September 20, 1930	*Brooklands*	*B.A.R.C. September Meeting – September Mountain Speed Handicap*	*4*	*Bugatti Type 43 43188 (YT 8241)*	*Harold Parker*	*DNA*	
October 04, 1930	Brooklands	B.R.D.C. 500	30	Talbot 90	with Hon. Brian Lewis	4th	Entered by Fox & Nicholl

1931

Date	Venue	Event	No.	Car	Co-Driver/ (Driver)	Result	Remarks
April 19, 1931	Monte Carlo	Grand Prix de Monaco	18	Bugatti Type 51 51121		Retired	Oil Pipe
May 25, 1931	Brooklands	B.A.R.C. Whitsun Meeting – Somerset Senior Short Handicap	4	Delage 15S8 21643 No. 3		D.N.S.	
May 25, 1931	Brooklands	B.A.R.C. Whitsun Meeting – 1 Lap Sprint Handicap	3	Delage 15S8 21643 No. 3		D.N.S.	
May 25, 1931	Brooklands	B.A.R.C. Whitsun Meeting – Gold Star Handicap	4	Delage 15S8 21643 No. 3		1st	
May 25, 1931	Brooklands	B.A.R.C. Whitsun Meeting – Somerset Senior Long Handicap	4	Delage 15S8 21643 No. 3		1st, Class F Record	
May 25, 1931	Brooklands	B.A.R.C. Whitsun Meeting – Second Mountain Whitsun Speed Handicap	2	Bugatti Type 51 51121		D.N.S.	
June 06, 1931	Phoenix Park	Irish Grand Prix	1	Mercedes SS 38/250 (UW 302)		14th Overall, 5th in Eireann Cup	Entered by Capt. Malcolm Campbell
June 13-14, 1931	Le Mans	24 Heures du Mans	16	Alfa Romeo 8C 2300 2111005	with Sir Henry Birkin	1st (Won Index & Biennial Cups)	Entered by Alfa Romeo S.A.
June 21, 1931	Montlhéry	Grand Prix de l'A.C.F.	30	Bugatti Type 51 51121	with Hon. Brian Lewis	12th	Ignition Fault – 90 minutes lost in pits
July 11, 1931	Shelsley Walsh	M.A.C. Hillclimb	18	Delage 15S8 21643 No. 3		4th in Racing cars up to 1500cc Class	47.8, 49.2
July 11, 1931	Shelsley Walsh	M.A.C. Hillclimb	40	Alfa Romeo 6C 1750 0312917 (UV 5647)		1st in Sports Cars to 2 litre Class	52.0, 54.2
July 11, 1931	Shelsley Walsh	M.A.C. Hillclimb	70	Mercedes SS 38/250 (UW 302)		1st in Class	46.8, 50.8
July 19, 1931	Nurbürgring	Grosser Preis von Deutschland	42	Bugatti Type 51 51121		11th	
July 26, 1931	Dieppe	Grand Prix de Dieppe	4	Delage 15S8 21643 No. 3		3rd, 1st in 1500cc Class	
August 22, 1931	Ards	R.A.C. Tourist Trophy	10	Alfa Romeo 8C 2300 2111005		Retired	Crash
September 05, 1931	*Brooklands*	*Brighton & Hove M.C. High Speed Trial*	*?*	*Bugatti Type 43 43188 (YT 8241)*	*Kenneth Evans*	*Retired*	*Engine*
October 03, 1931	Brooklands	B.R.D.C. 500	40	Bugatti Type 51 51121	with Clifton Penn-Hughes	Retired	Piston
October 17, 1931	Brooklands	B.A.R.C. October Meeting – Mountain Championship	5	Delage 15S8 21643 No. 3		Unplaced (Last)	Clutch Trouble delayed start

1932

Date	Venue	Event	No.	Car	Co-Driver/ (Driver)	Result	Remarks
February 26, 1932	Eynsham	O.U.A.C. Speed Trials	?	Mercedes SS 38/250 (UW 302)		2nd F.T.D., 2nd in Super-Sports Class	

Date	Venue	Event	No.	Car	Co-Driver/(Driver)	Result	Remarks
March 1-5, 1932	Torquay	R.A.C. Rally	127	Humber Snipe (KV 419)		33rd	
April 17, 1932	Monte Carlo	Grand Prix de Monaco	4	Bugatti Type 51 51121		4th	
April 30, 1932	Brooklands	British Empire Trophy	31	Delage 15S8 21643 No. 3		1st Heat 3, 3rd Final	
May 16, 1932	Brooklands	B.A.R.C. Whitsun Meeting – Nottingham Lightning Mountain Handicap	1	Bugatti Type 51 51121		1st	
May 16, 1932	Brooklands	B.A.R.C. Whitsun Meeting – Gold Star Handicap	2	Bugatti Type 54 54205		Retired	
May 22, 1932	AVUS	Avusrennen	1	Delage 15S8 21643 No. 3		1st	
June 3-4, 1932	Brooklands	J.C.C. 1000 Miles	15	Alfa Romeo 8C 2300 2111005	with Sir Henry Birkin	Retired	Con Rod & Electrical
June 18-19, 1932	Le Mans	24 Heures du Mans	9	Alfa Romeo 8C 2300 2211065	with Sir Henry Birkin	Retired	Gasket – Entered by Alfa Romeo S.A.
June 25, 1932	Shelsley Walsh	M.A.C. Hillclimb	67	Bugatti Type 51 51121		F.T.D., 1st in Class	44.0, 51.6
June 25, 1932	Shelsley Walsh	M.A.C. Hillclimb	85	Mercedes SS 38/250 (UW 302)		1st in Class	47.0, 56.0
July 03, 1932	Reims	Grand Prix de l'A.C.F.	28	Bugatti Type 54 54205	with Hugh Hamilton	9th	Carburettor & Brake Trouble, then lost 2nd & 3rd Gears
July 9-10, 1932	Spa-Francorchamps	24 Heures de Francorchamps	30	Alfa Romeo 8C 2300 2111005		3rd	
July 17, 1932	Nurbürgring	Grosser Preis von Deutschland	36	Delage 15S8 21643 No. 3		4th in 1500cc Class	
July 24, 1932	Dieppe	Grand Prix de Dieppe	1	Delage 15S8 18488 No. 4		5th, 2nd in up to 2 Litre Class	
August 6-7, 1932	Klausen	Klausenrennen	91	Bugatti Type 51 51121		7th Overall, 3rd in up to 2 Litre Class	
August 14, 1932	Pescara	Coppa Acerbo	22	Delage 15S8 21643 No. 3		7th, 1st in 1500cc Class	
August 26, 1932	Ards	R.A.C. Tourist Trophy	2	Alfa Romeo 8C 2300 2211065		4th, 1st in Class	Entered by Alfa Romeo S.A.
September 11, 1932	Monza	Gran Premio d'Italia	10	Delage 15S8 21643 No. 3		6th Heat 1, Repechage Retired	Crash, Car written off
September 24, 1932	Brooklands	B.R.D.C. 500	37	Bugatti Type 51 51121	with Hugh Hamilton	Retired	Axle Punctured Fuel Tank

1933

Date	Venue	Event	No.	Car	Co-Driver/(Driver)	Result	Remarks
April 8-9, 1933	Brescia	Mille Miglia	42	M.G. K3 3001 (JB 1472)	with Hugh Hamilton	22nd, 2nd in Class & Team Prize	Entered by M.G. Car Co.
April 23, 1933	Monte Carlo	Grand Prix de Monaco	6	Bugatti Type 51 51121		Retired – Lap 48	Rear Axle
May 06, 1933	Brooklands	J.C.C. International Trophy	15	M.G. K3 3001 (JB 1472)		4th	Entered by M.G. Car Co.
May 21, 1933	AVUS	Avusrennen – Voiturette Race	7	Delage 15S8 18488 No. 4		3rd	
May 28, 1933	Nurbürgring	Eifelrennen	24	Delage 15S8 18488 No. 4		7th, 1st in 1500cc Class	
June 11, 1933	Montlhéry	Grand Prix de l'A.C.F.	2	Bugatti Type 51 51121		Retired – Lap 19	Hit in the Eye by Stone
June 17-18, 1933	Le Mans	24 Heures du Mans	9	Alfa Romeo 8C 2300 2311201		D.N.A.	Eye Injury
July 12, 1933	Douglas	Mannin Beg	10	M.G. K3 3001 (JB 1472)		D.N.A.	Eye Injury – Entered by M.G. Car Co.
July 15, 1933	Dieppe	Grand Prix de Dieppe	34	Delage 15S8 18488 No. 4		4th, 2nd in up to 2 Litre Class	

Appendix One

Date	Venue	Event	No.	Car	Co-Driver/ (Driver)	Result	Remarks
July 30, 1933	Livorno	Coppa Ciano Junior	19	M.G. K3 3001 (JB 1472)		D.N.S.	Overturned in Practice – Entered by M.G. Car Co.
August 06, 1933	Nice	Grand Prix de Nice	12	Bugatti Type 51 51121		Retired	Carburettor Control
August 13, 1933	Pescara	Coppa Acerbo	28	Bugatti Type 51 51121		5th	
September 02, 1933	Ards	R.A.C. Tourist Trophy	4	Alfa Romeo 8C 2300 2311201		5th, 2nd in 2 to 5 litre Class	
September 10, 1933	Monza	Gran Premio d'Italia	38	Bugatti Type 51 51121		12th	
September 10, 1933	Monza	Gran Premio Monza	58	Bugatti Type 51 51121		5th in Heat 3, Retired in Final	Crashed
September 23, 1933	Brighton	Brighton Speed Trials	61	Bugatti Type 51 51121		2nd F.T.D, 2nd in 2 Litre Class	
September 30, 1933	Shelsley Walsh	M.A.C. Hillclimb	52	Alfa Romeo 8C 2300 2311201		8th in Class	47.6, 47.8
September 30, 1933	Shelsley Walsh	M.A.C. Hillclimb	61	Bugatti Type 51 51121		3rd in Class	44.0, 43.6
October 07, 1933	Donington	Donington Park Trophy	9	Bugatti Type 51 51121		1st	
October 21, 1933	Brooklands	B.A.R.C. Autumn Meeting – Mountain Championship	8	Bugatti Type 51 51121	Piero Taruffi	2nd	Tazio Nuvolari practiced, but was called to Paris on business

1934

Date	Venue	Event	No.	Car	Co-Driver/ (Driver)	Result	Remarks
April 02, 1934	Monte Carlo	Grand Prix de Monaco	2	Maserati 8CM 3013		10th	
April 08, 1934	Brescia	Mille Miglia	16	M.G. K3 K3017 (JB 3182)	with Percy Thomas	Retired	Crashed – Injured Arm – Entered by M.G. Car Co.
April 28, 1934	Brooklands	J.C.C. International Trophy	2	Bugatti Type 51 51121		5th, Team Prize	
May 06, 1934	Mellaha	Gran Premio di Tripoli	26	Maserati 8CM 3013		D.N.A.	
May 21, 1934	Brooklands	B.A.R.C. Whitsun Meeting – Gold Star Handicap	5	Bugatti Type 51 51121		1st	
May 27, 1934	AVUS	Avusrennen – Voiturette Race	12	Delage 15S8 18488 No. 4		D.N.S.	Withdrew from race
May 27, 1934	AVUS	Avusrennen	48	Maserati 8CM 3013		4th	
June 03, 1934	Nurburgring	Eifelrennen	37	Delage 15S8 18488 No. 4		D.N.S.	Withdrew from race
June 09, 1934	Shelsley Walsh	M.A.C. Hillclimb	49	Bugatti Type 51 51121		3rd in Class	43.6, 44.0
June 09, 1934	Shelsley Walsh	M.A.C. Hillclimb	70	Mercedes SS 38/250 (UW 302)		1st in Class (Won Garvagh Cup)	46.6, 46.2
June 16-17, 1934	Le Mans	24 Heures du Mans	6	Alfa Romeo 8C 2300 2311201	with Tim Rose-Richards	Retired	Clutch
June 23, 1934	Brooklands	British Empire Trophy	50	Maserati 8CM 3013		Retired	Spun out at Railway Snake damaging Front Axle & Wheels
July 08, 1934	Reims	Grand Prix de la Marne	20	Bugatti Type 51 51121		5th	
July 15, 1934	Vichy	Grand Prix de Vichy	18	Bugatti Type 51 51121		4th Heat 2, 7th Final	
July 22, 1934	Dieppe	Grand Prix de Dieppe	7	Maserati 8CM 3013		3rd in Heat 2, 3rd in Final	
August 12-13, 1934	Pescara	Targa Abruzzo	8	Alfa Romeo 8C 2300 2311201	with Tim Rose-Richards	4th Overall, 1st in Class & Group	
August 15, 1934	Pescara	Coppa Acerbo	56	Maserati 8CM 3013		Retired	Fuel Tank Burst
August 19, 1934	Nice	Grand Prix de Nice	18	Bugatti Type 51 51121		7th	

Date	Venue	Event	No.	Car	Co-Driver/(Driver)	Result	Remarks
August 26, 1934	Bremgarten	Preis von Bern	62	Delage 15S8 18488 No. 4		5th	
August 26, 1934	Bremgarten	Grosser Preis der Schweiz	16	Maserati 8CM 3013		9th	
September 01, 1934	Ards	R.A.C. Tourist Trophy	11	Talbot 105 (GO 54)		13th, 2nd in Class	Entered by Fox & Nicholl
September 09, 1934	Monza	Gran Premio d'Italia	16	Bugatti Type 51 51121		9th	
September 22, 1934	Brooklands	B.R.D.C. 500	41	Barnato Hassan Bentley	with Dudley Froy	Retired	Entered by Capt. Woolf Barnato
October 06, 1934	Donington	Donington Park Trophy	21	Bugatti Type 51 51121		3rd	
October 06, 1934	Donington	Nuffield Trophy	1	Delage 15S8 18488 No. 4		4th	
October 13, 1934	Brooklands	B.A.R.C. Autumn Meeting – Mountain Championship	2	Bugatti Type 51 51121		3rd	

1935

Date	Venue	Event	No.	Car	Co-Driver/(Driver)	Result	Remarks
April 22, 1935	Monte Carlo	Grand Prix de Monaco	8	Bugatti Type 51 51121		Retired – 34 Laps	Crashed – Brake Failure
May 06, 1935	Brooklands	J.C.C. International Trophy	1	Bugatti Type 59 59124	Hon. Brian Lewis	Retired	Valve Timing, Entered by Earl Howe & Noel Rees
May 12, 1935	Mellaha	Gran Premio di Tripoli	58	Maserati 8CM 3013		D.N.A.	
May 26, 1935	Péronne	Grand Prix de Picardie	22	Bugatti Type 59 59123		2nd	
May 31, 1935	Douglas	Mannin Moar	7	Bugatti Type 59 59123	Hon. Brian Lewis	1st	
June 15-16, 1935	Le Mans	24 Heures du Mans	10	Alfa Romeo 8C 2300 2311201	with Hon. Brian Lewis	Retired	Piston
July 07, 1935	Reims	Grand Prix de la Marne	36	Bugatti Type 59 59123		D.N.S.	Cracked Cylinder Head in Practice
July 14, 1935	Albi	Grand Prix d'Albi	4	Delage 15S8 18488 No. 4		3rd Overall – 5th Heat 1, 2nd Heat 2	
July 20, 1935	Dieppe	Grand Prix de Dieppe – Voiturette Race	20	Delage 15S8 18488 No. 4		Retired – Lap 10	Erratic Brakes
July 21, 1935	Dieppe	Grand Prix de Dieppe	2	Bugatti Type 59 59123		12th	Several Pit Stops
August 15, 1935	Pescara	Coppa Acerbo	44	Bugatti Type 59 59123		D.N.A.	
August 18, 1935	Nice	Grand Prix de Nice	10	Maserati 8CM 3013	Hon. Brian Lewis	Retired	Engine
August 25, 1935	Bremgarten	Preis von Bern	66	Delage 15S8 18488 No. 4		3rd	
August 25, 1935	Bremgarten	Grosser Preis der Schweiz	18	Bugatti Type 59 59123		10th	
August 25, 1935	Bremgarten	Grosser Preis der Schweiz	20	Maserati 8CM 3013	Hon. Brian Lewis	Retired – Lap 3	Mechanical
September 07, 1935	Ards	R.A.C. Tourist Trophy	5	Bugatti Type 57T 57222 (9219 NV2)		3rd, 2nd in Class	Entered by Earl Howe & Noel Rees
September 21, 1935	Brooklands	B.R.D.C. 500	35	Bugatti Type 59 59123	with Hon. Brian Lewis	3rd	57S Block probably used and GP engine without supercharger
October 05, 1935	Donington	Donington Grand Prix	1	Bugatti Type 59 59123		2nd	

1936

Date	Venue	Event	No.	Car	Co-Driver/(Driver)	Result	Remarks
January 01, 1936	East London	South African Grand Prix	23	Bugatti Type 59 59123		Retired	After a spin
April 04, 1936	Donington	British Empire Trophy	18	E.R.A. R6B	with Dudley Benjafield	8th	Entered by Dr. J.D. Benjafield
April 11, 1936	Monte Carlo	Coupe de Prince Rainier	56	E.R.A. R8B		5th	

Appendix One

Date	Venue	Event	No.	Car	Co-Driver/(Driver)	Result	Remarks
May 02, 1936	Brooklands	J.C.C. International Trophy	12	E.R.A. R8B		Retired	Oil Pipe
May 28, 1936	Douglas	R.A.C. Light Car Race	16	E.R.A. R8B		Retired – Lap 23	Split Fuel Tank
June 01, 1936	Brooklands	B.A.R.C. Whitsun Meeting – First Whitsun Long Handicap	2	Bugatti Type 59 59123		3rd	Broke Class C Lap Record
June 01, 1936	Brooklands	B.A.R.C. Whitsun Meeting – "The Star" Gold Trophy	1	Bugatti Type 59 59123		Unplaced	Threw Tyre Tread
June 01, 1936	Brooklands	B.A.R.C. Whitsun Meeting – Second Whitsun Short Handicap	1	Bugatti Type 59 59123		D.N.S.	
June 14, 1936	Nürburgring	Eifelrennen	72	E.R.A. R8B		8th	Plug Trouble
June 21, 1936	Péronne	Grand Prix de Picardie	44	E.R.A. R8B		2nd Heat 2, 3rd Final	
June 28, 1936	Montlhéry	Grand Prix de l'A.C.F.	30	Marendaz	with Tommy Wisdom	25th	Entered by Capt. D.M.K. Marendaz
July 04, 1936	Donington	Nuffield Trophy	27	E.R.A. R8B		6th	
July 12, 1936	Albi	Grand Prix d'Albi	6	E.R.A. R8B		Retired Heat 1, D.N.S. Heat 2	Gearbox
August 23, 1936	Bremgarten	Preis von Bern	66	E.R.A. R8B		4th	
August 23, 1936	Bremgarten	Grosser Preis der Schweiz	24	Bugatti Type 59 59123		Retired – Lap 25	Brakes – Left Road
August 29, 1936	Donington	J.C.C. 200	18	E.R.A. R8B		2nd	
September 05, 1936	Ards	R.A.C. Tourist Trophy	3	Lagonda LG45		5th	Entered by Fox & Nicholl
September 19, 1936	Brooklands	B.R.D.C. 500	21	Lagonda LG45 (EPE 97)	with Hon. Brian Lewis	3rd	
October 12, 1936	Roosevelt Raceway	Vanderbilt Cup	45	E.R.A. R8B		13th	

1937

Date	Venue	Event	No.	Car	Co-Driver/(Driver)	Result	Remarks
January 01, 1937	East London	South African Grand Prix	23	Bugatti Type 59 59123		6th	Handicap Race
January 16, 1937	Cape Town	Grosvenor Grand Prix	13	E.R.A. R8B		3rd	Handicap Race – Withdrew Bugatti Type 59 in favour of E.R.A. R8B
January 30, 1937	Lord Howe Circuit	Rand Grand Prix	14	E.R.A. R8B		2nd	Handicap Race
April 10, 1937	Donington	British Empire Trophy	17	E.R.A. R8B		D.N.A.	Car not prepared
May 01, 1937	Brooklands	Campbell Trophy	8	E.R.A. R8B		Retired	Accident – Serious Injuries
June 03, 1936	Douglas	R.A.C. Light Car Race	8	E.R.A. R8B		D.N.A.	Racing Injuries
August 28, 1937	Donington	J.C.C. 200	10	E.R.A. R8B		Retired	Brake Failure
October 02, 1937	Donington	Donington Grand Prix	9	E.R.A. R8B		7th	
December 16, 1937	Lord Howe Circuit	Rand Grand Prix	16	E.R.A. R8B		9th	Handicap Race
December 16, 1937	*Lord Howe Circuit*	*Rand Grand Prix*	*19*	*Maserati 6CM 1551*	*Bill Everitt*	*?*	*Handicap Race – Car bought by Howe for local driver Buller Meyer*

1938

Date	Venue	Event	No.	Car	Co-Driver/(Driver)	Result	Remarks
January 01, 1938	East London	South African Grand Prix	19	E.R.A. R8B		9th	
January 01, 1938	*East London*	*South African Grand Prix*	*20*	*Maserati 6CM 1551*	*Bill Everitt*	*5th*	
January 15, 1938	Cape Town	Grosvenor Grand Prix	16	E.R.A. R8B		1st	
January 15, 1938	*Cape Town*	*Grosvenor Grand Prix*	*15*	*Maserati 6CM 1551*	*Bill Everitt*	*4th*	

187

Date	Venue	Event	No.	Car	Co-Driver/(Driver)	Result	Remarks
April 09, 1938	Donington	British Empire Trophy	20	E.R.A. R8C		Retired	Valve Trouble
April 23, 1938	Carrigrohane	Cork Grand Prix	23	E.R.A. R8C		D.N.A.	
May 07, 1938	Brooklands	J.C.C. International Trophy	15	E.R.A. R8C		Retired	Gearbox
May 28, 1938	Shelsley Walsh	M.A.C. Hillclimb	37	E.R.A. R8C		4th F.T.D., 2nd in Class	41.25
June 12, 1938	Péronne	Grand Prix de Picardie	6	E.R.A. R8C		2nd Heat, Retired Final	Supercharger
July 02, 1938	Brighton	Brighton Speed Trials	38	E.R.A. R8C		2nd F.T.D. 2nd in up to 3 litre Class	22.94
July 02, 1938	Brighton	Brighton Speed Trials	38	E.R.A. R8C		1st in up to 1500cc Class	23.83
July 09, 1938	Donington	Nuffield Trophy	20	E.R.A. R8C		Retired	Engine
August 21, 1938	Bremgarten	Preis von Bern	16	E.R.A. R8C		2nd Heat, 4th Final	
August 27, 1938	Brooklands	J.C.C. 200	11	E.R.A. R8C		3rd	
September 17, 1938	Brooklands	B.R.D.C. Road Race	14	E.R.A. R8C		4th	
September 24, 1938	Brooklands	Dunlop Jubilee Meeting – Fourth Dunlop Road Handicap	1	E.R.A. R8C		Unplaced	
September 24, 1938	Brooklands	Dunlop Jubilee Meeting – Second Dunlop Jubilee Trophy	32	E.R.A. R8C		Unplaced	
October 10, 1938	Brooklands	Timed Runs	–	Lagonda V12 (FPK 550)		101.25 Miles covered in one hour	Average for 21 Laps 105.32 mph, Best Lap 108.27 mph

1939

Date	Venue	Event	No.	Car	Co-Driver/(Driver)	Result	Remarks
January 02, 1939	East London	South African Grand Prix	1	E.R.A. R8C		5th	
January 14, 1939	Cape Town	Grosvenor Grand Prix	6	E.R.A. R8C		Retired	Gearbox
May 06, 1939	Brooklands	J.C.C. International Trophy	10	E.R.A. R8C		Retired	Skidded and Hit Wall at Hill Bend – Howe's Final Competitive Event

Appendix Two

Lord Howe's Cars

The various chapters dealing with Francis Howe's racing years indicate that he drove many of the outstanding sports and racing cars produced during the inter-war period. Though some of these were works cars, the majority were bought by him and maintained by his mechanics. In three cases, the Type 51 Bugatti, the Delages and the E.R.A., they were used competitively over a number of racing seasons and became strongly associated with him.

The survival of cars from past eras of motoring matters, because it is the most powerful way in which those periods can be later evoked. Of course the written word and photographs are important but 'three-dimensional' evidence is likely to be the strongest demonstration of how things were in the past. Naturally one has to be aware of the 'woodman's axe' – an issue likely to be especially acute with racing cars where all the parts are stressed and therefore likely to need continued replacement if the car continues to race.

Bugattis

Francis Howe competed initially with Type 43 Bugattis but neither of the cars he used appears to have survived. T43s were expensive to maintain and by the mid-1930s they were not worth very much and prone to being broken up. The original T43 (c/no. 43188), which was registered YT 8241, was sold to Denis Evans, a member of the prominent motor racing family which also included Kenneth and Doreen Evans. Denis Evans competed with it at the 1932 Lewes Speed Trials where it was captured by the camera of W.J. Brunell. But there is no further record of the car beyond the early 1930s, or of the second T43 which carried the registration PH 9379.

Francis Howe's Type 51 Bugatti (c/no. 51121) was sold to Arthur Dobson in 1934, a member of another well-known motor racing family, the Dobson brothers. Dobson raced the car at Brooklands but switched allegiance to an E.R.A. the following year. The Bugatti then passed to Mervyn White who experienced two sensational accidents in successive years at the Cork races in Southern Ireland, most unfortunately the second proving fatal. Arthur Baron later acquired the car from White's executors and used it chiefly for sprints and hill climbs. He set FTD at the very first Prescott meeting when the course opened in May 1938.

In the post-war years the car was not active competitively and moved away from the limelight. In the early 1980s it was sold through an American dealer in Bugattis to a New Jersey-based owner.

The Type 54 which featured briefly in Howe's 1932 racing programme (c/no. 54205) was converted in 1936 into a sports car by Leslie Bachelier and road-registered DPJ 5. Bachelier chose a body style similar to that of the Type 55 roadster and in this form the car passed through a number of other U.K. owners – including John James who drove it at Prescott – during the early post-war period. After that the car was sold to America remaining there until 1987 when it was to Evert Louwman. It is now on display in the Louwman Museum in The Hague.

The Type 59 (59123) has had the 'ex-Howe' label attached to it much more than his other Bugattis. Francis Howe sold the car to a garage in Durban, South Africa, and in 1944 it was bought by H.B. Kelfkens. It had a broken crankshaft which Kelfkens replaced with a newly-made one from Laystalls in London. Kelfkens sold the car to fellow South African G.J.M. Hindle and after his death in 1962 the car returned to the U.K. where Doctor Tony Taylor, associated for many years with the Caesar Special, became the new owner. A celebrated 'exchange' took place after a few years with Sir Ralph Millais – Taylor taking Millais' 8C Monza Alfa Romeo in exchange for the Type 59. Neil Corner was the next U.K. owner of the T59 and when it left his ownership it passed to the Samsung Collection.

Alfa Romeos

Francis Howe's first Alfa Romeos were the 6C cars and at least one of these has survived, namely the 1750 SS, whose chassis number was 0312917. This car was originally registered UV 5647 and it was the car which Howe used to finish fifth in the 1930 Le Mans race. In 1965 Alan and Angels Cherrett bought the car from Philip Mann, a leading member of the V.S.C.C. Five years later, in September 1970,

Ronald Barker tested it and reported his experiences in the *Autocar*. Barker reported that the car's history in the immediate period after Howe's ownership was unknown, the log book only recording owners since 1939. By the time the Cherretts purchased it in 1965 The car was carrying a body of some crudity and Alan Cherrett undertook a major reconstruction aiming to restore the car as close as possible to its original appearance. Barker concluded his driving impressions by saying "It is responsive as an animal, responding best to a gentle touch – white knuckles never kept an Alfa on the road. Once you get the hang of it and the tension's off, you could be Campari, or Nuvolari, or Ramponi, or Lord Howe........." (*Autocar*, 10th September, 1970).

In 1931 Howe won the Le Mans race co-driving with Tim Birkin in one of the first 8 cylinder Alfas. The car which they shared carried chassis number 2111005 and it still survives, albeit after much international travel and modification. Simon Moore, the leading historian of the 2.3 Alfa cars, says that its log book does not record a post-Howe owner until 1945. Nonetheless Moore is fairly certain that it went from Howe to Malcolm Campbell who made an important change by fitting a preselector gearbox (Simon Moore: *The Legendary 2.3* (2000)). Shortly after the war it was sold along with a Tipo B to a New Zealand enthusiast and suffered the indignity with a subsequent Australasian owner of having a Ford back axle fitted and its chassis shortened. These 'modifications' remained in place for some years but during the 1980s and 1990s in the course of various changes of ownership it passed through the workshops of Alfa specialists such as Paul Grist, Neil Twyman and Jim Stokes. They all worked to restore the car by removing the pre-selector gearbox and the Ford back axle and by lengthening the chassis to restore it to its original *Lungo* specification. It then went to New Zealand again where one final change was made: the restoration work in the 1980s and 1990s had returned the car to its 1932 format which included the Howe colour scheme of blue and silver. The new New Zealand owner decided it would be more appropriate for the car to be red, as it had been when it first appeared at the 1931 Le Mans race. In this form the 8C was sold to a Japanese collector in mid-1995.

The second 8C Alfa which was bought by Lord Howe was chassis number 2311201. It was intended for the 1933 Le Mans race but due to his eye damage at Montlhéry Howe had had to withdraw his entry. He did use the car, however, for both the 1934 and 1935 Le Mans races and, as we noted in Chapter Three, although achieving a leading position in both races mechanical problems forced the car's retirement in both years. In 1935 the car was given a U.K. registration – CGP 901 – and it was sold to Commander Home Kidston, the younger brother of Glen Kidston. Home Kidston married Francis Howe's daughter, Georgiana, in October 1935, although this marriage unravelled during the Second World War.

Kidston used the car both on the road and for competition work, though most of his racing seems to have been in sprints and hill climbs rather than circuit events. He stored the car during the war and used it again afterwards but the car was finally sold in the 1950s. The next owner about whom Simon Moore is certain is another well-known figure, Major Richard Chichester of Wiscombe House – the drive to which has become one of the U.K.'s major hill climb venues. Chichester, in turn, sold the car to Sir Ralph Millais who won the V.S.C.C.'s Pomeroy Trophy with the car in 1965. Millais was persuaded to sell the car to Robin Ball in the early 1970s but, along with another Alfa he owned, both were dismantled and it was only when Bill Lake, a well-known collector, bought the car from Ball in the early 1980s that the car was put back together again. Subsequently the car was auctioned by Coys in 1989.

Delages

As indicated in Chapter Four the history of 1½ litre Delages is complicated. The principal difficulties arise because the cars have been dismantled, modified and then rebuilt with parts getting swapped around from one chassis to another. Furthermore, in 1937 two additional chassis were added to the original four cars which had been constructed ten years previously.

The late Alan Burnard did a sterling job unravelling these complexities. He says that Francis Howe's original Delage, purchased from Malcolm Campbell in 1931, was chassis no. 3. This was the car which was later written off in Howe's accident at Monza in 1932; although some components were salvaged, including the engine, the car never functioned again as a complete car. Before that accident Howe had purchased a second Delage, chassis no. 4. This was this car which he later sold to Dick Seaman at the end of 1935 and with which Seaman, following significant modifications by Giulio Ramponi, defeated the E.R.A.s and Maseratis in a number of major voiturette races in 1936 to make his name.

Seaman, in turn, sold the Delage to Prince Chula who hoped the car would continue to be the leading voiturette car when driven by Prince Bira. Although this hope was not fulfilled a considerable amount of money was spent on a modification project as Chula bought another of the Delage chassis, chassis no. 2 from Captain J.C. Davis, as well as commissioning two new chassis from the designer of the 1926 cars, Albert Lory. These new cars were distinguished by a system of independent front suspension (I.F.S.). During the Second World War Prince Chula sold the entire project to Reg Parnell – the ex-Davis and ex-Seaman cars plus the two new chassis, and a considerable stock of spare parts.

It is not very surprising that there was later some confusion as to exactly what was what when the various chassis and parts re-emerged into post-war racing. Although Howe's association was not wholly forgotten, it was the link to Dick Seaman that was most often recalled. The ex – Seaman car (chassis no. 4) did not enjoy particularly good fortune as it was seriously damaged by a garage fire in 1968 at Rob Walker's garage. The form in which the car has since been preserved incorporates the Ramponi modifications, so it differs significantly from the car which was raced by Francis Howe between 1932 and 1935.

E.R.A.

Like the second Delage, Howe's E.R.A. went through various changes since 1936 but, unlike the Delage, its last major reconstruction was designed to re-establish the car in the form in which Francis Howe had run it in 1938 and 1939. After the war it was sold to Reg Parnell who only kept it for a short while before it was bought by Cuth Harrison. Harrison made two major changes – substituting a D type chassis (bought from Prince Chula) for the C type and fitting a more rounded body. Harrison had a successful time – being placed in a number of major national races between 1948 and 1950, and when he retired from circuit work Brian Shawe-Taylor bought the car. After some excellent drives Shawe-Taylor's tenure was terminated by a serious accident at Goodwood at the end of the 1951 season. The damage to the chassis was sufficiently bad to cause its abandonment and a return to the C type unit which Cuth Harrison had put on one side.

By the time the car was re-built after Shawe-Taylor's accident E.R.A.s were no longer eligible for major races and were confined to smaller club events, though a few still ran competitively in the R.A.C. Hillclimb championship. Graham Whitehead took on R8C which externally still looked as it had during Cuth Harrison's ownership though no longer with the D type chassis. This different body style always made the car distinctive vis-à-vis other E.R.A.s and this style was retained by Derek Wilkinson and Bertie Brown, the next two owners. Bertie Brown was active for most of the 1960s but the car was stored during the following decade until it was eventually sold to Bruce Spollon.

Bruce decided on a complete re-build of the car, aiming to restore it to its 1938/9 specification. A new C type body shell was crafted and the car was sprayed in Lord Howe's colour scheme – dark blue bodywork with silver chassis rails and wheels, not forgetting the small union jacks on each side of the tail. There were

Above and following page – 1997 – Monte Carlo – The late Bruce Spollon seen in typical racing pose in the ex-Howe E.R.A. R8C at the 1997 Monaco Grand Prix Historique meeting. Photographs courtesy of Guy Spollon Collection

minor departures from the 1938 specification with rear axle radius rods and hydraulic shock absorbers – but the rods were subsequently removed and the hydraulic dampers replaced by Hartfords. One other change was made after the first season by increasing the engine size from 1½ to 2 litres.

Bruce first ran R8C in 1981 and until 1993 it was entered for both circuit events and hill climbs and sprints. Customarily the car was among the faster E.R.A.s on the circuits, if rarely the fastest; on the hills always among the fastest and very often setting FTD. Among many outstanding hill performances Bruce was the first person to climb Shelsley in an E.R.A. quicker than Ken Wharton – the latter had set a time in 1954 of 35.80 which Bruce lowered to 35.32 in 1985. There is a similar story at Prescott where Bruce's fastest time – 41.41 in 1993 – stands as one of the fastest E.R.A. ascents of the Gloucestershire hill.

While R8C never lost its identity, during the 50s, 60s and 70s as an ex-Howe car, since 1981 this has been powerfully re-asserted, partly because the car now *looks* like his car and partly because it has been one of the most prominent E.R.A.s in V.S.C.C. racing, especially on the hills.

Lagonda

Francis Howe drove a sports Lagonda in two long-distance races in 1936 – the T.T. and the Brooklands 500 Miles race. The T.T. car was one of three entered by Fox and Nichol – Howe's being one of the four-seaters originally prepared for the Le Mans race but not used due to the race's cancellation. It had, however been used at Spa in July for a twenty-four hours race but its life was brief as it was broken up after its fifth place in the T.T. It's not certain whether Fox and Nichol actually owned the cars it entered or whether they were lent by the works but there is no doubt of considerable works involvement both in the T.T. and in the 500 Miles race.

Howe's other Lagonda used for the 500 Miles was subsequently registered EPE 97 and unlike the four-seater it has enjoyed a lengthy life. It has not been a wholly undisturbed life however as at one stage it was subject to chassis shortening and lowering. Fortunately the shortening was done without cutting the original chassis and it was therefore possible to return the car to its original condition in the 1980s. Shortly after this restoration it was bought by Terry Cohn who owned until his premature death in the 1990s. It was sold to an American enthusiast after Cohn's death until coming up for auction in the summer of 2008.

Maserati

Maserati is not a marque strongly associated with Francis Howe as he only owned one example and the car was used for a single season – even then he was not exclusively 'faithful' to it as he continued to enter his T51 Bugatti for some Grand Prix races. Nonetheless he was the original owner of Maserati 8CM (c/no. 3013) a car that was, for a brief while, a leading grand prix contender and a number of which have survived to participate in other forms of motor racing.

As recounted in Chapter 4, Howe did not personally race his car after the end of the 1934 season but the car remained in his ownership until George Cholmondeley-Tapper bought it at the beginning of 1936. Tapper competed in a range of different events which included major U.K. races at Brooklands and Donington, the Shelsley Walsh hill climb as well as full continental grand prix races. Although he raced once in 1937 he had by that time decided to give up motor sport, and the car was sold to Arthur Hyde. Tapper had been seen as a promising driver, and he had been offered a test by Mercedes Benz, but he had decided against a career as a professional racing driver and he lacked the funds to continue as a private owner with up-to-date machinery.

The car re-appeared after the war with Kenneth McAlpine but he soon swapped the car for the ex-Bira 8CM (c/no. 3011) preferring the latter's narrower chassis. McAlpine had advertised the ex-Howe car as suitable for conversion to a sports car and that is exactly what happened to it. For some years, one converted, the naturalist writer Gavin Maxwell drove it on the road. The car was eventually acquired, in somewhat neglected condition, by Hon. Patrick Lindsay who passed it on to David Black and it was Black who restored it to single-seater status. David Heimann was its next owner and its attraction for him was that it facilitated the major rebuild he had commissioned of the ex – Straight and Bira 8CM, chassis number 3011. When that car was stripped

2012 – Goodwood – The ex-Howe Maserati 8CM 3013 being raced in anger in the hands of Frank Stippler at the Goodwood Revival in September 2012. *Photograph by Tim Scott – Fluid Images*

down its engine turned out to be numbered 3012, not 3011. At some stage McAlpine had made this change and he subsequently sold 3011's engine so that it could be used in the ex-Howe car after Gavin Maxwell had more or less destroyed the car's original engine during a road trip. David Heimann swapped the engines around, and both Maseratis were prepared for racing in 1986, 3013 appearing in the first Patrick Lindsay race at Silverstone in April, and 3011 in June driven by David Heimann himself. Tony Dron later drove 3013 and recorded some vivid impressions of the experience in *Thoroughbred and Classic Cars* (July 1986). The following year the car was used for a 'Track Test' by Willie Green (*Classic and Sports Car*, June 1987); by then Heimann had sold it to Dr. Thomas Bscher who drove a variety of Maseratis in historic racing. At that time the car was painted red, but by 2003, when the car was advertised for sale, it was in Earl Howe's colour scheme of dark blue bodywork and silver chassis.

1931 – London – Talbot Type 105 "GO 54" seen in the hands of its first private owner, Mr. George Wansbrough at its delivery in 1932
Photograph courtesy of Nick Pellett

Mercedes

Francis Howe was particularly attached to his ex-Caracciola 38/250 – as we have seen using it not only for competition work but also on the road. Before Francis acquired the 38/250 he had used a 36/250, the respective registrations being UW 302 and XV 3314.

Talbot

The specially-constructed single-seater based on the Talbot 90 sports car, which Howe shared with Hon. Brian Lewis made its first appearance in the 1930 500 Mile race in which it finished third overall and fourth on handicap. It raced again in 1931 at various club Brooklands meetings regularly picking up places. In 1932 it was converted into a four seater, then after a short while a two-seater sports car. The conversion was done by Roland Hebeler who worked at Fox and Nicholl and he used it as road-going transport rather than for competition. This was a very attractive car, clearly distinguished from other Talbot cars because it did not have the high-placed radiator characteristic of Talbot cars of this period. It was registered GX 68 and did some competition work after the Second World War. Its later owners have included John Rowley, a past president of the V.S.C.C. and Roy Beebee, another noted Midlands vintage exponent.

The other Talbot associated with Howe was a 1931 Fox and Nicholl team car, registered GO 54, a Type 105 powered by a 2.9 litre engine. During 1931 it was often used as a practice car but John Cobb drove it to third place in the 500 Mile race at Brooklands. It was also used for the Alpine Trial, gaining a Glacier Cup. The following year it was the sole Fox and Nicholl entry at Le Mans – and its third place, driven by Hon. Brian Lewis and Tim Rose-Richards, made it the highest placed British entry. It also appeared at Brooklands in some short races including the Ladies Race of 1932 in which Fay Taylour came second. Howe first experienced this car when he drove it on the road from Le Mans to Paris following its third place in the 1932 race; three years later he drove it into thirteenth place in the 1934 T.T. it having been loaned for the Ards race by George Wansbrough. The car was preserved through succeeding decades and a new phase occurred when it was acquired by Anthony Blight in 1965. Blight also bought the other 1931 Fox and Nicholl Talbots and they appeared in various V.S.C.C. events during his ownership. Blight's son-in-law, Stephen Curtis, who often drove the car, finally sold it in 2006.

Francis Howe's Road Cars

Francis Howe owned a large variety of cars for road travel in Britain and Europe. He did a lot of motoring within the London area and given the congestion and parking problems – one of his regular themes in Lords debates – smaller cars had a strong claim. Examples of these included various Austin Sevens and M.G.s and, after the 1939-45 war, Fiat 500s. He was running Austin Sevens almost from their inception and when he was asked about his experience he acknowledged that while a Mercedes or Bugatti would be quicker on the track or open road the same would not apply in the metropolis: "I can say with absolute truth that I can beat myself in practically any other make of car while driving my Austin in London" (*The Light Car and Cyclecar*, November 28th, 1930). At the time he made these comments his Austin had a Gordon England body and had just been fitted with a Whatmough head by A.F. Ashby which resulted in Howe's words in "an extraordinary degree of smoothness" (*ibid*).

The Austins were painted in Howe's personal colour scheme – described in the case of the Gordon England-bodied car as buff and marble blue with black wings and a similar combination was used for all his other road cars. Among the M.G.s he used were F and L type Magna Coupes, the latter with an unusual continental coupe body made by Barkers. Rivers Fletcher says of his L type that Howe "loved its bottom end performance, handy size and its strikingly smart appearance" (Rivers Fletcher: *Mostly Motor Racing*). Rivers also notes that Howe's mechanic, Sid Maslyn used to warn him that racing getaways from his Curzon Street home would damage the back axle and at least one occasion there was indeed an ominous clonk which betrayed a broken half shaft!

When Francis was in the Navy during the Second World War Francis was using a Fiat 500 Topolino, painted in his usual blue and black colour scheme. He had at least two of these cars and they continued to be part of his stable after the war. His youngest daughter, Lady Sarah Aspinall, remembers that they weren't always very reliable and it was necessary on occasion to help Francis' chauffeur push them to try and get them started when they failed.

So far as is known none of these Austin, M.G.s or Fiats have survived but the picture is rather different with some of Howe's larger cars. For longer journeys he chose cars with bigger engines which offered more performance in greater comfort. Examples of such cars were T57 Bugattis in the late 1930s and early post-war years, V12 Lagondas in 1938/9, a DB2/4 Aston Martin in the mid-1950s and a 300SL 'gullwing' Mercedes Benz in the later 1950s.

Howe's best known road cars are his Bugatti Type 57s, especially the first of these, a T57S with standard factory-built Atalante fixed head coupe coachwork. Although invoiced in November 1936 (probably ordered after the Olympia Motor Show) it was not completed until May 1937. It came to Howe via Col. Sorel, the London Bugatti agent, and was registered DYK 5 in July 1937. Howe had had it painted in his customary personal colour scheme of blue and black and he added one or two items such as mirrors and a luggage rack to the standard equipment. There are photographs of Howe sitting half in and half out of the car at a Donington meeting in 1938 – this posture being necessary so that he could use a rather splendid looking picnic basket for his lunch! Rivers Fletcher experienced some lively road trips with Howe in this car: "It was not the most practical tourer, as it was just like an oven in hot weather and so noisy that speech was difficult – but who would waste time talking when you could hear the music of that beautiful engine!" (*Old Motor*, April 1980).

Howe kept this car during the war years and it was the subject of another widely-reproduced photo when he used it to open the Cockfosters Rally in July 1945 – the first time competition cars were seen and heard again after their long silence during the war. Not long after this significant occasion Howe had a fairly serious accident and the Type 57S sustained some damage. After its repair it was sold by Continental Cars and changed its registration to EWS 73. Its next owner, John Tingay, who added a Marshall K200 blower, effectively turning it into a 57SC; after Tingay and an owner in Worcestershire it came to reside in the North East, first with Viscount Ridley – who changed its colour scheme to black and red – and then with a Tyneside doctor. There it was not seen for many years, only emerging publicly some time after the doctor's death in 2007. Its last tax disc expired in December 1960, after that it had literally been left to gather dust in a garage. The car was sold at auction in 2009.

Howe replaced the Type 57S with a Type 57C which he bought from the Marquess of Cholmondeley. Originally when the Marquess had taken delivery of this car it had been fitted with a standard Atalante coupe, but at some later stage a Gangloff Stelvio drop-head coupe body was substituted. Howe kept the car for a few years and although he told Rivers Fletcher that it was faster and better in every way than the 57S he never felt as enthusiastic about it (Rivers Fletcher: *Old Motor, ibid*). After one other British owner, in the early 1950s it crossed the

2010 – Ickford, Buckinghamshire – The ex-Francis Howe Bugatti Type 57S, the most famous of Howe's road cars, pictured before and after its restoration at the workshops of renowned Bugatti specialists, Ivan Dutton Ltd. *Photograph courtesy of Ivan Dutton Ltd.*

Atlantic where it has remained ever since.

The other road car Howe was running at the same time as the Bugatti was a Lagonda V12. He ordered this car in March 1938, taking delivery on 6th July, with a registration of GPK 780. He had chosen the short chassis model fitted with a sports saloon body and powered by a 4½ litre engine fitted with four S.U. carburettors. Just after delivery *The Motor* featured the car in a page of photographs under the by-line 'Fine Coachwork' highlighting the fact that the body was Lagonda's own design and build, not from a coachwork specialist. It also commented on the unusually narrow door pillars, the visors for reducing glare and Howe's personal colour scheme – blue and black with chromium wheels (*The Motor*, 12th July, 1938). A couple of months earlier when the magazine had road tested the model it said it could 'claim racing car performance' with 'all the necessary features of touring car comfort' (*The Motor*, May 17th, 1938).

Howe bought a second Lagonda V12 in August 1939 but the first car was also retained until March 1940. The original V12 (GPK 780) effectively disappeared for a period in the post-war period until the early 1980s when it was discovered, still in complete and original condition, by a professional engineer. He undertook a comprehensive restoration aiming to return the car to its 1939 condition and appearance. In 2007 Bonhams auctioned the car, its catalogue entry prominently advertising its Howe provenance 'Originally the property of Francis Curzon, the Fifth Earl Howe, C.B.E., P.C., V.D.'. The second V12, originally registered JPC 505, a registration Howe transferred to other road cars, went out to Malaya losing all its U.K. paperwork as it went through several hands. However the one element it did retain was its one-time connection with Lord Howe which was used to procure a new U.K. registration when it eventually returned to the U.K. in the 1980s. It was subsequently sold to an American owner where it has been subjected to various modifications to both its independent front suspension and its bodywork.

A similar prominence was given to Howe's Aston Martin DB2/4 when it was featured in the American series *Automobile Quarterly* (Vol. 38 (3), December 1998). Howe took delivery of this car in March 1954 using the registration JPC 505 which he had used on both the second V12 Lagonda and the Bugatti T 57C. At this stage Mulliners provided Aston Martin with its bodies and Howe's was painted in the familiar blue and black with a silver beading dividing the two colours. It also had polished Alfin brake drums and chrome-plated wire wheels. The DB2/4's predecessor, the DB2, had been fitted with a 2.6 litre engine and initially this continued with the 2/4 but a number of cars, including Howe's, were using the enlarged 3 litre unit (strictly 2922 cc) from the outset.

Howe retained the Aston until the end of his life although other cars such as the 300SL Mercedes were acquired. In the mid and late 1950s he was using it to travel to U.K. and continental race meetings: there are photos of him with the car in April 1954 at Oulton Park when he inaugurated extensions to the Cheshire circuit and, a month later, at Aintree's official opening. After four years use it was fitted with front disc brakes and was probably the first privately-owned Aston to be so equipped.

Following Howe's death the car was sold to a naval commander and after five years passed into other hands. Among its subsequent owners was David Holland, a well-known vintage enthusiast, who owned it at two different periods. In June 1998 the car was driven by the present Earl Howe up the approach road to Penn House, still with the slight banking that Francis House had instituted in the 1930s to practice his racing technique.

The Mercedes 300SL was a spectacular car both in performance and appearance.

The car first appeared in 1952 in fixed head coupe form where it was victorious in that year's Le Mans. It was Mercedes' first post-war sports car and utilised fuel injection for its six cylinder three litre engine. The bodywork incorporated large 'gull' doors which were hinged along the centre of the roof. Francis Howe acquired one in the 1950s and retained it until the end of his life. Lady Sarah Aspinall remembers accompanying her father in this car and that it was an 'exhilarating experience', with speeds well in excess of 100 mph being quite common. Other amusing vignettes of him 'in action' with the 300SL survive such as the occasion when he spoke to a meeting of the Eton College Automobile Club. Two of those who were present had similar memories of the occasion (quoted in Adam Cooper: *Piers Courage – Last of the Gentleman Racers*, 2003): the first said "The meeting ended at 9.55, and Lord Howe clambered into his 300SL – a laborious business for one of considerable circumference – and departed down the High Street at a terrifying rate of knots"; the second recalled "He was quite elderly then and the Mercedes had a great ledge you had to step over in order to get in the car. He said: 'It's great fun watching the girls get into this'. He was a great character".

Appendix Three
Lord Howe's Armbands

As is detailed in Chapter 7, Francis Howe played a major role as a steward at race meetings, particularly after his retirement from racing in 1939. Pictured above are the actual armbands which he wore at race meetings:- Top – CSI (Commission Sportive Internationale de la FIA), Centre – R.A.C. (Royal Automobile Club), Bottom – B.R.D.C. (British Racing Drivers Club). These armbands are visible in many of the photographs throughout the book. *Courtesy of Adam Ferrington Collection*

Index

Note:- For reasons of space and clarity only Chapters 4 to 7, which deal with Francis Howe's motor racing involvement, have been included in this index. In photograph captions drivers of preceding or following cars have not been indexed.

A

A.I.A.C.R. 57, 80, 85, 107
Aintree 44, 173, 177
Aitken, Hon. Peter 157
Aitken, Max 177
Albi 79, 123, 137
Alfa Romeo 40, 46, 48, 57, 58, 59, 61, 62, 63, 65, 66, 67, 74, 80, 82, 85, 89, 100, 116, 122, 127, 132, 134, 143, 158, 166, 175
Ards 37, 40, 44, 45, 53, 54, 65, 66, 67, 68, 69, 70, 71, 163, 165
Arnage 47, 60, 63
Ashby, Frank 157
Autocarrier 164
Automobile Association 171
Auto Union 99, 105, 107, 110, 117, 118, 129, 132, 142, 144, 147, 168
AVUS 90, 92, 93, 94, 97, 99, 103, 107, 110, 117, 119
Avusrennen 82, 93, 94, 103, 110

B

Ballystockart 53
Barnato Hassan Bentley 43
Barnato, Woolf 43, 169
"B. Bira" (Prince Birabongse Bhanutej Bhanubandh) 81, 110, 121, 123, 127, 132, 137, 139, 142, 143, 144, 145, 148, 152, 157, 158, 162, 167
Benjafield, Dr. Dudley 47, 133, 134, 162, 163, 164, 167, 179
Benoist, Robert 119, 121
Bentley 40, 43, 44, 47, 48, 52, 53, 57, 60, 68, 70, 71, 80, 81, 90, 91, 179
Berne 79, 108, 117, 123, 124, 131, 133, 138, 139, 149, 155
Berthon, Peter 133, 142, 150, 167
Birkin, Sir Henry ('Tim') 40, 44, 52, 53, 54, 55, 57, 58, 59, 60, 61, 62, 63, 69, 70, 75, 80, 90, 91, 100, 101, 166
Blight, Anthony 39, 44, 46, 50, 52, 65, 69, 77, 86, 117, 118
Boddy, Bill 76, 77, 114
Borzacchini, Baconin 85, 99, 114
Bouriat, Guy 85, 122
Brabazon, Lord 171, 172
Brackenbury, Charlie 109, 143, 145
Bradley, William Fletcher (W.F.) 38, 80, 91
Bradshaw's Brae 65, 68
Bremgarten 108, 123, 124, 139, 155
Briault, Douglas 140
Brighton Speed Trials 83, 103, 154
British Empire Trophy 92, 109, 111, 112, 114, 134, 150, 163, 164, 172
British Grand Prix 164, 173, 174, 175, 176, 177
British Racing Drivers Club 41, 43, 49, 90, 91, 124, 125, 126, 156, 157, 161, 162, 163, 164, 165, 166, 168, 169, 170, 172, 173, 174, 176, 179
Brivio, Antonio 114
Brooke, Leslie 158
Brooklands 37, 38, 39, 40, 41, 42, 43, 44, 46, 49, 50, 61, 62, 70, 71, 74, 75, 79, 81, 85, 88, 89, 90, 91, 92, 101, 102, 103, 107, 109, 111, 112, 114, 115, 117, 118, 124, 125, 126, 128, 131, 136, 137, 139, 142, 143, 144, 150, 151, 155, 156, 157, 158, 159, 161, 162, 163, 165, 166, 169, 170, 171, 172, 179, 180
Bugatti 37, 38, 39, 40, 41, 42, 44, 45, 46, 50, 51, 52, 57, 59, 65, 67, 68, 69, 73, 74, 79, 80, 81, 82, 84, 85, 86, 87, 88, 89, 90, 91, 94, 95, 97, 98, 99, 100, 101, 102, 103, 104, 105, 106, 107, 109, 110, 112, 114, 115, 116, 117, 119, 122, 123, 124, 125, 126, 127, 128, 132, 136, 142, 169, 173, 179
Bugatti, Ettore 38, 73, 117
Bugatti, Jean 59, 95, 97, 102
Burggaller, Ernst 103

C

Callingham, Leslie 40, 46, 48, 49
Cambridge University Automobile Club 173
Campari, Giuseppe 55, 64, 65, 85, 114
Campbell, Donald 178
Campbell, Sir Malcolm 39, 41, 42, 44, 46, 53, 74, 81, 169, 170
Campbell Trophy 143, 144
Canavesi, Carlo 71
Cape Town 142, 148, 149

199

Caracciola, Rudolf 46, 50, 52, 53, 54, 88, 90, 91, 98, 99, 114, 118, 123, 147, 168
Castagneto, Renzo 72
Chinetti, Luigi 63, 64
Chiron, Louis 59, 85, 89, 98, 99, 107, 121
Cholmondeley Tapper, T.P. 107, 123, 128, 140
Clutton, Cecil 50, 80
Cobb, John 69, 74, 91, 92, 111, 126, 168
Cockfosters Rally 173
Comber 53
Conway, Hugh 45, 65, 91
Cook, Humphrey 133, 135, 142, 143
Coppa Acerbo 90, 99, 101, 107, 133
Coppa Ciano 101
Cortese, Franco 157
Cotton, Major Sidney 142, 158
Coupe de Prince Rainier 134
Craigantlet 46, 50
Crystal Palace 44, 167, 169, 170, 172
Cushman, Leon 50
Czaykowski, Stanislas 89, 90, 103, 114

D

Dangerfield, Edmund 81, 83
Davis, Sammy (S.C.H.) 40, 45, 105, 117, 152, 163, 165
Desmond, Kevin 128
Dieppe 79, 81, 89, 99, 103, 104, 107, 112, 113, 117, 118, 119, 122, 123, 133
Divo, Albert 85, 91
Dixon, Freddie 68, 70, 116
D.K.W. 94, 142
Dobson, Arthur 116, 133, 138, 139, 143, 145, 146, 147, 157, 167
Donington 40, 44, 70, 79, 105, 106, 107, 114, 115, 116, 117, 126, 127, 129, 131, 133, 134, 137, 138, 139, 140, 144, 145, 146, 147, 148, 150, 152, 161, 162, 163, 169, 170, 171, 172, 173
Don, Kaye 163
Double Twelve 39, 40, 41, 42, 71, 81
Dreyfus, René 85, 110, 118, 121
Duesenberg 43
Dugdale, John 140
Dundonald 45, 54, 66, 67
Dunfee, Clive 46, 85

E

Eason-Gibson, John 177
East London 128, 166
Eccles, Lindsay 105, 109, 111, 117, 118, 121, 127
Eifelrennen 103, 133, 137
Eireann Cup 54, 55, 56, 57
Elstree 173
Embiricos, Nicky 139
E.R.A. 83, 117, 121, 127, 128, 131, 132, 133, 134, 135, 137, 138, 140, 141, 142, 143, 144, 145, 146, 147, 148, 149, 150, 151, 152, 153, 154, 155, 156, 157, 158, 159, 167, 175, 180
Esson-Scott, Aubrey 109, 114
Etancelin, Philippe 63, 89, 90, 107, 114, 118
Evans, Kenneth 117, 145, 157
Everitt, Bill 128, 149
Eyston, Capt. George 55, 71, 72, 73, 75, 92, 168

F

Fagioli, Luigi 85, 91, 101, 114, 118, 175
Fairfield, Pat 69, 70, 127, 128, 139, 140, 141, 142, 152, 167
Fane, A.F.P. 152, 153
Fangio, Juan Manuel 175
Farina, Giuseppe 118, 123, 127, 128, 132
Ferguson, Harry 44
Ferrari, Enzo 72
Feuereissen, Karl 168
Federation Internationale de l'Automobile (F.I.A.) 162, 169, 174
Finlayson, Jock 124
Follett, Charles 145
Fothringham, Thomas 114
Fox and Nicholl 47
Fox, Arthur 50, 64, 65, 70, 85
Froy, Dudley 43

G

Gallop, Clive 57
German Grand Prix 80, 85, 86, 87, 88, 90, 95, 97, 129
Glass, Zoltan 84, 87, 93, 95, 103
Grand Prix de Picardie 119, 122, 138, 139
Gransden Lodge 173
Grosvenor Grand Prix 148, 149, 158
Guidotti, Gianbattista 175
Guinness, Kenelm Lee 54, 163
Gunter, Sir Ronald 40, 41, 116

H

Hadley, Bert 152
Hall, Eddie 68, 70, 75
Hals, Frans 73
Hamilton, Hugh 73, 75, 91, 109, 110, 134
Hansgen, Walt 177
Hanson, Robin 145, 147, 157, 167
Hasse, Rudolf 168
Holgate, Stan 81
Houghton, Charles 146

Humber 165
Hunter, Hugh 154
Hutchison, Ken 175

I

International Trophy 70, 74, 75, 109, 114, 137, 150, 151, 157, 158, 159
Irish Grand Prix 37, 50, 52, 53, 54, 55, 57
Isle of Man 133, 135, 137, 164, 172
Italian Grand Prix 90, 91, 114
Ivanowsky, Boris 40, 59, 60, 85, 86

J

Jameson Aero Engines 159
Jameson, J.L. 159
Jamieson, Tom Murray 133, 159
Jersey International Road Race 174
Johannesburg 128, 142, 180

K

Kimber, Cecil 71
Klausen Pass 98
Klausenrennen 79, 97, 98
Kop Hill 52
Kroth, Ewald 103

L

Lagonda 43, 64, 65, 67, 69, 70, 71, 77
Lang, Hermann 168
Lea Francis 41, 45, 54
Lehoux, Marcel 90, 91, 104, 107, 137, 138
Le Mans 37, 46, 47, 48, 49, 57, 58, 59, 60, 61, 62, 63, 64, 65, 69, 85, 101, 152, 172

Lewis, Hon. Brian 43, 49, 50, 63, 64, 67, 68, 69, 70, 71, 74, 85, 86, 102, 107, 109, 118, 123, 124, 125, 126, 142
Lurani, Count Giovanni ('Johnny') 40, 71, 72, 73, 75, 76, 80, 99, 149

M

Maclure, Percy 126, 127, 145, 147, 157, 167
March, Freddie, Earl of Vickers 169
Marendaz, Capt. Donald 37, 76, 77, 132
Marinoni, Attilio 59
Martin, Charlie 116, 117, 118, 121, 127, 128, 152
Maserati 74, 75, 76, 80, 85, 86, 90, 91, 99, 100, 101, 102, 103, 107, 108, 109, 110, 112, 113, 114, 116, 117, 119, 123, 127, 128, 132, 135, 138, 140, 143, 144, 147, 148, 149, 150, 157, 158, 167, 174
Maslyn, Sidney 81, 83, 134, 159
Mathieson, T.A.S.O. (Taso) 105
Mays, Raymond 46, 52, 101, 102, 115, 117, 121, 123, 128, 133, 135, 138, 139, 142, 143, 145, 146, 148, 149, 150, 152, 154, 155, 156, 157, 175
Mazzacurati, Mario 128
McConnell, Hugh 66, 71, 72, 75
Mercedes Benz 51, 52, 57, 86, 105, 107, 110
M.G. 37, 43, 66, 71, 72, 73, 74, 75, 76, 101, 109, 114, 133
Mille Miglia 37, 71, 72, 73, 75, 76, 83, 84, 110, 117, 168, 169
Momberger, August 107, 110
Monaco Grand Prix 80, 90, 100, 108, 135
Monte Carlo Rally 73

Montlhéry 76, 77, 79, 85, 86, 88, 100, 101, 114
Monza 57, 79, 80, 81, 89, 90, 99, 102, 104, 108, 114, 115, 117, 134, 180
Morgan, John 145, 155
Morris, Sir William 71
Mortimer, Charles 154
Mosley, Oswald 76
Moss, Alfred and Aileen 77
Moss, Stirling 76, 177
Multi-Union 114
Mussolini, Benito 60

N

Neubauer, Alfred 168
Newtownards 45, 65, 66
Nice 79, 100, 101
Nickols, Ian 157
Nuffield Trophy 117, 123, 137, 138, 152
Nürburgring 79, 85, 86, 87, 88, 93, 95, 97, 103, 114, 137
Nuvolari, Tazio 66, 72, 91, 99, 101, 102, 107, 110, 118, 129
Nye, Doug 107

P

Pacey-Hassan 43
Panhard 92
Parnell, Reg 159
Pau 80
Penn House 71, 81, 82, 90, 97, 178
Penn Hughes, Clifton 75, 76, 108, 115
Percy Thomas, Percy 44, 45, 61, 75, 76, 81, 82, 89, 93, 126
Péronne 119, 122, 138, 139
Pescara 64, 79, 90, 99, 101, 117
Phoenix Park 52, 53, 55, 56, 57
Pitt's Head Mews 81, 159

Porsche 149

Prince Bertil of Sweden 111

Prince Chula Chakrabongse 81, 110, 121, 124, 132, 133, 141, 142

Purdy, Harold 50

R

Rabagliati, Duncan 85, 86, 101, 114

R.A.C. Rally 165

Ramponi, Guilio 117, 133, 140

Rand Grand Prix 142, 148

Rees, Noel 69, 118, 124

Reims 91, 110, 114, 118

Rest and Be Thankful 175

Richardson, Ken 145, 167

Riley 49, 74, 116, 126, 127, 147, 148, 157, 158, 167

Rivers Fletcher, A.F. 46, 50, 80, 83, 91, 103, 140, 141, 173

Roosevelt Raceway 141

Rosemeyer, Bernd 142, 147

Rose-Richards, T.E. ('Tim') 49, 63, 64, 67, 69, 108, 126

Rost, Maurice 59

Rovere, Gino 139

Royal Automobile Club 44, 45, 52, 53, 54, 65, 66, 67, 68, 69, 70, 135, 137, 162, 163, 164, 165, 171, 173, 174, 175, 176, 177, 178, 179

Rubin, Bernard 47, 75, 100

S

Scannell, Desmond 165, 173

Scott, W.B. ('Bummer') 81, 89

Scribbans, Dennis 133, 143, 144

Scuderia Ferrari 99, 106, 107, 110, 118, 123

Seaman, Dick 117, 121, 123, 124, 132, 133, 137, 139, 140, 141, 142, 168

Segrave, Sir Henry 54, 168

Sheldon, Paul 85, 86, 101, 114

Shelsley Walsh 37, 45, 46, 50, 51, 52, 62, 79, 89, 97, 98, 99, 101, 102, 103, 107, 114, 115, 116, 131, 150, 152, 153

Shuttleworth, Richard 116, 122, 127, 128

Siena, Eugenio 72

Silverstone 44, 164, 172, 173, 174, 175, 176, 177

Society of Motor Manufacturers and Traders 171

Sommer, Raymond 63, 65, 100, 118, 119, 123, 127, 128

Sorel, Col. W.L. 81

South African Grand Prix 128, 148, 157, 158, 166

Southport 37, 46

Stanford, J. 50, 80

Staniland, Chris 114, 116, 143

Stoffel, Henri 59, 60, 85, 86

Straight, Whitney 52, 66, 101, 103, 107, 110, 111, 114, 115, 116, 128

Stuber, Hans 98

Stuck, Hans 52, 93, 97, 102

Swiss Grand Prix 107, 123, 124, 155, 166

T

Talbot 46, 47, 49, 50, 59, 67, 69, 85, 86, 118, 124, 133

Targa Abruzzo 64, 65

Targa Florio 88

Taruffi, Piero 76, 101, 102, 148, 149

Taylor, Geoffrey 154

Thistlethwayte, Tommy ('Scrap') 46

Thomas, Sir Miles 174

Thomson and Taylor 107, 159

Tongue, Reggie 123, 133, 139, 145, 157, 158

Topham, Mrs. Mirabel 177

Tourist Trophy 37, 39, 40, 44, 45, 46, 50, 52, 53, 54, 65, 66, 67, 68, 69, 70, 86, 102, 106, 126, 132, 163, 165, 169

Trintignant, Louis 122

Tripoli 100

Trossi, Count Carlo 114, 139

Tubbs, D.B. ('Bunny') 50

V

Vanderbilt Cup 131, 141

Varzi, Achille 46, 57, 85, 98, 100, 101

Venables, David 83, 84, 94, 103, 123, 133, 159

Veyron, Pierre 103, 123

Vichy 114

Villiers, Amherst 102

Villoresi, Luigi 149, 150, 157

Vintage Sports Car Club 173

von Brauchitsch, Manfred 168

von der Becke, Bill 126

W

Wakefield, Johnnie 145, 150, 155, 157

Wheatcroft, F.B. ('Tom') 171

Whitehead, Peter 133, 140, 145, 157

Wilson Avenue, Brighton 50

Wilson, Norman 50, 157

Wimille, Jean-Pierre 119, 121, 128

Wisdom, Tommy 77

"W Williams" (Charles Grover-Williams) 45, 87, 90

Z

Zehender, Goffredo 59, 60, 85, 90, 107, 108, 118

Zoller 133, 134, 139, 142, 149, 150, 159

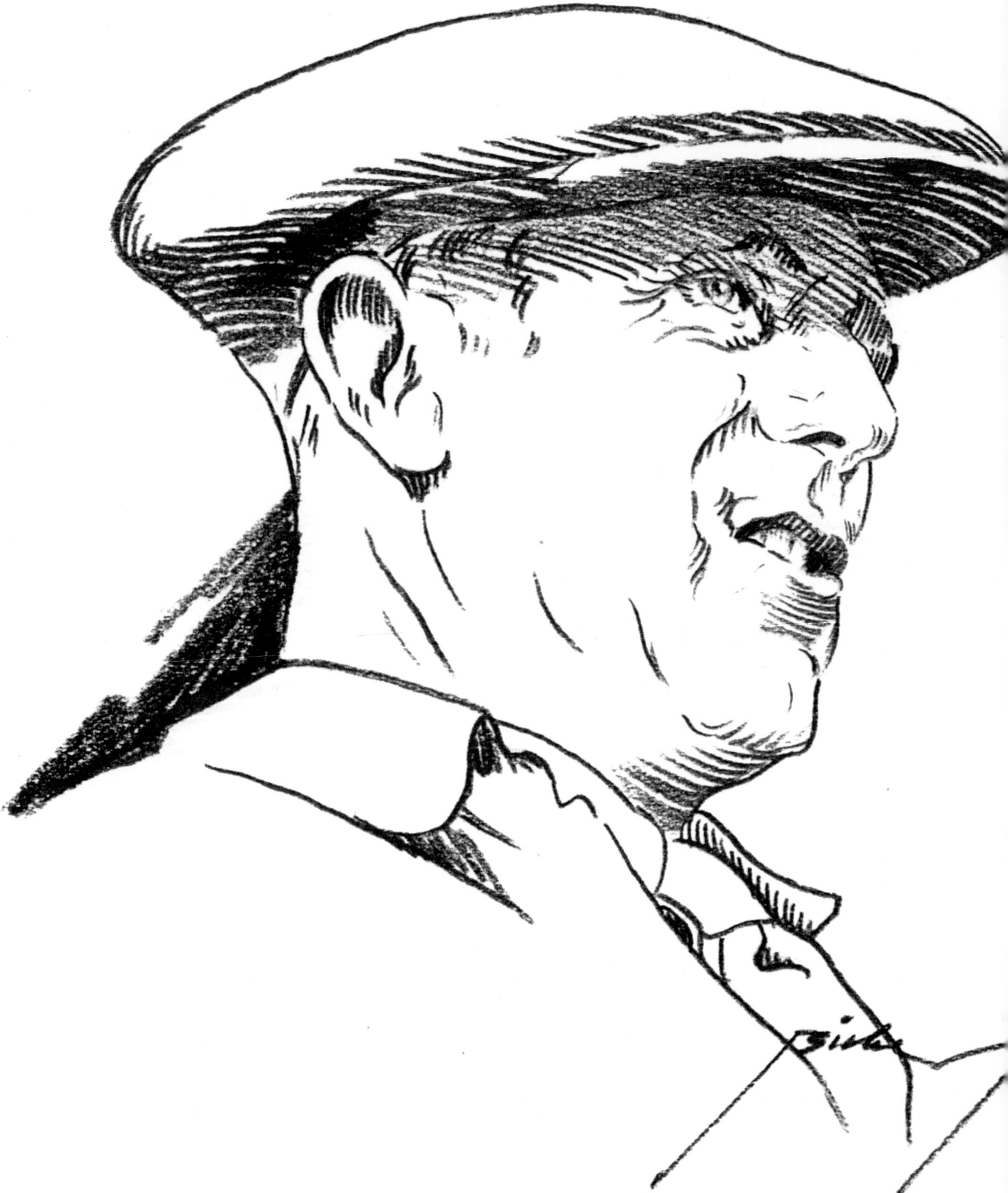